# THE LACANIAN SUBJECT

# THE LACANIAN SUBJECT

## BETWEEN LANGUAGE AND JOUISSANCE

*Bruce Fink*

PRINCETON UNIVERSITY PRESS    PRINCETON, NEW JERSEY

**Copyright © 1995 by Princeton University Press**
Published by Princeton University Press, 41 William Street,
Princeton, New Jersey 08540
In the United Kingdom: Princeton University Press, Chichester, West Sussex

*Library of Congress Cataloging-in-Publication Data*

Fink, Bruce, 1956–
The Lacanian subject: between language and jouissance / Bruce Fink.
p.     cm.
Includes bibliographical references and index.
ISBN 0-691-03760-4 (cloth : alk. paper)
1. Lacan, Jacques, 1901– . 2. Psychoanalysis. I. Title.
BF109.L28F56     1995
150.19′5—dc20     94-49033

This book has been composed in Times Roman

Princeton University Press books are printed
on acid-free paper and meet the guidelines
for permanence and durability of the Committee
on Production Guidelines for Book Longevity
of the Council on Library Resources

Printed in the United States of America by Princeton Academic Press

10  9  8  7  6  5  4  3  2

**Pour Héloïse**

# Contents _____

## PART FOUR: THE STATUS OF PSYCHOANALYTIC DISCOURSE

### Nine

### Ten

*Preface* _____

LACAN presents us with a radically new theory of subjectivity. Unlike most poststructuralists, who seek to deconstruct and dispel the very notion of the human subject, Lacan the psychoanalyst finds the concept of subjectivity indispensable and explores what it means to be a subject, how one comes to be a subject, the conditions responsible for the failure to become a subject (leading to psychosis), and the tools at the analyst's disposal to induce a "precipitation of subjectivity."

It is, however, extremely difficult to piece together the wide variety of things Lacan says about the subject, his theory of the subject being so "unintuitive" to most of us (consider the "definition" Lacan so often reiterates: the subject is that which one signifier represents to another signifier) and evolving quite significantly in the course of his work. Moreover, in the late 1970s and 1980s in the United States, Lacan was probably better known as a structuralist, due to the discussion of his work on language and on Edgar Allan Poe's "The Purloined Letter," and readers in the English-speaking world are often more familiar with a Lacan who uncovers the workings of structure at every turn—even at the very core of what we take to be our most precious, inalienable "selves"—seemingly leaving aside the problematic of subjectivity altogether.

In part 1 of this book, I retrace Lacan's extremely far-reaching examination of "otherness" as that which is alien or foreign to an as-yet-unspecified subject. That otherness runs the unlikely gamut from the unconscious (the Other as language) and the ego (the imaginary other [ideal ego] and the Other as desire [ego ideal]) to the Freudian superego (the Other as jouissance). We are alienated insofar as we are spoken by a language that functions, in certain respects, like a machine, computer, or recording/assembling device with a life of its own; insofar as our needs and pleasures are organized and channeled into socially acceptable forms by our parents' demands (the Other as demand); and insofar as our desire comes into being as the Other's desire. While Lacan incessantly invokes the subject in his seminars and written texts, the Other very often seems to steal the limelight.

Yet it is precisely the extension of the concept of structure or otherness in Lacan's work to its furthermost reaches that allows us to see where structure leaves off and something else begins, something that takes exception to structure. In Lacan's work, that which takes exception is twofold: the subject and the object (object *a* as cause of desire).

In part 2 of this book, I show that, departing from his early phenomenological notions, in the 1950s Lacan defines the subject as a position adopted with respect to the Other as language or law; in other words, the subject *is* a relationship to the symbolic order. The ego is defined in terms of the imaginary register, whereas the subject as such is essentially a positioning in relation to the Other. As Lacan's notion of the Other evolves, the subject is reconceptualized as a stance adopted with respect to the Other's desire (the mother's, parent's, or parents' desire), insofar as that desire arouses the subject's desire, that is, functions as object *a*.

Ever more influenced by Freud's earliest work[1] and his own psychoanalytic practice, Lacan begins (to cast his theoretical evolution in very schematic terms) to see that something in relation to which the subject adopts a stance as a primal experience of pleasure/pain or trauma. The subject comes into being as a form of attraction toward and defense against a primordial, overwhelming experience of what the French call *jouissance*: a pleasure that is excessive, leading to a sense of being overwhelmed or disgusted, yet simultaneously providing a source of fascination.

While in the late 1950s Lacan views "being" as something granted the human subject due only to its fantasized relation to the object which brought on that traumatic experience of jouissance, he eventually formulates the subject's primordial experience of jouissance as stemming from its *traumatic encounter with the Other's desire*. The subject—lacking in being—is thus seen to consist in a relation to, or a stance adopted with respect to, the Other's desire as fundamentally thrilling and yet unnerving, fascinating and yet overwhelming or revolting.

While a child wishes to be recognized by its parents as worthy of their desire, their desire is both mesmerizing and lethal. The subject's precarious existence is sustained by fantasies constructed to keep the subject at just the right distance from that dangerous desire, delicately balancing the attraction and the repulsion.

Nevertheless, that is, in my view, but one face of the Lacanian subject: the subject as fixated, as symptom, as a repetitive, symptomatic way of "getting off" or obtaining jouissance. The sense of being that is provided by fantasy is "false being," as Lacan refers to it in the mid-1960s, suggesting thereby that there is something more.

Predictably enough, the second face of the Lacanian subject appears in the overcoming of that fixation, the reconfiguring or traversing of fantasy, and the shifting of the way in which one gets one's kicks or obtains jouissance: that is, the face of *subjectivization*, a process of making "one's own" something that was formerly alien.

Through this process, a complete reversal occurs in one's position in relation to the Other's desire. One assumes responsibility for the Other's desire, that foreign power that brought one into being. One takes that causal alterity upon oneself, subjectifying what had previously been experienced as an external, extraneous cause, a foreign roll of the dice at the beginning of one's uni-

verse: destiny. Lacan suggests here a paradoxical move by the analysand, prepared by a specific approach on the analyst's part, to subjectify the cause of his
or her existence—the Other's desire that brought him or her into this world—
and to become the subject of his or her own fate. Not "it happened to me," but
"I saw," "I heard," "I acted."

Hence the gist of Lacan's multiple translations of Freud's "*Wo Es war, soll
Ich werden*": where the Other pulls the strings (acting as my cause), I must
come into being as my own cause.[2]

As for the object (discussed in detail in part 3 of this book), it evolves alongside the theory of the subject. Just as the subject is first viewed as a stance
adopted with respect to the Other, and then with respect to the Other's desire,
the object is first viewed as an other like oneself, and is eventually equated
with the Other's desire. The parents' desire brought the child into the world, in
a very material sense, serving as cause of the child's very being, and eventually
as cause of its desire. Fantasy stages the position in which the child would like
to see itself with respect to the object that causes, elicits, and incites its desire.

It is Lacan's theory of the object as *cause* of desire, not as something which
could somehow *satisfy* desire, that allows us to understand certain of Lacan's
innovations in analytic technique. Lacan reconceptualizes the analyst's position in terms of the roles the analyst must avoid (those of imaginary other and
of judgmental, all-knowing Other implicit in ego psychology approaches) and
the role s/he must position him or herself to play in the subject's fantasy (object *a*) in order to bring about ever greater subjectivization by the analysand of
the foreign causes that brought him or her into being.

In Lacan's view of the analytic setting, the analyst is not called on to play
the "good object," the "good enough mother," or the strong ego which allies
with the patient's weak one. Rather, the analyst must, by maintaining a position of enigmatic desire, come to serve as object in the subject's fantasy in
order to bring about a reconfiguration of fantasy, a new stance in relation to
jouissance, a new subject position. One of the tools for doing so at the analyst's disposal is time, the variable-length session being a means by which to
generate the tension necessary to separate the subject from its fantasized relation to the Other's desire.

The object is also elaborated by Lacan as the cause that upsets the smooth
functioning of structures, systems, and axiomatic fields, leading to aporias,
paradoxes, and conundrums of all kinds. It is the real which is encountered at
the points where language and the grids we use to symbolize the world break
down. It is the *letter* which insists whenever we try to use the signifier to
account for everything and to say it all.

The object thus has more than one function: as the Other's desire, it elicits
the subject's desire; but as the letter or signifierness (*signifiance*) of the signi-

fier, it has a materiality or substance associated with another kind of pleasure. It is, in a sense, the polyvalence of object *a* that leads Lacan to distinguish sexual desire (the pleasure of desire or desiring, which he refers to as "phallic jouissance," or more felicitously as "symbolic jouissance") from another kind of pleasure ("the Other jouissance").

These two faces of the object, *a* and S($\mathbb{A}$), allow for an understanding of sexual difference that has yet to be grasped in the English-language work on Lacan, and that goes far beyond current "interpretations" suggesting that, according to Lacan, masculine means subject and feminine means object, or that Lacan falls into the old Freudian trap of equating masculinity with activity and having, femininity with passivity and not having.

Two faces of the subject and two faces of the object. Parallel binary oppositions? I think not. Rather, a form of "Gödelian structuralism," as I call it, where every system is decompleted by the alterity or heterogeneity it contains within itself.

The status of psychoanalytic discourse, taken up in part 4 of this book, is an unavoidable issue for clinicians practicing in a scientistic context like the United States. In an environment in which the director of the National Institute of Mental Health in Washington can openly declare that the medical establishment is likely to "conquer" virtually all mental illness by the year 2000;[3] in which day after day the papers announce that the gene "responsible for" alcoholism, homosexuality, phobia, schizophrenia, or what have you has been found; and in which naive scientistic attacks on the foundations of psychoanalysis can be taken as serious blows to its credibility, analysts and the analytically inclined must become better equipped to intelligently discuss the epistemological status of their field.

For while psychoanalysis may not constitute a science, as "science" is currently understood, it has no need to seek legitimation from the existing medical or scientific establishment. Lacan's work provides us the wherewithal to constitute psychoanalysis as a discourse which is at once historically dependent on the birth of science and yet able to stand on its own two feet, so to speak. Psychoanalysis, as conceptualized by Lacan, is not only a discourse with its own specific grounding, but also one that is in a position to analyze the structure and workings of other "disciplines" (both academic and scientific), shedding new light on their mainsprings and blind spots.

Lacan points to the possibility of radicalizing or revolutionizing science, as it is usually understood, by introducing psychoanalytic notions therein—thus in a sense pushing back the frontiers of science in such a way as to redefine the *object* of scientific inquiry. Instead of claiming, as some do, that psychoanalysis is doomed to forever remain outside the field of science, Lacan's point is rather that *science is not yet equal to the task of accommodating psychoanalysis*.[4] Scientific discourse may, some day, be recast in such a way as to encompass psychoanalysis within its ambit, but in the meantime psychoanalysis can continue to elaborate its own distinctive praxis: clinical practice and theory building.

This thumbnail sketch indicates the general trajectory of my argument and will, I hope, serve the reader as something of a road map in reading this book, to be referred back to occasionally, as needed. For while subject, object, Other, and discourse are the main concepts developed here, to discuss them in context requires an explanation of a great many more of Lacan's basic concepts and of his earlier and later attempts to formulate psychoanalytic experience using them.

Some of the concepts that Lacan shaped and reshaped in the course of his career and that I am led to take up here, include the imaginary, symbolic, and real; need, demand, desire, and jouissance; the subject of the statement, the subject of enunciation (or speaking subject), the subject of the unconscious, the split subject, the subject as a defense, and the subject as metaphor; the paternal metaphor, primal repression, and secondary repression; neurosis, psychosis, and perversion; the signifier (the master or unary signifier and the binary signifier), the letter, and signifierness; the phallus (as the signifier of desire), the phallic function, sexual difference, phallic jouissance, Other jouissance, masculine structure, and feminine structure; alienation, separation, the traversing of fantasy, and the "pass"; punctuation, interpretation, the variable-length session, and the role of the analyst as pure desirousness; existence and ex-sistence; the four discourses (master's, hysteric's, analyst's, and university), their mainsprings, and the sacrifices they entail; knowledge, misrecognition, and truth; discourse, metalanguage, and suture; formalization, polarization, and transmission. The road map provided in this preface will hopefully help the reader distinguish the forest from the trees in my exposition of this broad range of concepts.

The chapters in part 1 aim at simplicity, assuming little if any previous knowledge of Lacan's work. Parts 2, 3, and 4 become progressively more complex, building upon the foundations laid in the earlier parts of the book. Certain readers may wish to skip some of the denser chapters the first time through (such as chapters 5, 6, and 8), moving, for example, directly from chapter 7, on object *a*, to chapters 9 and 10, on discourse. Many of the chapters can be read independently, even though they do build on, and occasionally refer back to, material that has come before. Readers with a good deal of prior knowledge of Lacan's work will probably want to skip chapter 1 altogether and perhaps even go directly to chapter 5, merely thumbing through the earlier material.

One of my more general aims in this book is to begin to resituate discussion of Lacan's work in a context which does not leave clinical considerations by the wayside. In America, the psychoanalytic community has resisted Lacan's thought for several decades now, whereas the more literary and linguistically minded have demonstrated the greatest and most enduring interest in his work. The historical and intellectual reasons for this situation are too well known to be reiterated here, but the result has, in my view, been a skewed or partial representation of his thought. While the present book was not written with clinicians specifically in mind,[5] my own experience with the praxis that is psychoanalysis does, I believe, form its backdrop.

I have made no pretense in this book of presenting a "balanced" view of Lacan's work. A balanced view would have to provide a great deal of historical perspective on Lacan's development—explaining his multifarious surrealist, Freudian, phenomenological, existential, post-Freudian, Saussurian, Jakobsonian, and Lévi-Straussian influences (just for starters)—and situate Lacan's forays into psychoanalytic theory in the context of debates going on in France and elsewhere at the time.

Instead I have attempted to present a view of Lacan's work which many will no doubt find overly static and closed, one of the many fascinations of his work lying precisely in its constant transformations, self-corrections, and reversals of perspective. I have endeavored to provide a view of several of Lacan's major concepts, not as they evolved from the 1930s on, but rather from a 1970s perspective. On occasion, I try to guide the reader through certain of Lacan's early ways of formulating psychoanalytic experience by "translating" them into Lacan's own later terms, but in general I provide a cut of Lacanian theory that I consider to be particularly powerful and useful to the clinician and theorist alike. Oppositions such as that between "full" and "empty" speech, found in Lacan's earliest seminars, are, to my way of thinking, superseded in his later work; thus as interesting as they may be in their own right, I have preferred to let others present them.[6]

My punctuation of Lacan's thought, which emphasizes certain developments and deemphasizes others, will, I hope, allow the reader to orient him or herself better in the voluminous mass of Lacan's published and yet-to-be published work. Having taught classes for a number of years on the basis of certain of Lacan's seminars, following the step-by-step development of a particular concept (like that of psychoanalytic ethics in Seminar VII or of transference in Seminar VIII), the excitement of seeing such an active and creative mind at work is often overshadowed by the difficulty involved in isolating an identifiable thesis. Working through Lacan's seminars is an important task for all serious students of psychoanalysis, and yet it is, in my experience, helpful to have a number of landmarks in what may otherwise be perceived as a somewhat amorphous field.

The task of interpreting Lacan's work is, like that of interpreting Plato's and Freud's, endless, and I make no pretense here of having the last word. It should be clear that what I am offering up here is an interpretation; in particular, the theory of the Lacanian subject presented in chapters 5 and 6 is my own, and my reading of Lacan's work on sexual difference in chapter 8 is likewise original.

The appendices include material too technical to maintain the general flow of the discussion here. They concern Lacan's detailed models of the structure of language, and the effects generated by the anomaly that arises within it (object *a*).

In the glossary provided at the end of this book, the reader will find short explanations of the major symbols (known as "mathemes") discussed in these pages. Lacan's mathemes condense and embody a considerable quantity of conceptualization, and while I have attempted in the glossary to summarize their most salient aspects, their proper use requires a firm overall grasp of Lacan's theoretical framework.

When quoting Lacan's work, I have, wherever possible, provided references to the English editions, but I have taken considerable liberties with the existing translations: their inadequacies are becoming ever more glaring. "*Écrits* 1966" refers to the French edition of the *Écrits* published by Seuil in Paris, while "*Écrits*" alone refers to Alan Sheridan's 1977 English selection published by Norton.[7] Page references to Seminars I, II, VII, and XI always correspond to the English translations published by Norton. I refer to the Seminars by their numbers alone; full references are found in the bibliography. When quoting Freud's work, I have provided volume and page numbers from the Standard Edition (abbreviated SE), but I have often modified the translations on the basis of far more interesting or striking "nonstandard" translations.

April 1994

# Part One ————————————————

## STRUCTURE: ALIENATION AND THE OTHER

The self is an other.

# 1

## Language and Otherness

### A Slip of the Other's Tongue

A patient walks into his analyst's office and sits down in the armchair. He looks the analyst right in the eye, picks up the thread where he left off at the end of his last session, and immediately makes a blunder, saying "I know that in my relationship with my father there was a lot of tension, and I think it came from the fact that he was working much too hard at a schnob he couldn't stand and took it out on me." He meant to say "job" but "schnob" came out instead.

Discourse is never one-dimensional. A slip of the tongue immediately reminds us that more than one discourse can use the same mouthpiece at the same time.

Two distinct levels can be identified here: an intentional discourse consisting of what the speaker was *trying* to say or *meant* to say and an unintentional discourse which in this case takes the form of a deformed or garbled word, a kind of conflation of "job," "snob," and perhaps other words as well. The analyst may already know, for example, that the speaker thinks of the eldest child in the family, say, his older brother or sister, as an effete snob and feels that their father doted on that older sibling excessively—to a fault, as far as the patient or analysand (i.e., the person engaged in analyzing him or herself) is concerned. The analysand may also think of the word "schnoz," and recall that as a young child he was afraid of his father's nose, which reminded him of a witch's nose; the word "schmuck" may then also pass through his mind.

This simple example already allows us to distinguish between two different types of discourse or, more simply stated, two different types of talk:[1]

- *ego talk*: everyday talk about what we consciously think and believe about ourselves
- and *some other kind of talk.*

Lacan's Other is, at its most basic level, related to that *other kind of talk.*[2] For we can tentatively assume that there are not only two different kinds of talk, but that they come, roughly speaking, from two different psychological places: the ego (or self) and the Other.

Psychoanalysis begins with the presupposition that that Other kind of talk stems from *an other* which is locatable in some sense; it holds that unintentional words that are spoken, blurted out, mumbled, or garbled come from *some other place*, some other agency than the ego. Freud called that Other place the unconscious, and Lacan states in no uncertain terms that "the unconscious is the Other's discourse,"[3] that is, the unconscious consists of those words which come from some other place than ego talk. At this most basic level then, the unconscious is the Other's discourse (table 1.1).

Table 1.1

| EGO/SELF DISCOURSE | OTHER DISCOURSE/<br>THE OTHER'S DISCOURSE |
|---|---|
| conscious<br>intentional | unconscious<br>unintentional |

Now how did that Other discourse wind up "inside" of us? We tend to believe that we are in control, and yet at times something extraneous and foreign speaks, as it were, through *our* mouths. From the viewpoint of the self or ego, "I" runs the show: that aspect of us that we call "I" believes that it knows what it thinks and feels, and believes that it knows why it does what it does. The intruding element—that Other kind of talk—is shoved aside, considered random, and thus ultimately of no consequence. People prone to making slips of the tongue often just figure that they get tongue-tied now and then or that their brains simply work faster than their mouths and wind up trying to get two words out of that one slow-working mouth at the same time. While slips of the tongue are recognized in such cases as foreign to the ego or self, their importance is pushed aside. While in most cases a person who just made a slip would probably endorse the following statement, "I just made a random, meaningless goof," Freud's retort would be "The truth has spoken."

Whereas most people attach no particular importance to that Other discourse that breaks through and interrupts ego discourse, psychoanalysts hold that there is method in the seeming madness, an altogether identifiable logic behind those interruptions, in other words, that there is nothing random about them whatsoever. Analysts seek to discover the method in that madness, for it is only by changing the logic that governs those interruptions, only by impacting that Other discourse, that change can come about.

Freud spent a great deal of time in *The Interpretation of Dreams*, *Jokes and Their Relation to the Unconscious*, and *The Psychopathology of Everyday Life* unraveling the mechanisms governing what he daringly called "unconscious thought."[4] In his widely read article entitled "The Agency of the Letter in the Unconscious" (*Écrits*), Lacan pointed out the relationship between Freud's concepts of displacement and condensation typical of dream work and the

linguistic notions of metonymy and metaphor. But Lacan by no means left off
there; he went on to seek models for deciphering unconscious mechanisms in
the then developing field of cybernetics. In chapter 2, I examine in detail
Lacan's juxtaposition of ideas contained in Edgar Allan Poe's story "The Purloined Letter" and ideas inspired by the cybernetics of the 1950s. Lacan's work
on Poe has been commented upon by myriad literary critics,[5] but few authors
have followed Lacan's own speculations on the workings of the unconscious
that stemmed from it.

In this chapter my focus is not so much on how this Other discourse works,
but rather on how it got there: How did it get "inside" of us? How did something which seems so extraneous or foreign wind up speaking through *our*
mouths?

Lacan accounts for the foreignness as follows: we are born into a world of
discourse, a discourse or language that precedes our birth and that will live on
after our death. Long before a child is born, a place is prepared for it in its
parents' linguistic universe: the parents speak of the child yet to be born, try
to select the perfect name for it, prepare a room for it, and begin imagining
what their lives will be like with an additional member of the household. The
words they use to talk about the child have often been in use for decades, if
not centuries, and the parents have generally neither defined nor redefined
them despite many years of use. Those words are handed down to them by
centuries of tradition: they constitute the Other of language, as Lacan can call
it in French (*l'Autre du langage*), but which we may try to render as the linguistic Other, or the Other *as* language.

If we draw a circle and posit that it represents the set of all words in a
language, then we can associate it with what Lacan calls the Other (figure 1.1).
It is the Other as the collection of all the words and expressions in a language.
This is a rather static view, as a language such as English is always evolving,
new words being added almost every day and old ones falling into disuse, but
as a first gloss it will serve our present purposes well enough.[6]

Figure 1.1

A child is thus born into a preestablished place in its parents' linguistic
universe, a space often prepared many months, if not years, before the child
sees the light of day. And most children are bound to learn the language spoken by their parents, which is to say that, in order to express their wishes, they
are virtually obliged to go beyond the crying stage—a stage in which their

parents must try to guess what it is their children want or need—and try to say what they want *in so many words*, that is, in a way that is comprehensible to their primary caretakers. Their wants are, however, molded in that very process, for the words they are obliged to use are not their own and do not necessarily correspond to their own particular demands: their very desires are cast in the mold of the language or languages they learn (table 1.2).

Table 1.2

| NEED   —>   THE OTHER AS LANGUAGE   —>   DESIRE |
|---|

Lacan's view is more radical still in that one cannot even say that a child *knows* what it wants prior to the assimilation of language: when a baby cries, the *meaning* of that act is provided by the parents or caretakers who attempt to name the pain the child seems to be expressing (e.g., "she must be hungry"). There is perhaps a sort of general discomfort, coldness, or pain, but its meaning is imposed, as it were, by the way in which it is interpreted by the child's parents. If a parent responds to its baby's crying with food, the discomfort, coldness, or pain will retroactively be determined as having "meant" hunger, as hunger pangs. One cannot say that the true meaning behind the baby's crying was that it was cold, because meaning is an ulterior product: constantly responding to a baby's cries with food may transform all of its discomforts, coldness, and pain into hunger. Meaning in this situation is thus determined not by the baby but by other people, and on the basis of the language they speak. I'll come back to this point a little further on.

The Other as language is assimilated by most children (autistic children are the most notable exception to the rule) as they attempt to bridge the gap between inarticulate need that can only cry out and be interpreted for better or for worse, and the articulation of desire in socially understandable, if not acceptable, terms. The Other, in this sense, can be seen as an insidious, uninvited intruder that unceremoniously and unpropitiously transforms our wishes; it is, however, at the same time that which enables us to clue each other in to our desires and "communicate."

Since time immemorial, people have expressed nostalgia for a time before the development of language, for a supposed time when *homo sapiens* lived like animals, with no language and thus nothing that could taint or complicate man's needs and wants. Rousseau's glorification and extolment of the virtues of primitive man and his life before the corrupting influence of language is one of the best known nostalgic enterprises.

In such nostalgic views, language is deemed the source of a great many evils. People are considered to be naturally good, loving, and generous, it being language that allows for perfidy, falsehood, lying, treachery, and virtually every other fault with which human beings and hypothetical extraterrestrials have ever been taxed. From such standpoints, language is clearly viewed as a foreign element inopportunely foisted upon or grafted onto an otherwise wholesome human nature.

Writers like Rousseau have beautifully expressed what Lacan calls man's *alienation in language.* According to Lacanian theory, every human being who learns to speak is thereby alienated from her or himself—for it is language that, while allowing desire to come into being, ties knots therein, and makes us such that we can both want and not want one and the same thing, never be satisfied when we get what we thought we wanted, and so on.

The Other seems then to slip in the back door while children are learning a language that is virtually indispensable to their survival in the world as we know it. Though widely considered innocuous and purely utilitarian in nature, language brings with it a fundamental form of alienation that is part and parcel of learning *one's mother tongue.* The very expression we use to talk about it—"mother tongue"—is indicative of the fact that it is some Other's tongue first, the mOther's tongue, that is, the mOther's language, and in speaking of childhood experience, Lacan often virtually equates the Other with the mother. (Alienation will be discussed at much greater length in chapter 5.)

## The Unconscious

Now while this accounts for the foreignness of the mother tongues that we usually consider to be altogether ours, which we have, in other words, tried to make our own as far as possible—and those mother tongues are constitutive of ego discourse, which thus turns out to be far more foreign and alienating than is generally thought (table 1.3)—we have yet to account for that Other discourse which somehow seems still more foreign: the unconscious. We have seen that ego discourse, that discourse we have about ourselves in ordinary conversation with ourselves and other people, is already a lot further from being truly reflective of ourselves than we thought, permeated as it is by this Other presence that is language. Lacan puts that in no uncertain terms: *the self is an other*, the ego is an other.[7]

Table 1.3

| EGO/SELF DISCOURSE | OTHER DISCOURSE/ THE OTHER'S DISCOURSE |
|---|---|
| conscious intentional alienated due to language | unconscious unintentional |

Is it any less foreign ultimately to the individual in question than to an outside person, another person? What we think we know about our most intimate selves may in fact really be as far off track as our wildest imaginings about other people. The understanding we have of ourselves may be just as wrongheaded, just as farfetched, as other people's views of us. Others may in fact know us much better than we really know ourselves. The very notion of the self, as some sort of innermost part of a person, seems to break down here; we will return to this point about the foreignness or otherness of the ego, or self as I have been calling it, in chapter 4. Let us try to account here for that "most foreign" of all others: the unconscious.

Lacan states very simply that *the unconscious is language*, meaning that language is that which makes up the unconscious.[8] Freud is mistakenly thought by many people to have held that feelings can be unconscious, whereas for the most part he held that what is repressed is what he called the *Vorstellungsrepräsentanzen*, commonly translated into English as ideational representatives.[9] On the basis of the German philosophical tradition underlying Freud's work and close study of Freud's texts themselves, Lacan translates it into French as *représentants de la représentation*, representatives of (the) representation, and concludes that these representatives can be equated with what are referred to in linguistics as signifiers.[10]

Thus, according to Lacan's interpretation of Freud, when repression takes place, a word, or some part of a word, "sinks down under," metaphorically speaking.[11] The word does not thereby become inaccessible to consciousness, and it may indeed be a word that a person uses perfectly well in everyday conversation. But by the very fact of being repressed, that word, or some part thereof, begins to take on a new role. It establishes relations with other repressed elements, developing a complex set of connections with them.

As Lacan says over and over again, *the unconscious is structured like a language*;[12] in other words, the same kinds of relationships exist among unconscious elements as exist in any given language among the elements that constitute it. To return to our earlier example: "job" and "snob" are related because they contain a certain number of identical phonemes and letters, the basic building blocks of speech and writing, respectively. Thus they may be associated in the unconscious, even though they are not associated consciously by the individual whose unconscious we are examining. Take the words "conservation" and "conversation." They are anagrams: they contain the same letters, only the order in which they appear being different. While ego discourse may totally neglect the *literal equivalence* of such terms—the fact that they contain the same letters—the unconscious pays attention to details like that in substituting one word for another in dreams and fantasies.

Now by saying the unconscious is structured like a language, Lacan did not assert that the unconscious is structured in exactly the same way as English, say, or some other ancient or modern language, but rather that language, as it operates at the unconscious level, obeys a kind of grammar, that is, a set of rules that governs the transformation and slippage that goes on therein. The unconscious, for example, has a tendency to break words down into their smallest units—phonemes and letters—and recombine them as it sees fit: to express the ideas of job, snob, schnoz, and schmuck all in the same breath, for instance, as we saw in the word "schnob" above.

As we shall see in the next chapter, the unconscious is nothing but a "chain" of signifying elements, such as words, phonemes, and letters, which "unfolds" in accordance with very precise rules over which the ego or self has no control whatsoever. Rather than being the privileged seat of subjectivity, the unconscious, as understood by Lacan (except in the expression "subject of the unconscious," which we shall come to later), is itself Other, foreign, and unassimilated. Most of us probably tend to think, as did Freud, that the analysand who blurts out "schnob" instead of "job" is revealing his or her true colors: a gripe against a father who paid too much attention to an older sibling and not enough to the analysand, and a wish that it had been otherwise. And yet, while that desire may be considered *truer*, in some sense, than other desires expressed by the analysand in "ego mode" (e.g., "I really want to become a better person"), it may nevertheless be a foreign desire: the Other's desire. The analysand who says "schnob" may go on to say that it was, in fact, his mother who felt that his father was a schmuck and who repeatedly told him that his father was neglecting him; he may come to realize that he stopped himself from loving his father and began resenting him only to please his mother. "I wasn't the one who wanted to reproach him," he may conclude, "she was." In this sense, we can think of the unconscious as expressing, through its irruptions into everyday speech, a desire that is itself foreign and unassimilated.

Insofar as desire inhabits language—and in a Lacanian framework, there is no such thing as desire, strictly speaking, without language—we can say that the unconscious is full of such foreign desires. Many people sense at times that they are working towards something they do not even really want, striving to live up to expectations they do not even endorse, or mouthing goals they know perfectly well they have little if any motivation to achieve. The unconscious is, in that sense, overflowing with *other people's desires*: your parents' desire, perhaps, that you study at such and such a school and pursue such and such a career; your grandparents' desire that you settle down and get married and give them great-grandchildren; or peer pressure that you engage in certain activities that do not really interest you. In such cases, there is a desire that you take to be "your own," and another with which you grapple that seems to pull the strings and at times force you to act but that you do not feel to be altogether your own.

Other people's views and desires flow into us via discourse. In that sense, we can interpret Lacan's statement that the unconscious is the Other's discourse in a very straightforward fashion: *the unconscious is full of other peo-*

*ple's talk, other people's conversations, and other people's goals, aspirations, and fantasies* (insofar as they are expressed in words).

That talk takes on a sort of independent existence within "our*selves*," as it were. Clear examples of the internalization of the Other's discourse—other people's talk—are found in what is commonly called conscience or guilty conscience, and in what Freud called the superego. Let us imagine, and this a purely fictional account, that Albert Einstein overheard a conversation, which perhaps was not intended for his ears, wherein his father said to his mother, "He'll never amount to anything,"[13] and his mother concurred, saying, "That's right; he's lazy like his father." We can imagine that Albert was not yet even old enough to either understand what all the words meant or divine their sense. Nevertheless, they wound up being stored somewhere and lay dormant for many years, only to be reactivated and plague him relentlessly when he was trying to make headway in high school. The words finally took on meaning and took their toll when he failed math in high school—that part of the story is apparently true—even though he certainly did not lack the ability to grasp the material.

Now we can imagine two different situations. In the first, whenever Albert sat down to take a test, he heard his father's and mother's voices saying, "He'll never amount to anything" and "That's right; he's lazy like his father" and was so distracted, now that he finally understood what all the words meant, that he could never answer any of the questions on the test. In the second situation, none of that talk would be consciously remembered, but it would nevertheless have a similar effect on Albert. In other words, those disparaging remarks would be circulating in his unconscious, working, distracting, and torturing the young Einstein, short-circuiting consciousness. Albert would see the test in front of him on the desk and suddenly find himself in something of a daze and have no idea why. Perhaps he knew the material backwards and forwards five minutes before the test, and yet was suddenly inexplicably incapable of concentrating on anything whatsoever. Thus he unknowingly fulfilled a prophecy he did not even consciously know his father had made, the prediction "He'll never amount to anything." And, irony of ironies, let us suppose that, in this fictional account, his father had in fact been talking about the next door neighbor's son at the time!

Lacan sets out to explain how such situations are possible: the unconscious as a chain of signifying elements which unfolds in accordance with very precise rules (the likes of which will be indicated in the following chapter) constitutes a memory device such that while Albert is unable to remember how many times his father said "No, the boy will never amount to anything," it is remembered *for* "him." He may not remember his father ever having said that about anyone at all, but the chain of signifiers remembers in his stead. The unconscious counts, records, takes it all down, stores it, and can call up that "information" at any time. That's where Lacan's cybernetic analogies come in.[14]

Freud says of unconscious elements that they are indestructible. Is it grey matter that is so constituted that certain neuronal pathways, once established, can never be eradicated? Lacan's answer is that only the symbolic order, through its combinatory rules, has the wherewithal to hold onto snatches of conversation forever.[15]

At this most basic level, then, the Other is that foreign language we must learn to speak which is euphemistically referred to as our "native tongue," but which would be much better termed our "mOther tongue": it is the discourse and desires of others around us insofar as the former are internalized. By "internalized" I do not mean to suggest that they become our own; rather, albeit internalized, they remain foreign bodies in a sense. They may very well remain so foreign, so estranged, so cut off from subjectivity that an individual would choose to take his or her life in order to be rid of such a foreign presence. That is obviously an extreme case, but it indicates the overwhelming importance of the Other within oneself.

## Foreign Bodies

The Other corresponds here to what goes by the name of structure in the movement known as structuralism. Here I would like to pursue structure insofar as we find it at work in the body, not in the sense of bone structure or the organization involved in the nervous system, but in the sense of that which proves that the body is at the mercy of language, at the mercy of the symbolic order. A former analysand of mine complained of a plethora of psychosomatic symptoms which changed all the time, albeit slowly enough so that each symptom had ample time to get him quite worried and to prompt a visit to his doctor. At one point this analysand heard that a friend of his had had an acute case of appendicitis that came on very suddenly and led to a close call in the emergency room. The analysand asked his spouse which side of the body the appendix was on, and she told him. Some time thereafter, the analysand, strangely enough, began feeling pains on that very side of his body. The pains persisted; the analysand became surer and surer every day that his appendix was soon going to burst and finally decided to go see his doctor. When the analysand showed the doctor where it hurt, the doctor burst out laughing and said, "But the appendix is on the other side: your appendix is on the right, not on the left!" The pain immediately vanished, and the analysand felt obliged to explain that his wife must surely have been mistaken, then, in telling him that the appendix was on the left. He shuffled out of the examining room feeling rather silly.

The point of the story is that knowledge, knowledge as embodied in the words "appendix," "left," and so on, allowed a psychosomatic symptom to develop on a side of the body where even the worst informed of doctors could divine the error. The body is written with signifiers. If you believe that the appendix is on the left, and by identification with someone else or as part of a wide array of psychosomatic symptoms—which are just as rife nowadays as in nineteenth century Vienna, though they often take different forms—you are bound to come down with appendicitis, it's going to hurt, not in your biological organ, but where you *believe* the organ to be located.

Analysts of Freud's generation often related cases of anesthesia—numbness or lack of all feeling in certain parts of the body—which were in no way, shape, or form regulated by the location of a particular nerve's endings in some part of the body, but which instead clearly obeyed popular notions about where a part of the body, as defined in common speech, started and stopped. Whereas one and the same nerve might flow through all of a person's arm and down to the tip of the fingers, someone might feel nothing at all at one particular point on the arm, or might feel sharp pain (pseudo-neuralgia) at that point, for no apparent physiological reason. It might well turn out that, during some war, the person's father had been shot at that very point in the arm. And we might perfectly well imagine that, as a child, the person had been misinformed concerning which arm the father had been shot in, and that the lack of feeling or sharp pain showed up in the wrong arm!

These anecdotes illustrate the notion that the body is written with signifiers and is thus foreign, Other. Language is "encrusted upon the living," to borrow Bergson's expression. The body is overwritten/overridden by language.

Freud shows us how the polymorphously perverse child's libido is progressively channeled into (thereby creating) specific erogenous zones—oral, anal, and genital—through socialization and toilet training, that is, through verbally expressed demands made on the child by its parents and/or parental figures. The child's body is progressively subordinated to those demands (perhaps never entirely so, but rebellion against them simultaneously demonstrates their centrality), the different parts of the body taking on socially/parentally determined meaning. The body is subdued; "the letter kills"[16] the body. The "living being" (*le vivant*)—our animal nature—dies, language coming to life in its place and living us. The body is rewritten, in a manner of speaking, physiology giving way to the signifier, and our bodily pleasures all come to imply/involve a relationship to the Other.

Our sexual pleasures are thus also intimately tied to the Other. Not necessarily to other "individuals"; indeed, there are many people who sense that they are unable to have intimate relations *with* other people, those other people being little more than peripheral props for their fantasies, scenarios, and so on, or material manifestations of the particular body types that turn them on. Any time we talk about body *types*, *scenarios*, or *fantasies*, we're talking about linguistically structured entities. They may take the form of images in one's mind, but they are at least in part ordered by the signifier, and thus at least potentially signifying and meaningful. (In later chapters, I will explain at length why images and the imaginary in general rarely function independently of the symbolic in speaking beings.)

Our very fantasies can be foreign to us, for they are structured by a language which is only tangentially or asymptotically our own, and they may even be someone else's fantasies at the outset: one may find that one has a fantasy which is in fact one's mother's or father's fantasy, and that one does not even know how it wound up knocking around in one's own head. That is one of the things that people find the most alienating: even their fantasies do not seem to be their own.

I certainly do not mean to suggest that they necessarily wind up in one's head through no doing of one's own. It seems to me that there is no such thing as a symptom or fantasy without some subjective involvement, in other words, without the subject being somehow implicated, without the subject somehow having had a hand in it. Bringing an analysand to the point of realizing the part she or he played in the "choice" of her or his symptom is often quite a feat, and indeed at times it seems as if there is no subjective involvement whatsoever in certain symptoms and fantasies prior to analysis; subjectification is only brought about after the fact. This conundrum will be discussed at length in chapters 5 and 6.

One can already begin to distinguish different possible subject positions,[17] that is, the different clinical structures (neurosis, psychosis, and perversion) and their subcategories (e.g., hysteria, obsession, and phobia under neurosis), on the basis of different relations to the Other. Indeed, in Lacan's early work, the subject *is* essentially a relationship to the symbolic order, that is, the stance one adopts with respect to the Other as language or law. But since the Other as elaborated by Lacan has many faces or avatars—

- The Other as language (i.e., as set of all signifiers)
- The Other as demand
- The Other as desire (object *a*)
- The Other as jouissance

—and since demand, desire, and jouissance will not be examined in any depth until parts 2 and 3 of this book, such a schematization is best left aside for now.[18] The different facets of the Other should not be viewed as entirely separate and unrelated, yet their articulation is a complex task not to be undertaken at this stage.

I will turn now to an examination of the functioning of language in the unconscious.

# 2

## The Nature of Unconscious Thought, or
## How the Other Half "Thinks"

LANGUAGE functions. Language "lives" and "breathes," independently of any human subject. Speaking beings, far from simply using language as a tool, are also used by language; they are the playthings of language, and are duped by language.

Language has a life of its own. Language as Other brings with it rules, exceptions, expressions, and lexicons (standard vocabularies and jargons, lingoes, specialized technospeak, and subcultural dialects). It evolves over time, its history related to that of the beings who speak it, who are not simply cast and recast by it but have an impact upon it as well, introducing new terms, new turns of phrase, new constructions, and so on. Shakespeare has been credited with introducing into English hundreds of new metaphors and turns of phrase, and Lacan himself has had a substantial impact upon the French spoken by at least a significant percentage of French intellectuals, having forged original translations for many of Freud's terms and introduced many new terms and expressions of his own into French psychoanalytic discourse.

Yet language also operates independently, outside of our control. While we have the feeling, much of the time, of choosing our words, at times they are chosen for us. We may be unable to think and express something except in one very specific way (that being the only formulation our language—or at least that part of the language we have assimilated and have, as it were, at our disposal—provides); and words are occasionally blurted out that we do not have the impression of having chosen (far from it!). Certain words and expressions *present themselves* to us while we are speaking or writing—not always the ones we want—sometimes so persistently that we are virtually forced to speak or write them before being able to move on to others. A certain image or metaphor may *come to mind* without our having sought it out or in any way attempted to construct it and thrust itself upon us so forcibly that we can but reproduce it and only then try to tease out its meaning.

Such expressions and metaphors are selected in some Other place than consciousness. Lacan suggests that we view the process as one in which there are two chains of discourse which run roughly parallel to each other (in a figurative sense), each "unfolding" and developing chronologically along a timeline, as it were, one of which occasionally interrupts or intervenes in the other.

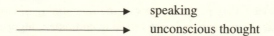

speaking

unconscious thought

We might refer to the upper line as a chain of spoken words, that is, a chain of speaking, enunciation, or enunciating. Lacan uses the word "chain" to remind us of the grammatical and contextual links between each word uttered and the ones that come before and after: no one word in a statement has any fixed value except insofar as it is used in a particular context. (Lacan's approach to linguistics rebukes any strictly referential theory of language whereby each word uttered would have a strict one-to-one relation with a thing existing in "reality.")[1]

The lower line in the figure represents the movement of unconscious thought processes, which occurs contemporaneously with the movement of speech in time, but is for the most part independent thereof. In a conversation, you might be talking with a friend about a blister you got on your foot while running, the parapraxal slip to "sister" indicating that another thought is preoccupying you at some other level—at the level of the unconscious. Something your interlocutor said might have reminded you of your sister, but it might alternatively be the case that nothing in the present speech situation activated thoughts of her, and that a certain unconscious rumination had been going on since earlier in the day when you spoke to her on the phone or dreamt about her.

How does thinking go on at the unconscious level?[2] And what kind of thought processes occur there? In *The Interpretation of Dreams*, Freud showed that condensation and displacement are fundamental characteristics of unconscious thought processes, and Lacan went on, in "The Agency of the Letter in the Unconscious, or Reason Since Freud" (*Écrits*), to demonstrate the relation between condensation and metaphor on the one hand, and between displacement and metonymy on the other, metaphor and metonymy being linguistic tropes that have been discussed at great length in works on rhetoric for centuries (Gracian, Perelman, etc.). Virtually every analysand is astonished early on in the analytic process, in his or her initial attempts to understand dreams and fantasies, by the complexity of the process that gives rise to such unconscious products (or "unconscious formations," as Lacan calls them).[3]

Yet Lacan went much further still in his exploration of what occurs at the unconscious level, attempting to provide models by which to conceptualize the autonomous functioning of language in the unconscious and the uncanny "indestructibility" of unconscious contents.

These models were first developed during his 1954–55 seminar, *The Ego in Freud's Theory and in the Technique of Psychoanalysis*, and considerably expanded in the afterword to his "Seminar on 'The Purloined Letter' " (*Écrits* 1966). Few attempts have yet been made to outline the ramifications of these models, and indeed, they present a view of the functioning of language that is quite unfamiliar to anyone who is not versed in computer languages or combinatories as used in mathematics. Lacan's models begin here, not with "natural languages" (as they are called in linguistics: languages as they are actually spoken), but with artificial languages (most notably their syntactic rules). The latter have a good deal to teach us about the symbolic order itself: about its "stuff" or substance, its relation to the reality it ostensibly describes, and its byproducts.

Lacan's models require a bit of mental gymnastics on our part, and it should be viewed as neither superfluous nor gratuitous. For it is perfectly in keeping with Lacan's view of the nature of unconscious thought processes: as we shall see, they involve various degrees of *ciphering*.[4] "Heads or Tails," below, presents a simplified model of the "language" Lacan develops, and that model should suffice for the more conceptual discussion beginning in the subsequent section.

## Heads or Tails

Lacan's models can be understood through the use of a simple example. Those readers interested in seeing why Lacan picked these particular kinds of models are referred to chapters 15 and 16 of Seminar II as well as the "Seminar on 'The Purloined Letter'" and its postface.

The artificial language Lacan develops takes a "real event" as its point of departure: the flipping of a well-balanced, unloaded coin. (As we shall see, this "real event" could equally well be the comings and goings—alternating presence and absence—of a child's mother, and is thus more than tangentially related to the "Fort-Da" game played by Freud's grandson, described in *Beyond the Pleasure Principle*.) With such a coin, there is no way to predict, at any one toss, whether the result will be heads or tails. Following Lacan's nonarbitrary choice of + and − for heads and tails, a random string of toss results can be broken down in a variety of ways. Consider, for example, the following chain:

$$1 \quad 2 \quad 3 \quad 4 \quad 5 \quad 6 \quad 7 \quad 8 \quad 9 \quad \text{Toss Numbers}$$
$$+ \quad + \quad - \quad - \quad + \quad - \quad - \quad - \quad + \quad \text{Heads/Tails Chain}$$

The "toss numbers" refer to the first toss of the coin, the second toss, the third toss, and so on, while the "heads/tails chain" presents the result of each toss: + stands for heads and − for tails.

The rationale for referring to this string of toss throws as a chain, whereas their results are a priori altogether independent (the second throw has the same fifty-fifty chance of showing up heads or tails, regardless of the result of the first throw), derives from the fact that we proceed to group the signs by pairs along the chain. There are four possible pair combinations: $+ +, - -, + -,$ and $- +$.

$$
\begin{array}{ccccccccc}
1 & 2 & 3 & 4 & 5 & 6 & 7 & 8 & 9 \quad \text{Toss Numbers} \\
\underline{+ \ +} & \underline{- \ -} & \underline{+ \ -} & \underline{- \ -} & + \quad \text{Heads/Tails Chain} \\
1 & & 3 & & 2 & & & 2 & \quad \text{Numeric Matrix Category}
\end{array}
$$

Let us assign the pair $+ +$ the number 1 (see the "numeric matrix category" line above). This is the first level of coding we are going to introduce, and it marks the origin of the symbolic system we are creating here; I will refer to this first level as our numeric matrix. The two alternating combinations ($+ -$ and $- +$) will be designated by the number 2. And the pair $- -$ will receive the designation 3 (table 2.1).

Table 2.1

| 1 | 2 | 3 |
|---|---|---|
| ++ | + −<br>− + | − − |

However, a still more chainlike aspect will result if we group the toss results by *overlapping* pairs.

$$
\begin{array}{c}
\quad\quad\quad \underline{\ \ 2\ \ } \\
\quad\quad \underline{\ \ 2\ \ } \\
\underline{+\ \ +}\ \ -\ \ -\ \ +\ \ -\ \ -\ \ -\ \ + \quad \text{Heads/Tails Chain} \\
\ 1\ \ \underline{\quad\quad} \\
\quad\quad 3
\end{array}
$$

In the above chain, we see that our first element is $+ +$, a combination we have decided to designate as 1; taking the second and third toss results, we have $+ -$, to be denoted as 2; the third and fourth toss results, $- -$, constitute a 3 combination; the fourth and fifth toss results, $- +$, a 2; and so on.

Following Lacan's notation (*Écrits* 1966, p. 47, n. 1), we can write these figures just below the heads/tails chain; here each numeric matrix category (1, 2, or 3) refers to the plus or minus sign directly above it, taken in conjunction with the plus or minus sign immediately to that sign's left.

$$
\begin{array}{ccccccccc}
+ & + & - & - & + & - & - & - & + \quad \text{Heads/Tails Chain} \\
& 1 & 2 & 3 & 2 & 2 & 3 & 3 & 2 \quad \text{Numeric Matrix Category}
\end{array}
$$

It is already clear at this point that a category 1 set of tosses ($+ +$) cannot be immediately followed in the lower line (i.e., the line representing category numbers) by a category 3 set, as the second throw in a category 1 is necessarily a plus, whereas the first throw in a category 3 has to be a minus. Similarly, though a category 2 can be followed by a 1, 2, or 3, a category 3 cannot be immediately followed by a category 1, for the former ends in a minus while the latter must begin with a plus.

We have thus already come up with *a way of grouping tosses* (a "symbolic matrix") *which prohibits certain combinations* (viz., 1 followed by 3, and 3 followed by 1). This obviously does not in the least require that a heads toss be followed by any one particular kind of toss: in reality, a heads may still just as easily be followed by another heads as by a tails. We have generated *an impossibility in our signifying chain*, even though we have not determined the outcome of any particular toss. This amounts to a spelling rule, akin to *i* before *e* except after *c* (except that the rule we have just created knows no exception); note that most rules of spelling and grammar concern the way letters and words are strung or *chained* together, dictating what can and cannot precede one letter or term and what can and cannot follow it.

Suppose, now, that we know that the first pair of tosses fell into category 1 and that the third pair was a category 3. The series can be easily reconstructed: $+ + - -$, and we can have no doubt but that the second pair of tosses fell into category 2. If we suppose anew that we began with a 1 (i.e., a category 1 pair) and that position four (i.e., the fourth overlapping pair) was occupied by a 1, there are clearly only two possibilities open to us (figure 2.1).

Figure 2.1

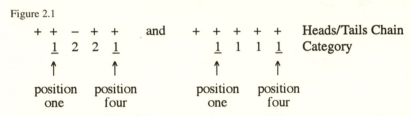

And in neither of them is a category 3 combination visible: a type 3 combination is, in fact, impossible here. It is also clear that, if there are not simply 1s in the "numeric chain," there must be *an even number of 2s* if we are to ever find a 1 in the chain again after the first one, the first 2 introducing a minus sign $(+ -)$, the second (or even-numbered 2) moving the chain back to positive from negative $(- +)$.

```
 +  +  -  -  +  -  +  +
 1  2  3  2  2  2  1  = four 2s.
 +  +  -  -  -  +  -  -  +  -  -  -  -  +  -  +  -  -  -  +  +
 1  2  3  3  2  2  3  2  2  3  3  3  3  2  2  2  2  3  3  2  1  =  ten 2s.
```

Here the chain prohibits the appearance of a second 1 until an even number of 2s has turned up. In this sense we may say that *the chain remembers or keeps track of its previous components.*

The example found in Lacan's afterword is far more complicated than the one I have provided here, as it groups the coin tosses into triplets instead of pairs, and proceeds to superimpose upon them a second symbolic matrix. The simpler 1,2,3 matrix described above

- results in impossibilities related to the *order* in which the category numbers can appear as well as to *which* of them can appear if certain positions are predefined, and
- records within itself or "remembers" its previous components. Thus we have at our disposal a simple symbolic coin-toss overlay which suits our needs. For it not only comports an elementary though consequent grammar, but a built-in memory function as well, primitive as it may be.[5]

A restriction in terms of possibility and impossibility has arisen, it seems, ex nihilo. Important too, though, is the *syntax* produced, which allows certain combinations and prohibits others. The similarities between this kind of apparatus and language will be explored further on.


## Randomness and Memory

Now what is the point of Lacan's ciphering? As I mentioned above, Lacan is interested, in Seminar II and the postface to the "Seminar on 'The Purloined Letter,'" in constructing a symbolic system that brings with it a syntax—a set of rules or laws—that is not inherent in the "pre-existing reality." *The resulting possibilities and impossibilities can thus be seen to derive from the way in which the symbolic matrix is constructed*, that is, the way it ciphers the event in question. It is not so much the fact of ciphering, in this particular instance, as the method of ciphering which gives rise to laws—syntactic laws—that were not "already there." The method of ciphering Lacan employs here is by no means the simplest imaginable, and a far simpler method yields no syntax whatsoever; but his method seems to significantly mimic the ciphering of natural languages and dream processes.[6]

Let us note another feature of the symbolic system Lacan develops. I have shown above that the numeric chains "keep track of" numbers, that in a certain sense they *count* them, not allowing one to appear before enough of the others, or certain combinations of the others, have joined the chain. This keeping track of or counting constitutes a type of memory: the past is recorded in the chain itself, determining what is yet to come. Lacan points out that "the remembering [*mémoration*] in question in the unconscious—and I mean the Freudian unconscious—is not the same as that assumed to be involved in memory, insofar as this latter would be the property of a living being" (*Écrits* 1966, p. 42).

The implication here is twofold: in the first place, grey matter, or the nervous system as a whole, is incapable of accounting for the *eternal and indestructible nature of unconscious contents*. Matter seems to behave in such a way as to necessarily lead to a gradual decay or decrease in the amplitude or quality of impressions. It cannot be the guarantor of their everlastingness. And in the second place, rather than being remembered by the individual (in an active way, i.e., with some sort of *subjective* participation), things are "remembered" for him or her by the signifying chain. As Lacan says in the "Seminar on 'The Purloined Letter' ": "Such is the case of the man who retreats to an island to forget, what? he has forgotten—such is the case of the minister who, by not using the letter, winds up forgetting it. . . . But the letter, no more than the neurotic's unconscious, does not forget him" (*Écrits* 1966, p. 34; *The Purloined Poe*, p. 47).

We see here a clear connection between the letter (or signifying chain) and the unconscious. The unconscious *cannot* forget, composed of "letters" working, as they do, in an autonomous, automatic way; it preserves in the present what has affected it in the past, eternally holding onto each and every element, remaining forever marked by all of them. "For the moment, the links of this [constituting order that is the symbolic] are—as concerns what Freud constructs regarding the indestructibility of what his unconscious conserves—the only ones that can be *suspected of doing the trick*" (*Écrits* 1966, p. 42), that is, of guaranteeing indestructibility.

## The Unconscious Assembles

This characterization of unconscious thought[7] was by no means a passing fancy of Lacan's, representative at best of his "structuralist" years. In Seminar XX, Lacan says that, in his vocabulary, "the letter designates an assemblage . . . [or rather] letters *make up* assemblages; not simply *designating* them, they *are* assemblages, they are to be taken as functioning as assemblages themselves" (p. 46). He later adds, "The unconscious is structured like the assemblages in question in set theory, which are like letters" (p. 47).

Freud has accustomed psychoanalysts to the notion that "thinking," as we commonly understand it, plays a far smaller role in the determination of human action than previously thought. We may believe, feel, and claim that we have done A for reason B; or when we seem unable to immediately explain our behavior, we grope around for ad hoc explanations: rationalizations. Psychoanalysis seems, in a sense, to intervene by asserting the existence of reason C which we had not even considered or had been deliberately ignoring. Not to mention the flood of ulterior motives D, E, and F which slowly but surely "raise their ugly heads" in the course of analytic work.

But this is to liken unconscious thought processes to conscious ones, whereas Lacan insists, instead, upon a dichotomy. Conscious thought is grounded in the realm of meaning, in a striving to make sense of the world. Lacan proposes that unconscious processes have little if anything whatsoever to do with meaning. We can, it seems, completely ignore the whole issue of meaning, that is, the whole of what Lacan calls the signified or signification, in discussing the unconscious.

According to Lacan, the unconscious is structured like a language, and a natural language (unlike speech) is structured like a formal language. As Jacques-Alain Miller says, "the structure of language is, in a radical sense, ciphering,"[8] the type of ciphering or coding Lacan engages in when he superimposes numeric and alphabetic matrices on chains of pluses and minuses (altogether akin to the type of ciphering used in the machine language "assembler" to go from open and closed circuit paths to something resembling a language with which one can program). To Lacan's mind, the unconscious consists in chains of quasi-mathematical inscriptions, and—borrowing a notion from Bertrand Russell, who in speaking of mathematicians said that the symbols they work with *don't mean anything*[9]—there is thus no point talking about the *meaning* of unconscious formations or productions.

The kind of truth "unveiled" by psychoanalytic work can thus be understood to have nothing whatsoever to do with meaning, and while Lacan's mathematical "games" may seem to be merely recreational, his belief was that an analyst gains a certain agility in working them through, in deciphering them, and in discovering the logic behind them. It is the kind of deciphering activity required by any and every encounter with the unconscious. Language in the unconscious, and as the unconscious, ciphers. Analysis thus entails a significant deciphering process that results in truth, not meaning.

Consider, for example, Lacan's enthusiasm in Seminar XI over Serge Leclair's reconstruction of the assemblage "Poordjeli" as the key to the whole configuration of unconscious desire and identification in one of his patients. Though letters themselves are not decomposed in this example, it is clear that, while we can provide glosses "accounting for" specific elements, the assemblage as a whole—for example, the order of its components and the logic of its construction—remains as impenetrable as a dream's navel. According to Lacan, Leclaire was able to "isolate the unicorn sequence [Poordjeli], not, as was suggested in the discussion [following his talk], in its dependence on meaning, but precisely in its irreducible and insane character as a chain of signifiers" (Seminar XI, p. 212). Here, as elsewhere in the same seminar, Lacan notes that interpretation does not so much aim at revealing meaning as at "reducing signifiers to their nonmeaning (lack of meaning) so as to find the determinants of the whole of the subject's behavior" (p. 212). Interpretation brings forth an irreducible signifier, "irreducible, signifying elements" (p.

250). What must be glimpsed by the analysand, beyond the meaning inherent in interpretation itself, is "the signifier—which has no meaning, and is irreducible and traumatic—to which he, as subject, is subjected" (p. 251).[10]

Let us consider a better known example: Freud's "Rat Man." As a child, the Rat Man identified with rats (*Ratten*) as biting creatures that are often treated cruelly by humans, he himself having been severely beaten by his father for having bitten his nurse. Certain ideas then become part of the "rat complex" due to meaning: rats can spread diseases such as syphilis, just like a man's penis. Hence rat = penis. But other ideas become grafted onto the rat complex due to the word *Ratten* itself, not its meanings: *Raten* means installments, and leads to the equation of rats and florins; *Spielratte* means gambler, and the Rat Man's father, having incurred a debt gambling, becomes drawn into the rat complex. Freud refers to these links as "verbal bridges" (SE X, p. 213); they have no meaning per se, deriving entirely from literal relations among words. Insofar as they give rise to symptomatic acts involving payment (for the pince-nez/father's debt), it is the signifier itself that subjugates the Rat Man, not meaning.

Let us assume that the latter overheard a snatch of his parents' conversation including *Spielratte*, and though he was still too young to understand it, it was nevertheless recorded, indelibly etched in his memory. There it took on a life of its own, forming links with other "purloined letters"—scenes witnessed and words overheard not intended for his eyes or ears. His unconscious was irremediably transformed by what he heard, and "what you hear is the signifier," not meaning (Seminar XX, p. 34). Here the signifier is not so much signify*ing*—devoted to making sense—as nonsensical substance (see chapter 3).

Meaning, in this example, like subjective involvement in the choice of a symptom (as discussed in chapter 1), is only constituted after the fact.

## Knowledge without a Subject

> Once the structure of language is recognized in the
> unconscious, what sort of subject can we conceive
> of for it?
> —Lacan, *Écrits*, p. 298

> There is perfectly well articulated knowledge for
> which no subject is, strictly speaking, responsible.
> —Lacan, Seminar XVII, p. 88

Now this way of conceptualizing the unconscious apparently leaves *no room for a subject of any kind*. There is a type of structure automatically and autonomously unfolding in/as the unconscious, and there is absolutely no need to postulate any kind of consciousness of this automatic movement (Lacan, in any case, breaks with the association, made by so many philosophers, of subjectivity and consciousness). The unconscious contains "indelible knowledge" which at the same time is "absolutely not subjectivized" (Seminar XXI, February 12, 1974).

The unconscious is not something one knows, but rather something that is known. What is unconscious is known *unbeknownst to* the "person" in question: it is not something one "actively," consciously grasps, but rather something which is "passively" registered, inscribed, or counted. And this unknown knowledge is locked into the connection between signifiers; it consists in this very connection. *This kind of knowledge has no subject, nor does it need one.*

And yet Lacan speaks constantly about *the* subject: the subject of the unconscious, of unconscious desire, the subject in its phantasmatic relation to object *a*, and so on. Where can the subject possibly fit in?

Before turning to that question, to be discussed in part 2 of this book, I take up in the next chapter the overriding importance of the symbolic order for speaking beings.

# 3

## The Creative Function of the Word:
## The Symbolic and the Real

THINKING always begins from our position within the symbolic order; in other words, we cannot but consider the supposed "time before the word" from within our symbolic order, using the categories and filters it provides. We may try to think ourselves back to a time before words, to some sort of presymbolic or prelinguistic moment in the development of *homo sapiens* or in our own individual development, but as long as we are thinking, language remains essential.

In order to conceive of that time, we give it a name: the real. Lacan tells us that "the letter kills": it kills the real which was *before* the letter, before words, before language. It is, of course, the letter itself—which, at the stage at which Lacan formulates this (1956, "Seminar on 'The Purloined Letter'"), is not distinguished from the signifier, words, or language—that informs us of its own lethal properties,[1] and thus of the real that would have been but for the letter's advent.

The real is, for example, an infant's body "before" it comes under the sway of the symbolic order, before it is subjected to toilet training and instructed in the ways of the world. In the course of socialization, the body is progressively written or overwritten with signifiers; pleasure is localized in certain zones, while other zones are neutralized by the word and coaxed into compliance with social, behavioral norms. Taking Freud's notion of polymorphous perversity to the extreme, we can view the infant's body as but one unbroken erogenous zone, there being no privileged zones, no areas in which pleasure is circumscribed at the outset.

So too, Lacan's real is without zones, subdivisions, localized highs and lows, or gaps and plenitudes: the real is a sort of unrent, undifferentiated fabric, woven in such a way as to be full everywhere, there being no space between the threads that are its "stuff."[2] It is a sort of smooth, seamless surface or space which applies as much to a child's body as to the whole universe. The division of the real into separate zones, distinct features, and contrasting structures is a result of the symbolic order, which, in a manner of speaking, *cuts into* the smooth facade of the real, creating divisions, gaps, and distinguishable entities and laying the real to rest, that is, drawing or sucking it into the symbols used to describe it, and thereby annihilating it.

Canceling out the real, the symbolic creates "reality," reality as that which is named by language and can thus be thought and talked about.[3] The "social construction of reality"[4] implies a world that can be designated and discussed with the words provided by a social group's (or subgroup's) language. What cannot be said in its language is not part of its reality; it does not *exist*, strictly speaking. In Lacan's terminology, existence is a product of language: language brings things into existence (makes them part of human reality), things which had no *existence* prior to being ciphered, symbolized, or put into words.[5]

The real, therefore, does not *exist*, since it precedes language; Lacan reserves a separate term for it, borrowed from Heidegger: it "ex-sists."[6] It exists outside of or apart from our reality. Obviously, insofar as we name and talk about the real and weave it into a theoretical discourse on language and the "time before the word," we draw it into language and thereby give a kind of existence to that which, in its very concept, has only ex-sistence (I shall explore this point further in chapter 8).

But we need not think in strictly temporal terms: the real need not be understood as merely *before* the letter, in the sense of disappearing altogether once a child has assimilated language (as if, in any case, a child could ever assimilate all of language, or all at once). The real is perhaps best understood as *that which has not yet been symbolized*, remains to be symbolized, or even resists symbolization; and it may perfectly well exist "alongside" and in spite of a speaker's considerable linguistic capabilities. In that sense, part of the psychoanalytic process clearly involves allowing an analysand to put into words that which has remained unsymbolized for him or her, to verbalize experiences which may have occurred before the analysand was able to think about them, speak of them, or formulate them in any way at all. The verbal apparatus at the analysand's disposal later in life enables the analysand to transform those earlier unspoken, never conceptualized or incompletely conceptualized experiences by talking—hence the "talking cure," as Anna O. called it back in the earliest days of psychoanalysis.

Lacan's distinction between reality and the real allows us to isolate an ideological or ethical difference between certain forms of psychoanalysis and Lacanian psychoanalysis. Every person's *reality* differs by the mere fact that every cultural and religious group, subculture, family, and set of friends develops its own words, expressions, and idiosyncratic meanings. And every analysand's reality is colored or permeated by notions about the world—about human nature, the gods, magic, business, education, music, and so on—that may in no way coincide with any particular analyst's notions. Now while certain psychoanalysts have taken it upon themselves to "straighten their patients out" regarding reality—attempting to influence or change their beliefs about a wide range of subjects—Lacan insists again and again that it is an analyst's job to intervene in the patient's real, not in the patient's view of reality.[7]

From a Lacanian perspective, the presupposition of psychoanalysis has always been that the symbolic can have an impact upon the real, ciphering and thereby transforming or reducing it. Depicted schematically, the symbolic bars the real, overwriting and erasing it:

$$\frac{\text{Symbolic}}{\text{Real}}$$

## Trauma

One of the faces of the real that we deal with in psychoanalysis is trauma. If we think of the real as everything that has yet to be symbolized, language no doubt never completely transforms the real, never drains all of the real into the symbolic order; a residuum is always left. In analysis, we are not interested in just any old residuum, but in that residual experience that has become a stumbling block to the patient. The goal of analysis is not to exhaustively symbolize every last drop of the real, for that would make of analysis a truly infinite process, but rather to focus on those scraps of the real which can be considered to have been traumatic. By getting an analysand to dream, daydream, and talk, however incoherently, about a traumatic "event," we make him or her connect it up with words, bring it into relation with ever more signifiers.

To what end? Trauma implies fixation or blockage. Fixation always involves something which is not symbolized, language being that which allows for substitution and displacement—the very antithesis of fixation.[8] To oversimplify momentarily, imagine a man fascinated by blue eyes, his mother having had blue eyes: while no two sets of eyes are ever absolutely identical, and no two shades of blue either, for that matter, the word "blue" allows him to equate his mother's blue eyes with a partner's blue eyes and thus to transfer his fascination with the former to the latter. Language allows for such equations, and thus for the substitution of one loved object for another or the displacement of cathexis from one object to another. When, as is the case in melancholia, no such substitution or displacement is possible, fixation is at work, and some part of the real remains to be symbolized. By inciting the analysand to say it and bring it into relation with ever more signifiers, it undergoes "dialectization,"[9] being drawn into the dialectic or movement of the analysand's discourse and set in motion.

This is a fairly simplistic account that does not attempt to account for the constitution of trauma ex post facto or to distinguish between fixation and the fundamental fantasy, but it can perhaps serve our purposes momentarily, allowing us to begin with the straightforward model in table 3.1.

We can think of the real as being *progressively symbolized* in the course of a child's life, less and less of that "first," "original" real (call it $R_1$) being left

Table 3.1

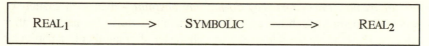

behind, though it can never all be drained away, neutralized, or killed. *There is thus always a remainder which persists alongside the symbolic.*

We can, however, also show that the symbolic order itself gives rise to a "second-order" real. One way of describing this process is found in a part of Lacan's postface to the "Seminar on 'The Purloined Letter'" that was left in abeyance in the preceding chapter, the part where Lacan introduces the cause.[10] For the symbolic order, as modeled by Lacan's numeric and alphabetic matrices, produces something, in the course of its autonomous operation, that goes beyond the symbolic order itself.

I will try to show how in just a moment, but note first that this allows us to postulate two different levels of the real: (1) a real before the letter, that is, a presymbolic real, which, in the final analysis, is but our own hypothesis ($R_1$), and (2) a real after the letter which is characterized by impasses and impossibilities due to the relations among the elements of the symbolic order itself ($R_2$), that is, which is generated by the symbolic.[11]

In what does this real "after the letter" consist? It has several faces, one of which I will illustrate on the basis of the 1,2,3 chain discussed in chapter 2. In the simplified model of overlapping symbol application, we saw that a 3 could not directly follow a 1. Thus in the position immediately following the 1, we can view 3 as a sort of a *residue*: it cannot be used in the circuit and amounts to a simple leftover or scrap. At every step, at least one number is excluded or pushed aside; we can thus say that the chain works around it, that is, that the chain forms by circumventing it, tracing thereby its contour. Lacan calls these excluded numbers or symbols the *caput mortuum* of the process, likening them thereby to the remainder left at the bottom of a test tube or beaker as an alchemist attempted to create something worthy from something lowly.

The *caput mortuum* contains what the chain does not contain; it is in a sense the other of the chain. The chain is as unequivocally determined by what it excludes as by what it includes, by what is within it as by what is without. The chain never ceases to *not* write the numbers that constitute the *caput mortuum* in certain positions, being condemned to ceaselessly write something else or say something which keeps avoiding this point, as though this point were the truth of everything the chain produces as it beats around the bush. One could go so far as to say that what, of necessity, remains outside the chain *causes* what is inside; something must, structurally speaking, be pushed outside for there to even be an inside.[12]

The excluded symbols or letters comprising the *caput mortuum* take on a certain materiality, akin to that of the letter the minister swipes from the queen in the story of "The Purloined Letter," and it is less what the letters say—and *insofar as they are letters they do not say anything*—than their matter- or *object*-like nature which has an effect on one character in the narrative after another. The letter in the tale fixates one character after another in a particular position: it is a real object, signifying nothing.

The "first" real, that of trauma and fixation, returns in a sense in the form of a center of gravity around which the symbolic order is condemned to circle, without ever being able to hit it. It gives rise to impossibilities within the chain itself (a given word cannot appear randomly, but only after certain other words) and creates a sort of lump that the chain is forced to skirt. This will constitute for us a first approach to the "second" real, and to Lacan's concept of cause.

## Interpretation Hits the Cause

Lacan's theory of interpretation is based, to some extent, on a formulation similar to that of the *caput mortuum*: an analysand speaking in the analytic setting is often unable to say, formulate, or come out with certain things; certain words, expressions, or thoughts are unavailable to him or her at a particular moment and he or she is forced to keep circling around them, beating around the bush, as it were, never enunciating what he or she senses to be at issue. The analysand's discourse traces a contour around that which it hovers about, circles, and skirts. Those words or thoughts may become accessible to the analysand in time, in the course of analysis, but they may also be introduced by the analyst in the form of an interpretation. That is what Lacan means when he says that "interpretation hits the cause": it hits that around which the analysand is revolving without being able to "put it into words."

What is unspeakable from the analysand's vantage point or position need not be unspeakable from the analyst's. Through the analyst's intervention, the analysand may be able to speak the signifier to which he or she as subject had been subjected, as Lacan puts it. By interpolating or bringing the analysand to pronounce the word or words (or conflation of words: assemblage) around which he or she had been circling, that inaccessible, untouchable, immovable cause is impacted, the avoidance of that absent center is mitigated, and the cause is on the road to "subjectivization" (this term will be explained in chapter 5).

That does not necessarily imply that the cause—the traumatic cause—was a word or an expression (though it may well be a formulation the analysand is loath to express); nevertheless, the analyst may jolt the analysand into taking a leap towards the word: perhaps but a garbled or mumbled sound at first, speech with no apparent meaning, but a first step towards symbolization notwithstanding.

Garbled speech and conflated words bring us closer to the "stuff" of language than well articulated phrases, and serve as something of a bridge between the symbolic and the real. For while many sounds humans can produce have no socially recognized meaning, they may nevertheless have an impact: they may be libidinally cathected and have a deeper effect on the subject than words can ever tell.[13] They may have a certain materiality and weight, and Lacan in fact includes phonemes on his multifarious list of causes.

## Incompleteness of the Symbolic Order: The (W)hole in the Other

Let us consider another tack Lacan takes regarding the "second" real described above. The real is also associated by Lacan with logical paradoxes, such as the anomalous catalogue of all catalogues that do not include themselves, to which we shall turn momentarily.[14]

It should first be pointed out, however, that the image provided for the symbolic order in chapter 1, a circle, is but a kind of shorthand, and as such misleading. For what could it possibly mean to speak of the set of *all* signifiers?

As soon as we attempt to designate such a set, we add a new signifier to the list: the "Other" (with a capital "O"). That signifier is not yet included within the set of all signifiers (figure 3.1).

Figure 3.1

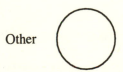

Let us include that new signifier within the set. We change the set in so doing and can now justifiably rename it, as it is no longer the same set. Suppose we call it the "complete Other" (figure 3.2).

Figure 3.2

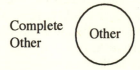

This new name, however, is not yet part of the set. To include it would involve changing the set, and once again call for a new name (figure 3.3).

The process can be repeated endlessly, proving that *the supposed set of all signifiers can never be complete*. If nothing else, there is always the very name

Figure 3.3

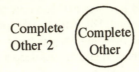

Complete
Other 2

Complete
Other

of the set that forever remains outside of the set. If we try to imagine a set that includes its own name, we find ourselves in a situation whereby *the set includes itself* as one of its own elements, which is a paradoxical result, at least on the face of it.

The argument here can be related to Gödel's theorem concerning the incompleteness of arithmetic, generalizable (in theory) to all axiomatic systems: an axiomatic system can never decide upon the validity of certain statements that can be formally expressed within it using the definitions and axioms that constitute it. Such systems are thus structurally untotalizable, as is language (i.e., the Other) in Lacan's view, for the set of all signifiers does not exist. The attempt to axiomatize various fields (and Lacan can be seen as undertaking the first steps of axiomatization with his introduction of the mathemes $S_1$, $S_2$, $\mathbb{S}$, $a$, $S(\mathbb{A})$, etc.) is usually made in order to account for every possible statement that can be made in those fields. Lacan's position here is that something anomalous *always* shows up in language, something unaccountable, unexplainable: an aporia. These aporias point to the presence within or influence on the symbolic of the real. I refer to them as *kinks in the symbolic order*.

## Kinks in the Symbolic Order

An argument Bertrand Russell puzzled over in the early twentieth century constitutes just such an aporia. He attempted to examine the status of a catalogue of all catalogues that do not include themselves as entries.[15] An art catalogue which mentions itself in a long list of other art catalogues is perfectly imaginable, for example, and there are no doubt some which do. Consider, however, the dilemma of someone trying to create a catalogue which includes only those catalogues which make *no* mention of themselves within their own covers (in other words, a catalogue would be selected only if it did *not* include its own title in the list it provides of other catalogues). Should that person include the title of the catalogue he or she is making in the latter's list? If he or she decides not to include it, then it too will be a catalogue which does not contain itself as an entry and which therefore should be included. If, on the other hand, he or she decides to include it, then it will be a catalogue which *does* include itself as an entry and which therefore should not be included.[16] What is the catalogue maker to do?

The precise status of the catalogue of all catalogues that do not include themselves ultimately remains paradoxical: it is impossible to ascertain what it contains and what it does not. Lacan's second-order real—the Lacanian cause—is of precisely that nature. Its status is always akin to that of a logical exception or paradox.

## Structure versus Cause

The aspects of the cause outlined above constitute but one approach to the concept of cause (and of object *a* as cause) in Lacanian theory, and I shall supply many others in the course of this book. Here I would like to ensure that two levels are carefully distinguished, those of "structure" and "causation." One could, certainly, consider them to be ultimately equivalent to two different levels of structure or two separate levels of causation, but one would then be likely to miss the point of their radical heterogeneity.

There is, on the one hand, the level of the *automatic functioning of the signifying chain*, illustrated by the 1,2,3 matrix discussed above. (Note here that Lacan translates Freud's *Wiederholungszwang*—generally translated as "repetition compulsion" in English—as *automatisme de répétition*, repetition automatism or repetition automaton.)

There is, on the other, *that which interrupts the smooth functioning of this automatism*, namely, the cause. Working in isolation, the signifying chain seems to need neither a subject nor an object; but, almost in spite of itself, it produces an object and subjugates a subject.[17]

Lacan parts ways with structuralism here, as structuralists attempt to explain everything in terms of the first level, that is, in terms of a more or less mathematically determinate combinatory which plays itself out without any reference whatsoever to subjects or objects. While structure plays a very important role in Lacan's work—and we have begun to see to what extent it pervades conscious and unconscious "thought processes"—it is never the whole story at any point in Lacan's development.

In Seminar X, Lacan associates the supposed progress of science (and structuralism's scientific pretensions were rarely kept secret) with our increasing inability to think the category "cause." Continually filling in the "gap" between cause and effect, science progressively eliminates the content of the concept "cause," events being viewed as leading smoothly, in accordance with well-known "laws," to other events. Science, attempting to suture the subject (as we shall see in chapter 10)—that is, trying to evict subjectivity from its field—tends also towards a suturing of the cause. The challenge of Lacanian psychoanalysis is, in part, to maintain and further explore these two primordial concepts, however paradoxical they may seem.

I turn now, in part 2, to the role assigned by Lacan to the subject and the subject's situation "outside" signification.

# Part Two

## THE LACANIAN SUBJECT

Something with the essential property of defining the conjunction of identity and difference—that is what seems most appropriate to me to structurally account for the function of the subject.
   —Lacan, Seminar XIII, January 12, 1966

Once the subject himself comes into being, he owes it to a certain nonbeing upon which he raises up his being.
   —Lacan, Seminar II, p. 192

# 4

## The Lacanian Subject

EVEN WHEN structuralism was alive and well, subjectivity was often taken to be incompatible with the notion of structure. Structure seemed to exclude the very possibility of the existence of a subject, and the assertion of subjectivity seemed to undermine a structuralist position. With the advent of "poststructuralism," the very concept of subjectivity seems to be have become unfashionable, and Lacan is one of the few contemporary thinkers to have devoted considerable effort to its elaboration.

Lacan, while dubbed a "structuralist" by certain people and a "poststructuralist" by others, maintains and defends *both* concepts—structure and subject—in a rigorous theoretical framework. Nevertheless, as he strips the subject of so many of the characteristics usually attributed to it in Western thought and relentlessly exposes the workings of structure in psychoanalytic and literary contexts, it is not always easy to see what role is left to the subject in Lacan's work. The difficulty for the reader of Lacan's texts is compounded by the fact that his attempt to isolate the subject takes many different forms at different points in his teaching, not all of which seem to converge on any easily recognizable conception of subjectivity.

I will not try to *demonstrate* the existence of the Lacanian subject, for no such demonstration is possible. As Lacan says in Seminar XXIII, "the subject is never more than supposed"; in other words, the subject is never more than an assumption on our part. It does, however, seem to be a necessary assumption for Lacan, a construct without which psychoanalytic experience cannot be accounted for. In that sense its status is similar to that of what Freud calls the "second phase" of the fantasy "A Child is Being Beaten," the "second phase" being the thought "I am being beaten by my father." Freud remarks, "This second phase is the most important and the most momentous of all. But we may say of it in a certain sense that it has never had a real existence. It is never remembered, it has never succeeded in becoming conscious. It is a construction of analysis, but it is no less a necessity on that account" (SE XVII, p. 185).

My hope is to lend credence to this Lacanian construct by discussing a whole series of tacks Lacan takes in his endeavor to close in on it from the 1950s on, thereby indicating where structure leaves off and subjectivity begins. A number of illustrations and metaphors will be provided which I hope will furnish a basic grasp of the notion; its more theoretical underpinning will be explained further on. I will begin my discussion with an indication of what the Lacanian subject is not, as it seems to me that nothing should be taken for granted in understanding Lacan's use of the term.

## The Lacanian Subject Is Not the "Individual" or Conscious Subject of Anglo-American Philosophy

It should be mentioned right from the outset that, whereas in English, one would usually speak of an analysand as a "patient," an "individual," or (in certain schools of psychology) as a "client," in French one would quite naturally refer to him or her as a "subject." There is nothing specifically conceptual or theoretical about the use of the term "subject" in such contexts; it refers no more to the Lacanian subject I will attempt to isolate here than does the appellation *le malade*, the patient (or more literally translated, the sick person, the person who is ill). Such nontheoretical terms are used more or less interchangeably in Lacan's early work in particular.

The Lacanian subject is neither the individual nor what we might call the conscious subject (or the consciously thinking subject), in other words, the subject referred to by most of analytic philosophy. The consciously thinking subject is, by and large, indistinguishable from the ego as understood in the school of ego psychology, which is prevalent in the same countries in which analytic philosophy predominates. This should come as no surprise: dominant conceptions in most cultures cross disciplinary boundaries.

Now the ego, according to Lacan, arises as a crystallization or sedimentation of ideal images, tantamount to a fixed, reified object with which a child learns to identify, which a child learns to identify with him or herself. These ideal images may consist of those the child sees of him or herself in a mirror, and they are ideal in the sense that, at the stage at which mirror images begin to play an important role (six to eighteen months),[1] the child is quite uncoordinated and truly but an unorganized jumble of sensations and impulses, the mirror image presenting a unified surface appearance similar to that of the child's far more capable, coordinated, and powerful parents.

Such images are invested, cathected, and internalized by a child because his or her parents make a great deal of them, insisting to their infant that the image in the mirror *is* him or her: "Yes, baby, that's you!" Other ideal images are similarly assimilated by the child which stem from the image of him or herself reflected back from the parental Other: "a good girl" or a "bad girl," "a model son," and so on. Such "images" derive from how the parental Other "sees" the child and are thus linguistically structured. Indeed, it is the symbolic order that brings about the internalization of mirror and other images (e.g., photographic images), for it is primarily due to the parents' reaction to such images that they become charged, in the child's eyes, with libidinal interest or value—which is why mirror images are not of great interest to the child prior to about six months of age, in other words, prior to the functioning of language in the child (which occurs well before the child is able to speak).[2]

Once internalized, these various images fuse, in a manner of speaking, into a vast global image which the child comes to take for him or her *self*; this *self-image* can, of course, be added to in the course of a child's life, new images being grafted upon the old. In general, it is this crystallization of images which allows for a coherent "sense of self" (or does not allow for it in cases in which the images are too contradictory to fuse in any way), and a great deal of our attempt to "make sense" of the world around us involves juxtaposing what we see and hear with this internalized self-image: How does what happens reflect upon us? Where do we fit in? Is it a challenge to our view of ourselves?

This self or ego is thus, as Eastern philosophy has been telling us for millennia, a construct, a mental object, and though Freud grants it the status of an agency (*Instanz*), in Lacan's version of psychoanalysis the ego is clearly not an active agent, the agent of interest being the unconscious. Rather than qualifying as a seat of agency or activity, the ego is, in Lacan's view, the seat of fixation and narcissistic attachment. Moreover, it inevitably contains "false images," in that mirror images are always inverted images (involving a right-left reversal), and in that the "communication" which leads to the internalization of linguistically structured ideal "images"—such as "You're a model son"—is, like all communication, prone to miscommunication: the son may understand/misunderstand that appraisal in terms of model cars and planes, viewing himself thereafter as but a miniaturized, plastic version of the real thing, instead of a genuine son. The point of analysis is not to strive to give the analysand a "true" or correct image of him or her self, for the ego is by its very nature a distortion, an error, a repository of misunderstanding.

While the ego or self is what we generally refer to when we say "*I* think that . . ." or "*I'm* the kind of person who . . . ," that "I" is anything but the Lacanian subject: it is no more than the subject of the statement.

## The Lacanian Subject Is Not the Subject of the Statement

In the late 1950s and early 1960s, Lacan set out to pinpoint the subject as precisely as possible, and seemed to hold out for himself a hope that *a signifier of the subject* could be found in statements, that is, in what is said. He was looking for a precise manifestation of the subject in discourse, and began by considering the work of grammarians and linguists concerning the subject of a sentence.

Lacan makes explicit reference on a number of occasions to Roman Jakobson's paper on "shifters."[3] In that paper, Jakobson presents the concept of *code* as the set of signifiers used in speaking or writing—in a sense what Lacan calls the "treasure" or "battery" of signifiers—and the concept of message as what a speaker in fact says.

Jakobson points out that there are: (1) messages that refer to other messages—quotations, for example, in which a previous message is included in a current one (message ⟹ message); (2) messages that refer to the code—as, for example, "'puppy' designates a young dog," which provides the meaning of an element of the code, in other words, its definition (message ⟹ code); (3) elements of the code that refer to the code itself, such as proper names, for "'Jerry' refers to a person named Jerry"—that name designates whoever it is that bears or is called by that name (code ⟹ code).[4] Lastly, Jakobson points out that one can find (4) elements in a code that refer to the message, the example he provides being that of personal pronouns, such as "I," "you," "he," "she," and so on (code ⟹ message). The meaning of these latter elements cannot be defined without reference to the messages in which they appear, "I" designating the message sender and "you" the message receiver or addressee. Borrowing Jespersen's term,[5] Jakobson refers to these elements as "shifters," since what they designate changes or shifts with each new message.

Jakobson's four combinations—quotations, definitions, proper names, and shifters—exhaust the possibilities offered by the concepts code and message, but do not purport to cover all parts of speech, as the vast majority of these latter are simply elements of the code. Nouns, verbs, prepositions, and so on are part and parcel of the code.

Qualifying as a shifter, the grammatical subject of a sentence, such as "I am the kind of person who . . . ," designates the message sender, and insofar as it can be said to signify that message-sending subject, it signifies the ego: the conscious subject who thinks of him or her self as X and not Y, as generous and not miserly, as open-minded and not bigoted, and so on. The personal pronoun "I" designates the person who identifies his or her self with a specific ideal image. Thus the ego is what is represented by the subject of the statement. What then of the agency or instance that interrupts the ego's fine statements, or botches them up?

## The Lacanian Subject Appears Nowhere in What Is Said

Ever seeking a precise manifestation of the subject in discourse, in the early 1960s Lacan often attempted to peg the subject's appearance to the French word *ne*, literally "not," one half of the French *ne pas*, but used in many cases alone, not so much to negate in a full-fledged way (though *ne* alone suffices to signify negation when used with *pouvoir*) as to do something a bit vaguer, which Damourette and Pichon call introducing "discordance."[6] In certain expressions, the isolated use of this supposedly expletive *ne* is grammatically necessary or at least more correct and more forceful than leaving it out (e.g., *avant qu'il n'arrive, pourvu qu'il ne soit arrivé, craindre qu'il ne vienne*), but it seems to introduce a certain hesitation, ambiguity, or uncertainty into the utterance in which it appears, as if to suggest that the speaker is denying the very thing he is asserting, afraid of the very thing he claims to wish, or wishing for the very thing he seems to fear. In such cases, we get the impression that the speaker *both wants and does not want* the event in question to take place or the person in question to show up.

In English we have a somewhat similar situation with the word "but" in expressions like "I can't help but think that . . . ," meaning "I can't help thinking that . . . ," where the "but" seems almost superfluous—though if we translate this expression as "I can't stop myself from thinking that . . . ," it slips towards the double negative "I can't not think that. . . ." "But" often has the meaning of "only," "simply," or "just," yet in certain expressions it seems to go beyond these meanings, taking on a connotation of negation which can be confusing in certain circumstances even to native speakers, for example, "I can't but not wonder at his complacency," "I can't but not suspect him of having done it; after all he is my best friend," "I can't but imagine he won't call." What allows us to clearly distinguish the meaning of "I can but hope he won't call" from that of "I cannot but hope he won't call"? The *Oxford English Dictionary* provides a plethora of examples of this highly polyvalent three-letter signifier, which can be used as a conjunction, preposition, adverb, adjective, or noun. Among those which interest us here, one finds:

> "You say you are tied hand and foot. You will never be but that in London."
> "Not but that I should have gone if I had had the chance."
> "I will not deny but that it is a difficult thing."
> "I cannot deny but that it would be easy."
> "She cannot miss but see us."
> "I do not fear but that my grandfather will recover."[7]

A conflict seems to be played out in such expressions between a conscious or ego discourse, and another "agency" which takes advantage of the "possibility" offered by English grammar (and French grammar in the case of *ne*) to manifest itself. This other agency, this non-ego or unconscious "discourse," interrupts the former—almost saying "No!"—much in the same way as does a slip of the tongue. Lacan suggests that, in such cases, we can take the French *ne*—and I would suggest that in English we can take the somewhat ambiguous, or at least at times confusing, use of "but"—as *signifying* the speaking or enunciating subject.[8] Why as "signifying"? "But" here is not the *name* of the subject of enunciation; rather, it points to a sort of "no-saying," a saying-"No" (Lacan's term is *dit-que-non*).

This "but" is a very strange bird, so strange indeed that there may be no other example like it in the whole English language, nor any other example like *ne* in the French language (cf. *non* in Italian).

Can we see any way of categorizing the word "but" as used in this kind of "no-saying"? The word is clearly part of the code, and insofar as it appears in the message, it seems to say something about the message and, more precisely, about the speaker. But instead of simply designating *who* is speaking, it seems to tell us something about the speaker, in other words, that he or she is not entirely in agreement with what he or she is saying. It seems to point to an ambivalent speaker who says yes and no at the same time, who while saying one thing, insinuates another.

Whereas a shifter is the grammatical subject of the statement, the word "but" is a sort of "nay-saying" that occurs in the act of speaking, that is, during enunciation. "No!" is said, and Lacan can be seen, in a sense, to be breaking down such messages or statements into two parts (figure 4.1).

Figure 4.1

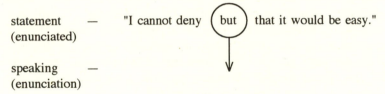

The concepts "code" and "message" do not suffice here; to qualify the term "but" in this instance, we are forced to refer to a sort of interference between the enunciated and enunciation, in other words, between that which is stated (the "content") and the very act of stating or enunciating.

The only subject Lacan allots to the statement is the conscious subject of the enunciated, represented here by the personal pronoun "I." To qualify this subject, we need look no further than the linguistic categories code and message, that is, no further than strictly structural categories. The subject of the statement, "I," is a shifter: an element of the code that refers to the message.

The word "but" remains in a class by itself, announcing the unconscious subject of enunciation, and thereby showing that the subject is split—of two minds, so to speak, for and against, conscious and unconscious. Slips of the tongue also prove that there are two levels, but the Lacan of the early 1960s suggests that it is only in the case of *ne* (and "but") that we seem to have constant or regular signifiers of the subject—regular in that they appear regularly and often tag this "other" subject. Needless to say, many expressions in French and English that employ *ne* and "but" have become formulaic and fixed over time, to such a degree that one is virtually obliged to use them in tandem with certain other words (in French, for example, the verb *craindre* almost always requires one to use *ne* in the same breath). Nevertheless, every speaker in some sense chooses such pat expressions from the variety of ways of "saying the same thing" provided by the language in question.

## The Fleetingness of the Subject

Now this "other" subject—this enunciating subject signified by "but" in certain statements—is *not* something which or someone who has some sort of permanent existence: it only appears when a propitious occasion presents itself. It is *not* some kind of underlying substance or substratum (*hupokeimenon* or *subjectum*).[9]

The unconscious as a continual playing out of a signifying chain excluded from consciousness (as described in chapter 2 and appendices 1 and 2), in which knowledge of a certain kind is embodied, is permanent in nature; in other words, it subsists throughout an individual's life. Yet its subject is in no sense permanent or constant. The unconscious as chain is not the same as the *subject* of the unconscious.

In his "Seminar on 'The Purloined Letter,'" Lacan states that a signifier marks the cancellation of what it signifies: *ne* and "but" sign the death sentence of the *subject of the unconscious*. The latter subsists only long enough to protest, to say "No." Once the subject has said his or her piece, what he or she has said usurps his or her place; the signifier replaces him or her; he or she vanishes. It is in that sense that we can say that *ne* and "but" are signifiers of the subject. The subject, as represented by Lacan's symbol $\$$ (S for "subject," / for "barred": the subject as barred by language, as alienated within the Other), vanishes "beneath" or "behind" the signifier *ne* (designated here by $S_1$—a first signifier):

$$\frac{S_1}{\$}$$ (substitution of a signifier, $S_1$, for the barred subject, $\$$)

That signifier takes the subject's place, standing in for the subject who has now vanished. *This subject has no other being than as a breach in discourse.* The subject of the unconscious manifests itself in daily life as a fleeting irruption of something foreign or extraneous. Temporally speaking, the subject appears only as a pulsation, an occasional impulse or interruption that immediately dies away or is extinguished, "expressing itself," as it does, by means of the signifier.

## The Freudian Subject

This provisional "definition" of the subject as *breach* applies, however, more specifically to what one might call the "Freudian subject" than to the Lacanian subject.

In his early study of Freud's *The Interpretation of Dreams*, *The Psychopathology of Everyday Life*, and *Jokes and Their Relation to the Unconscious*, Lacan accustoms us to the idea of something which "surges forth," as he says, at a particular conjuncture. In slips of the tongue, as in bungled actions and parapraxes of all kinds, some sort of alien *intention* seems to arrive on the scene or break its way in. Freud leads us to associate such intrusions with the unconscious, and thus it is quite natural that we attribute some sort of intentionality, agency, or even subjectivity to it. We could provisionally consider this intruder as being, in a sense, "the Freudian subject." Freud, of course, never introduces such a category, but I will use it here as a sort of shorthand for talking about a Freudian approach to the subject of the unconscious.

For Freud at one stage makes the unconscious into a full-fledged agency (*Instanz*), an agency seemingly endowed with its own intentions and will—a sort of second consciousness built, in some ways, on the model of the first. While Lacan certainly presents the unconscious as that which interrupts the normal flow of events, he never makes an agency of the unconscious; it remains a discourse divorced from consciousness and subjective involvement— the Other's discourse—even as it interrupts the ego's discourse that is based on a false sense of self. To attribute subjectivity to Freud's unconscious as a breach, interruption, or irruption in discourse and other "intentional" activities in no way accounts for the specificity of Lacan's subject.[10] Who then is the subject of the unconscious, and how can it be situated?

Before answering that question directly, let us continue to discern what that subject is not.

## The Cartesian Subject and Its Inverse

One of the things that is so unusual about the Freudian subject is that it surges forth only to disappear almost instantaneously. There is nothing substantial about this subject; it has no *being*, no substratum or permanence in time, in short nothing we are accustomed to look for when speaking of subjects. We have a sort of flash in the pan, and then it is over.

Lacan points out that Descartes' subject—the cogito—has a similarly short-lived existence. The Cartesian subject concludes that he *is* every time he says to himself, "I am thinking."[11] He must repeat to himself the words "I am thinking" in order to be able to convince himself that he exists. And as soon as he stops repeating those words, his conviction inevitably evaporates. Descartes is able to secure more permanent being for his subject by introducing God—the guarantor of so many things in the Cartesian universe—but Lacan focuses his analysis on the punctual, evanescent nature of the Cartesian subject.

I will use two circles to illustrate what Descartes can be understood to have done here.[12] He conceptualizes a point at which thinking and being overlap: when the Cartesian subject says to himself, "I am thinking," being and thinking coincide momentarily (figure 4.2). It is the fact that he thinks that serves as the foundation for his being; therein he joins thought to the speaking subject "I."

Figure 4.2

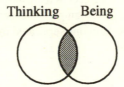

To Lacan's mind, such a view is rather utopian. The subject, as he understands the term, cannot take refuge in an idyllic moment where thought and being coincide but is, rather, forced to choose one or the other. He can "have" either thought or being, but never both at the same time. Figure 4.3 shows how one might schematize the Lacanian subject.

Figure 4.3

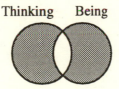

Why does Lacan thus turn Descartes' subject inside out, employing everything the cogito is not? Well, for one, Lacan's view of thought, like Freud's, revolves around unconscious thought, not the conscious thought studied by Descartes the philosopher. Freud generally associates conscious thought with *rationalization*, and Lacan hardly grants it any more elevated a status.

Secondly, Descartes' subject who says "I" corresponds to the level of the ego, a constructed self taken to be the master of its own thoughts and whose thoughts are believed to correspond to "external reality." Such a one-dimensional self believes that it is the author of its own ideas and thus has no qualms about affirming "*I* think." This Cartesian subject is characterized by what Lacan calls "false being" (Seminar XV), and this false being manifests itself every time an analysand says, "I'm the kind of person who's independent and free-thinking"; or "I did what I did because it was the magnanimous thing to do, and I always strive to be not only fair but generous." A fixed self is posited in such statements, the unconscious being rejected; it is as though such an analysand were saying to his or her analyst, "I can tell you all about myself because *I know*. I don't kid myself, I know where I stand."

While thus beginning with the punctual (or pointlike) Cartesian subject, that is, the fleeting coincidence of thinking and being, Lacan turns Descartes on his head: ego thinking is mere conscious rationalization (the ego's attempt to legitimate blunders and unintentional utterances by fabricating after-the-fact explanations which agree with the ideal self-image), and the being thus engendered can only be categorized as false or fake. Lacan thus seems to hold out for us some sort of prospect of a subject with true or real being that would be diametrically opposed to the false being of the ego, but this is not ultimately the case. The Lacanian subject remains separated from being, except in a sense that I shall come to further on.

## Lacan's Split Subject

Keeping in mind Lacan's own use of the term "thinking" to refer to unconscious thought as it unfolds in isolation from subjectivity (as discussed in chapter 2), let us consider one of Lacan's clearest graphic illustrations of what he calls the split or divided subject. It appears in Seminars XIV and Seminar XV and is presented here in figure 4.4.

Figure 4.4

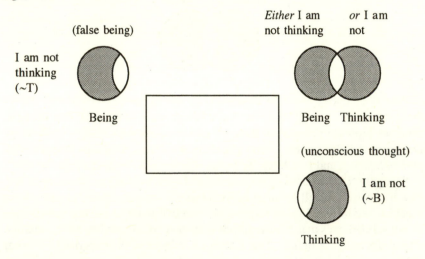

This schema will be discussed at length in the course of this chapter and chapter 6. Here I shall confine myself to noting some of its most striking features. The initial position in the schema (upper right-hand corner) provides one of Lacan's "definitions" of his subject: "either I am not thinking or I am not"—the second "am" to be taken in the absolute sense of "I am beingless." The either/or alternative means that one is obliged to situate oneself in some other corner of this schema. The path of least resistance, so to speak, is to refuse the unconscious (to refuse to pay attention to the thoughts unfolding in the unconscious), a sort of indulgence in false being (upper left-hand corner). Analysis, however, requires the individual to forego, as far as possible, this false being, to let unconscious thought have full sway.

The subject is split between ego (upper left) and unconscious (lower right), between conscious and unconscious, between an ineluctably false sense of self and the automatic functioning of language (the signifying chain) in the unconscious.

Our first attempt, then, to say what the Lacanian subject is comes down to the following: *The subject is nothing but this very split.* Lacan's variously termed "split subject," "divided subject," or "barred subject"—all written with the same symbol, $S$—consists entirely in the fact that a speaking being's two "parts" or avatars share no common ground: they are radically separated (the ego or false being requiring a refusal of unconscious thoughts, unconscious thought having no concern whatsoever for the ego's fine opinion of itself).

This momentous split is a product of the functioning of language in us as we first begin to speak as children. It is equivalent to what I have been referring to as our alienation in language (discussed in detail in chapter 5), and Lacan takes his lead here from Freud's concept of *Spaltung*, as set forth in his 1938 paper "*Die Ichspaltung im Abwehrvorgang*," translated in the Standard Edition as "Splitting of the Ego in the Process of Defence," but better rendered as "Splitting of the I."

The splitting of the I into ego (false self) and unconscious brings into being a surface, in a sense, with two sides: one that is exposed and one that is hidden. Though the two sides may not ultimately be made of radically different material—linguistic in nature—at any given point along the surface there is a front and a back, a visible face and an invisible one. Their value may only be local, as in the case of the Möbius strip, where, if you draw a long enough line along any side, you eventually wind up on the flip side due to the twist in the strip. Yet there is an at least locally valid split between front and back, conscious and unconscious.

The split, while traumatic for each new speaking being, is by no means an indication of madness. On the contrary, Lacan states that in psychosis this split cannot be assumed to have occurred at all, the "unconscious" being "*à ciel ouvert*," exposed for all the world to see. Unconscious-like thought processes are not *hidden* in psychosis as they are in the case of neurosis, demonstrating that the split generally brought on by language assimilation has not occurred, and that there is something different about the psychotic's being in language. The very notion of splitting as produced by our alienation within language can serve as a diagnostic tool, enabling the clinician to distinguish, in certain cases, neurosis from psychosis.

While this split has nothing in common with the kind of agency we tend to associate with subjectivity, it is nevertheless already a first step beyond structure. Language as Other does not *automatically* make a subject of a *homo sapiens* child; it can misfire, as it does in psychosis. This split is not something that can be explained in strictly linguistic or combinatory terms. It is thus in excess of structure. Though *the subject is nothing here but a split between two forms of otherness*—the ego as other and the unconscious as the Other's discourse—the split itself stands in excess of the Other. As we shall see in the next chapter, the advent of the split subject signals a corresponding division or breakdown of the Other.[13]

## Beyond the Split Subject

Now *the split subject is by no means Lacan's last word on subjectivity*, there being a further aspect to the subject which I will first attempt to illustrate graphically and then explain in the next two chapters. Let us return to the illustration of the split subject presented in figure 4.4 and note, firstly, that not only is the subject split here between ego and unconscious, it is further split in each of the two opposing corners of the schema (upper left and lower right). For the moment, let us simply take up the split at the level of the unconscious.

In the excluded (unshaded) portion of the circle in the lower right-hand corner, Lacan writes "I." In this case, it is not the reified "I" of conscious discourse, found in statements of the "I am like this and not like that" type; nor is it the empty shifter, a signifier whose referent changes with each new person who pronounces it.[14] It is rather the I of Freud's "*Wo Es war, soll Ich werden,*" a veritable leitmotif in Lacan's work. The gist of Lacan's many glosses on it involves a morally dictated movement from the impersonal "it" form (and not the id per se—for Freud says neither *das Es* nor *das Ich* here, as he usually does when designating the agencies of the id and the ego) to I. I must become I where "it" was or reigned; I must come to be, must assume its place, that place where "it" was. I here appears as the subject that analysis aims to bring forth: an I that assumes responsibility for the unconscious, that arises there in the unconscious linking up of thoughts which seems to take place all by itself, without the intervention of anything like a subject (figure 4.5).

This I, or subject of the unconscious, as we might call it, is in general excluded at the level of unconscious thought. It comes into being, so to speak, only momentarily, as a sort of pulselike movement towards the lower left-hand corner of the schema (figure 4.6).

Figure 4.5

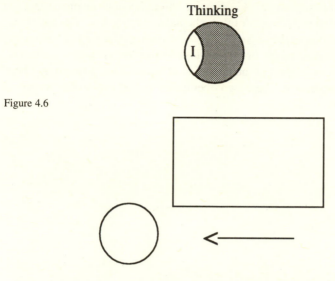

Figure 4.6

But while it is just as evanescent or short-lived a subject as was that of the interruptions known as slips of the tongue and bungled actions, *this specifically Lacanian subject is not so much an interruption as the assumption thereof,* in the French sense of the term *assomption,* that is, an acceptance of responsibility for that which interrupts, a taking it upon oneself.

For Lacan claims that "one is always responsible for one's position as subject."[15] His concept of the subject thus has an ethical component that finds its founding principle in Freud's "*Wo Es war, soll Ich werden.*"

Thus we begin with an alienated subject that is no other than the split itself (figure 4.7).

Figure 4.7

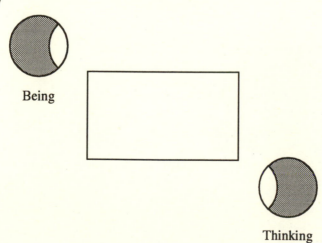

But there is a sense in which the split subject, the subject as "alienated," is able to go "beyond" or "overcome" this division through a shift or movement towards the lower left-hand corner of the schema (see figure 4.6). *The split is, in a sense, the condition of the possibility of the existence of a subject, the pulsation-like shift seeming to be its realization.* While the split corresponds to alienation, the second aspect of the Lacanian subject as I am presenting it here corresponds to separation. These two operations will be explored at length in the next chapter.

# 5

## The Subject and the Other's Desire

IN CHAPTER 1, I spoke in very general terms about our alienation in and by language, language preceding our birth, flowing into us via the discourse that surrounds us as infants and children, and shaping our wants and fantasies. Without language there would be no desire as we know it—exhilarating, and yet contorted, contradictory, and loath to be satisfied—nor would there be any subject as such.

In this chapter I outline Lacan's view of the advent of the subject in more theoretical terms. I begin with a brief general discussion of the two processes Lacan refers to as "alienation" and "separation" and then go on to describe them more fully in terms of the Other's desire. Afterwards, I turn to the operation Lacan regards as a *further* separation, or a going beyond of separation: the traversing of the fundamental fantasy. Lastly, I illustrate the workings of these three operations in the analytic setting.

### Alienation and Separation

In Lacan's concept of alienation, the two parties involved, the child and the Other, are very unevenly matched, and the child almost inevitably loses in the struggle between them.[1] By submitting to the Other, the child nevertheless gains something: he or she becomes, in a sense, one of language's subjects, a subject "of language" or "in language." Schematically represented, the child, submitting to the Other, allows the signifier to stand in for him or her.

$$\frac{\text{Other}}{\text{child}}$$

The child, coming to be as a divided subject (as illustrated in chapter 4), disappears beneath or behind the signifier, S.

$$\frac{S}{\$}$$

The child need not absolutely be vanquished in his or her "struggle" with the Other, and psychosis can be understood as a form of victory by the child over the Other, the child *foregoing* his or her advent as a divided subject so as not to submit to the Other as language. Freud speaks of the *choice* or *election* of neurosis,[2] and Lacan suggests that a choice of some kind is involved in the child's acceptance to submit to this Other—a "forced choice," as he calls it (which is something of an oxymoron), the decision not to allow oneself to be subdued by the Other entailing the loss of oneself. The latter decision forecloses the possibility of one's advent as a subject. The choice of submission is necessary *if* one is to come to be as a subject, but it maintains its status as a choice since it is nevertheless possible to refuse subjectivity.

Thus, in Lacan's concept of alienation, the child can be understood to in some sense choose to submit to language, to agree to express his or her needs through the distorting medium or straightjacket of language, and to allow him or herself to be represented by words.

Lacan's second operation, *separation, involves the alienated subject's confrontation with the Other, not as language this time, but as desire.*

The cause of the subject's physical presence in the world was a desire for something (pleasure, revenge, fulfillment, power, immortality, and so on) on the part of the child's parents. One or both of them wanted something, and the child results from that wanting. People's motivations for having children are often very complex and multilayered, and a child's parents may be very much at odds concerning their motives. One or both parents may have not even wanted to have a child at all, or may have wanted only a child of one particular sex.

Whatever their complex motives, they function in a very straightforward way as a cause of the child's physical presence in the world, and their motives continue to act upon the child after his or her birth, being responsible, to a great extent, for his or her advent as a subject within language. In this sense, *the subject is caused by the Other's desire*. This can be understood as a description of alienation in terms of desire, not simply in terms of language, though they are clearly but warp and woof of the same fabric, language being ridden with desire and desire being inconceivable without language, being made of the very stuff of language.

If, then, alienation consists in the subject's causation by the Other's desire which preceded his or her birth, by some desire not of the subject's own making, separation consists in the attempt by the alienated subject to come to grips with that Other's desire as it manifests itself in the subject's world. As a child tries to fathom its mOther's desire—which is ever in motion, desire being essentially desire for something else—it is forced to come to terms with the fact that it is not her sole interest (in most cases, at least), not her be-all and end-all. There is rarely, if ever, a total mother-child unity, whereby the child can fulfill all of the mother's wants in life, and vice versa. Indeed, the mother is often led to momentarily neglect her child's wants precisely because her attention is drawn to other centers of interest; a child is often obliged to await its mother's return, not only because of the demands of reality (she must procure food and other necessities for her child, not to mention the money with which to buy them), but also because of priorities and desires of her own that do not involve her child. The child's unsuccessful attempt to perfectly complement its mother leads to an expulsion of the subject from the position of wanting-to-be and yet failing-to-be the Other's sole object of desire. The why and wherefore of this expulsion, this separation, will be described at some length further on.

## The Vel of Alienation

Alienation is not a permanent state of affairs; rather it is a process, an operation that takes place at certain times. Rather than trace the historical development of Lacan's concept of alienation throughout his writings—it already appears in his 1936/1949 article on the mirror stage—I will present it here as a fully developed notion.[3]

We could imagine a concept of alienation involving an either/or—a *vel*, as the Latin would have it—amounting to an *exclusive* choice between two parties, to be decided by their struggle to the death. Such a vel would allow for the possibility of only one of the parties surviving (but either one), or perhaps also the possibility of *neither* party surviving. Yet Lacan's "vel of alienation" always *excludes* the survival of one and the same party.

Lacan's classic example of his vel of alienation is the mugger's threat: "Your money or your life!" (Seminar XI, p. 212). As soon as you hear those words pronounced, it is clear that your money is as good as gone. Should you be so foolhardy as to try to hold onto your money, your trustworthy mugger will unburden you of your life, proceeding, no doubt, to unburden you of your money as well shortly thereafter. (And even if he doesn't, you won't be around to spend it.) You will thus, no doubt, be more prudent and hand over your wallet or purse; but you will nonetheless suffer a restriction of your enjoyment, insofar as money buys enjoyment. Uncertainty only really remains around the question of whether you will struggle with him and thus perhaps get yourself killed in the bargain.

The parties to the vel of alienation that concern us here are not, however, your money and your life, but the subject and the Other, the subject being assigned the losing position (that of money in the previous example, which you had no choice but to lose). In Lacan's vel, the sides are by no means even: in his or her confrontation with the Other, the subject immediately *drops out* of the picture. While alienation is the necessary "first step" in acceding to subjectivity, this step involves choosing "one's own" disappearance.

Lacan's concept of the subject as *manque-à-être* is useful here: the subject fails to come forth as a someone, as a particular being; in the most radical sense, he or she is not, he or she has no being. The subject *exists*—insofar as the word has wrought him or her from nothingness, and he or she can be spoken of, talked about, and discoursed upon—yet remains beingless. Prior to the onset of alienation there was not the slightest question of being: "it's the subject himself who is not there to begin with" (Seminar XIV, November 16, 1966); afterwards his or her being is strictly potential. *Alienation gives rise to a pure possibility of being,* a place where one might expect to find a subject, but which nevertheless remains empty. Alienation engenders, in a sense, a place in which it is clear that there is, as of yet, no subject: a place where something is conspicuously lacking. *The subject's first guise is this very lack.*

Lack in Lacan's work has, to a certain extent, an ontological status:[4] it is the first step beyond nothingness. To qualify something as empty is to use a spatial metaphor implying that it could alternatively be full, that it has some sort of existence above and beyond its being full or empty. A metaphor often used by Lacan is that of something *qui manque à sa place,* which is out of place, not where it should be or usually is; in other words, something which is missing. Now for something to be missing, it must first have been present and localized; it must first have had a place. And something only has a place within an ordered system—space-time coordinates or a Dewey decimal book classification, for example—in other words, within some sort of symbolic structure.

*Alienation represents the instituting of the symbolic order*—which must be realized anew for each new subject—*and the subject's assignation of a place therein.* A place he or she does not "hold" as of yet, but a place designated for him or her, and for him or her alone. When Lacan says (in Seminar XI) that the subject's being is eclipsed by language, that the subject here slips under or behind the signifier, it is in part because the subject is completely submerged by language, his or her only trace being a place-marker or place-holder in the symbolic order (figure 5.1).

Figure 5.1

Other

The process of alienation may, as J.-A. Miller suggests, be viewed as yielding the subject as empty set, {Ø}, in other words, a set which has no elements, a symbol which transforms nothingness into something by *marking* or *representing* it. Set theory generates its whole domain on the basis of this one symbol and a certain number of axioms. Lacan's subject, analogously, is grounded in the naming of the void. The signifier is what founds the subject;

the signifier is what wields ontic clout, wresting existence from the real that it marks and annuls. What it forges is, however, in no sense substantial or material.

The empty set as the subject's place-holder within the symbolic order is not unrelated to the subject's proper name. That name is often selected long before the child's birth, and it inscribes the child in the symbolic. A priori, this name has absolutely nothing to do with the subject; it is as foreign to him or her as any other signifier. But in time this signifier—more, perhaps, than any other— will go to the root of his or her being and become inextricably tied to his or her subjectivity. It will become the signifier of his or her very absence as subject, standing in for him or her.[5]

Let us now turn to an operation that "complements" alienation.

## Desire and Lack in Separation

Alienation is essentially characterized by a "forced" choice which rules out *being* for the subject, instituting instead the symbolic order and relegating the subject to mere *existence* as a place-holder therein. Separation, on the other hand, gives rise to being, but that being is of an eminently evanescent and elusive ilk. While alienation is based on a very skewed kind of *either/or*, separation is based on a *neither/nor*.

Separation implies a situation in which both the subject and the Other are excluded. The subject's *being* must thus come, in a sense, from "outside," from something *other* than the subject and the Other, something that is neither exactly one nor the other.

One of the essential ideas involved in separation is that of *a juxtaposition, overlapping, or coincidence of two lacks*. This is not to be confused with a lack of lack: a situation in which lack is lacking. Consider the following passage from Seminar X:

> What provokes anxiety? Contrary to what people say, it is neither the rhythm nor the alternation of the mother's presence-absence. What proves this is that the child in-dulges in repeating presence-absence games: security of presence is found in the possibility of absence. What is most anxiety-producing for the child is when the relationship through which he comes to be—on the basis of lack which makes him desire—is most perturbed: when there is no possibility of lack, when his mother is constantly on his back. (December 5, 1962)

This example fails to conform to Lacan's notion of separation, for the nega-tives here (the lacks) both apply to the same term: the mother, in other words, the Other. The mOther must show some sign of incompleteness, fallibility, or deficiency for separation to obtain and for the subject to come to be as $; in other words, the mOther must demonstrate that she is a desiring (and thus also

a lacking and alienated) subject, that she too has submitted to the splitting/
barring action of language, in order for us to witness the subject's advent. The
mother, in the above example from Seminar X, monopolizes the field: it is not
clear whether she herself has come to be as a divided subject.

In separation we start from a barred Other, that is, a parent who is him or
herself divided: who is not always aware (conscious) of what he or she wants
(unconscious) and whose desire is ambiguous, contradictory, and in constant
flux. The subject has—to change metaphors somewhat—gained, via alienation, a foothold within that divided parent: *the subject has lodged his or her
lack of being (manque-à-être) in that "place" where the Other was lacking.*
In separation, the subject attempts to fill the mOther's lack—demonstrated by
the various manifestations of her desire for something else—with his or her
own lack of being, his or her not yet extant self or being. The subject tries to
excavate, explore, align, and conjoin those two lacks, seeking out the precise
boundaries of the Other's lack in order to fill it with him or her self.

The child latches onto what is indecipherable in what its parent says. It is
interested in that certain something which lies in the interval between the parent's words. The child tries to read between the lines to decipher *why*: She says
X, but why is she telling me that? What does she want from me? What does she
want in general? Children's endless *why*s are not, to Lacan's mind, the sign of
an insatiable curiosity as to how things work but rather of a concern with
where they fit in, what rank they hold, what importance they have to their
parents. They are concerned to secure (themselves) a place, to try to be the
object of their parents' desire—to occupy that between-the-lines "space"
where desire shows its face, words being used in the attempt to express desire,
and yet ever failing to do so adequately.

Lack and desire are coextensive for Lacan. The child devotes considerable
effort to filling up the whole of the mother's lack, her whole space of desire;
the child wants to be everything to her. Children set themselves the task of
excavating the site of their mother's desire, aligning themselves with her every
whim and fancy. Her wish is their command, her desire their demand.[6] Their
desire is born in complete subordination to hers: "*Le désir de l'homme, c'est
le désir de l'Autre*," Lacan reiterates again and again.[7] Taking the second *de* as
a subjective genitive (*Écrits*, p. 312) for the moment, the following translations
are possible here: "Man's desire is the Other's desire," "Man's desire is the
same as the Other's desire," and "Man desires what the Other desires," all of
which convey part of the meaning. For man not only desires *what* the Other
desires, but he desires it *in the same way*; in other words, his desire is structured exactly like the Other's. Man learns to desire *as an other*, as if he were
some other person.

What is posited here is a tendency to totally superimpose the mother's lack
and the child's, which is to say that an attempt is made to make their desires
completely coincide (figure 5.2).

Figure 5.2

**Other**

**Subject**

This is, however, a chimerical, unrealizable moment. For the fact is that, try as it might, a child can rarely and is rarely allowed (or forced) to completely monopolize the space of its mother's desire. The child is rarely her only interest and the two lacks can thus never entirely overlap: the subject is prevented or barred from holding at least part of the "space" of desire.

### The Introduction of a Third Term

Separation may be seen here as involving an attempt by the subject to make these two lacks thoroughly coincide, that attempt being abruptly thwarted. We can begin to understand how and why that attempt is thwarted by examining Lacan's reconceptualization of psychosis in Seminar III and "On a Question Preliminary to any Possible Treatment of Psychosis" in *Écrits*, for it seems to me that his notion of separation, as formulated in 1964, is in some respects equivalent to what Lacan in 1956 referred to as the operation of the "paternal metaphor" or "paternal function."[8]

Psychosis, according to Lacan, results from a child's failure to assimilate a "primordial" signifier which would otherwise structure the child's symbolic universe, that failure leaving the child unanchored in language, without a compass reading on the basis of which to adopt an orientation. A psychotic child may very well *assimilate* language, but cannot *come to be in* language in the same way as a neurotic child. Lacking that fundamental anchoring point, the remainder of the signifiers assimilated are condemned to drift.

That "primordial" signifier is instated through the operation of what Lacan calls the paternal metaphor or paternal function. If we hypothesize an initial child-mother unity (as a logical, i.e., structural, moment, if not a temporal one), the father, in a Western nuclear family, typically acts in such a way as to disrupt that unity, intervening therein as a third term—often perceived as foreign and even undesirable. The child, as yet a sort of undifferentiated bundle of sensations, lacking in sensory-motor coordination and all sense of self, is not yet distinguishable from its mother, taking the mother's body as a simple extension of its own, being in a kind of "direct, unmediated contact" with it. And the mother may be inclined to devote virtually all of her attention to the child, anticipate its every need, and make herself 100 percent accessible and available to the child. In such a situation, the father or some other member of the household, or some other interest of the mother's, can serve a very specific function: that of annulling the mother-child unity, creating an essential space or gap between mother and child. Should the mother pay no attention to the father or other member of the household, granting him or her no importance, the mother-child relationship may never become triangulated. Or should the father or other member of the household be unconcerned, tacitly allowing the unity to go undisrupted, a third term may never be introduced.

Lacan calls this third term the Name-of-the-Father or the Father's Name, but by formalizing its action in the form of the paternal metaphor or function, he makes it clear that it is not inescapably tied to either biological or de facto fathers, or, for that matter, to their proper names. In Seminar IV, Lacan goes so far as to suggest that the only signifier that is able to serve a paternal function in the case of Freud's "Little Hans" is the signifier "horse." "Horse" is, clearly in Little Hans' case, *a* name of the father, but certainly not his "proper" name. It stands in for Hans' father, who is unable to serve a paternal function because he is incapable of separating his son from his wife.[9]

As indicated in chapter 3, the symbolic order serves to cancel out the real, to transform it into a social, if not socially acceptable, reality, and here the name that serves the paternal function bars and transforms the real, undifferentiated, mother-child unity. It bars the child's easy access to pleasurable contact with its mother, requiring it to pursue pleasure through avenues more acceptable to the father figure and/or mOther (insofar as it is only by her granting of importance to the father that the father can serve that paternal function). In Freudian terms, it is correlated with the reality principle, which does not so much negate the aims of the pleasure principle as channel them into socially designated pathways.[10]

The paternal function leads to the assimilation or instating of a name (which, as we shall see, is not yet a "full-fledged signifier," as it is not displaceable) that neutralizes the Other's desire, viewed by Lacan as potentially very dangerous to the child, threatening to engulf it or swallow it up. In a striking passage in Seminar XVII, Lacan sums up in very schematic terms what he had been saying for years:

> The mother's role is her desire. That is of capital importance. Her desire is not something you can bear easily, as if it were a matter of indifference to you. It always leads to problems. The mother is a big crocodile, and you find yourself in her mouth. You never know what may set her off suddenly, making those jaws clamp down. That is the mother's desire.
>
> So I tried to explain that there was something reassuring. I am telling you simple things—indeed, I am improvising. There is a roller, made of stone, of course, which

is potentially there at the level of the trap and which holds and jams it open. That is what we call the phallus. It is a roller which protects you, should the jaws suddenly close. (p. 129)

It should be kept in mind that the French words I am translating by mother's desire (*désir de la mère*) are inescapably ambiguous, suggesting both the child's desire for the mother and the mother's desire per se. Whichever of the two we choose to dwell on, or whether we prefer to view the situation as a whole, the point is the same: language protects the child from a potentially dangerous dyadic situation, and the way this comes about is through the substitution of a name for the mother's desire.

Name-of-the-Father
_____
Mother's Desire

Read quite literally, this kind of formulation (*Écrits*, p. 200) suggests that the mother's desire is for the father (or whatever may be standing in for him in the family), and that it is thus his name which serves this protective paternal function by naming the mOther's desire.

Now a name is, according to Saul Kripke, a rigid designator;[11] in other words, it always and inflexibly designates the same thing. We might refer to a name as a signifier, but only with the caveat that it is an unusual kind of signifier, a "primordial" signifier. A further step is required for that which replaces or stands in for the mOther's desire to function as a "full-fledged" signifier: it must become part and parcel of the dialectical movement of signifiers, that is, become displaceable, occupying a signifying position that can be filled with a series of different signifiers over time. This requires a "further separation" of the kind discussed later in this chapter, and it is only that further separation that allows Lacan to refer to the symbolic element operative in the paternal function in a variety of ways: as the Father's Name (*le nom du père*), the father's no-saying (*le non du père*) or prohibition, the phallus (as signifier of desire), and the *signifier* of the Other's desire, S(Å).

Signifier
_____
Mother's Desire

The substitution implied by the paternal metaphor is only made possible by language, and thus it is only insofar as a "second" signifier, $S_2$, is instated (the Father's Name, at the outset, and then more generally the signifier of the Other's desire) that the mother's desire is retroactively symbolized or transformed into a "first" signifier ($S_1$):

$$\frac{S_2}{S_1}$$

$S_2$ here is thus a signifier which plays a very precise role: it symbolizes the mOther's desire, transforming it into signifiers. By doing so, it creates a rift in the mOther-child unity and allows the child a space in which to breathe easy, a space of its own. It is through language that a child can attempt to mediate the Other's desire, keeping it at bay and symbolizing it ever more completely. While in the 1950s Lacan spoke of the $S_2$ involved here as the Name-of-the-Father, and in the 1960s as the phallus, we can understand it most generally as the signifier that comes to signify (to wit, replace, symbolize, or neutralize) the Other's desire. The symbol Lacan provides us for it (see, in particular, Seminars VI and XX) is S($A$), which is usually read "the signifier of the lack in the Other" but, as lack and desire are coextensive, can also be read "the signifier of the Other's desire." (The phallic signifier and S($A$) are discussed at length in chapter 8 below.)

The result of this substitution or metaphor is the advent of the subject as such, the subject as no longer just a potentiality, a mere place-holder in the symbolic, waiting to be filled out, but a desiring subject. (As we shall see in the discussion of substitutional metaphors in the next chapter, every such metaphor has a similar effect of subjectification.) Graphically speaking, separation leads to the subject's expulsion from the Other, in which he or she was still nothing but a place-holder. Simplistically described, this can be associated with Freud's view of the outcome of the Oedipus complex (at least for boys), whereby the father's castration threats—"Stay away from Mom or else!"—eventually bring about a breaking away of the child from the mOther. In such a scenario, the child is, in a sense, kicked out of the mOther (figure 5.3).

Figure 5.3

child         mOther

This logically discernable moment (which is generally quite difficult to isolate at any particular chronological moment of an individual's history, and is likely to require many such moments to come about, each building on the ones before) is a fundamental one in Lacan's metapsychology, all of the crucial elements of his algebra—$S_1$, $S_2$, $\mathcal{S}$, and $a$—arising simultaneously here. As $S_2$ is instated, $S_1$ is retroactively determined, $\mathcal{S}$ is precipitated, and the Other's desire takes on a new role: that of object $a$.

## Object a: *The Other's Desire*

In the child's attempt to grasp what remains essentially indecipherable in the Other's desire—what Lacan calls the X, the variable, or (better) the unknown—the child's own desire is founded; the Other's desire begins to function as the cause of the child's desire. That cause is, on the one hand, the Other's desire (based on lack) for the subject—and here we encounter the other meaning of Lacan's dictum "*Le désir de l'homme, c'est le désir de l'Autre*," which we can translate here as, for example, "Man's desire is for the Other to desire him" or "Man desires the Other's desire for him." His desire's cause can take the form of someone's voice or of a look someone gives him. But its cause also originates in that part of the mOther's desire which seems to have nothing to do with him, which takes her away from him (physically or otherwise), leading her to give her precious attention to others.

In a sense we can say that it is the mother's very desirousness that the child finds desirable. In Seminar VIII, Lacan points to Alcibiades' fascination with "a certain something" in Socrates which Plato (in the *Symposium*) terms "agalma": a precious, shiny, gleaming something which is interpreted by Lacan to be Socrates' desire itself, Socrates' desiring or desirousness. This highly valued "agalma"—inspiring desire in its detectors—can serve us here as an approach to what Lacan calls object *a*, the cause of desire (which will be discussed at length in chapter 7).

This second formulation of Lacan's dictum, involving man's desire to be desired by the Other, exposes the Other's desire *as* object *a*. The child would like to be the sole object of its mother's affections, but her desire almost always goes beyond the child: there is something about her desire which escapes the child, which is beyond its control. A strict identity between the child's desire and hers cannot be maintained; her desire's independence from her child's creates a rift between them, a gap in which her desire, unfathomable to the child, functions in a unique way.

This approximate gloss on separation posits that a rift is induced in the hypothetical mother-child unity due to the very nature of desire and that this rift leads to the advent of object *a*.[12] Object *a* can be understood here as the *remainder* produced when that hypothetical unity breaks down, as a last trace of that unity, a last *reminder* thereof. By cleaving to that rem(a)inder, the split subject, though expulsed from the Other, can sustain the illusion of wholeness; by clinging to object *a*, the subject is able to ignore his or her division.[13] That is precisely what Lacan means by fantasy, and he formalizes it with the matheme $\$ \lozenge a$, which is to be read: the divided subject in relation to object *a*. It is in the subject's complex relation to object *a* (Lacan describes this relation as one of "envelopment-development-conjunction-disjunction" [*Écrits*, p. 280]) that he or she achieves a phantasmatic sense of wholeness, completeness, fulfillment, and well-being.

When analysands recount fantasies to their analyst, they are informing the analyst about the way in which they want to be related to object *a*, in other words, the way they would like to be positioned with respect to the Other's desire. Object *a*, as it enters into their fantasies, is an instrument or plaything with which subjects do as they like, manipulating it as it pleases them, orchestrating things in the fantasy scenario in such a way as to derive a maximum of excitement therefrom.

Given, however, that the subject casts the Other's desire in the role most exciting to the subject, that pleasure may turn to disgust and even to horror, there being no guarantee that what is most exciting to the subject is also most pleasurable. That excitement, whether correlated with a conscious feeling of pleasure or pain, is what the French call *jouissance*. Freud detected it on the face of his Rat Man, interpreting it as *"horror at pleasure of his own of which he himself was unaware"* (SE X, p. 167). And Freud states in no uncertain terms that "patients derive a certain satisfaction from their sufferings" (p. 183). This pleasure—this excitation due to sex, seeing, and/or violence, whether positively or negatively viewed by conscience, whether considered innocently pleasurable or disgustingly repulsive—is termed jouissance, and that is what the subject orchestrates for him or herself in fantasy.

Jouissance is thus what comes to substitute for the lost "mother-child unity," a unity which was perhaps never as united as all that since it was a unity owing only to the child's sacrifice or foregoing of subjectivity. We can imagine a kind of jouissance before the letter, before the institution of the symbolic order ($J_1$)—corresponding to an unmediated relation between mother and child, a *real* connection between them—which gives way before the signifier, being canceled out by the operation of the paternal function. Some modicum or portion of that real connection is refound in fantasy (a jouissance after the letter, $J_2$), in the subject's relation to the leftover or byproduct of symbolization (table 5.1): object *a* (that which is produced as $S_2$ retroactively determines $S_1$ and precipitates out a subject, as we shall see).

Table 5.1

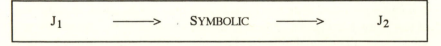

| $J_1$ | $\longrightarrow$ | SYMBOLIC | $\longrightarrow$ | $J_2$ |
|---|---|---|---|---|

This second-order jouissance takes the place of the former "wholeness" or "completeness," and fantasy—which stages this second-order jouissance—takes the subject beyond his or her nothingness, his or her mere existence as a marker at the level of alienation, and supplies a sense of being. It is thus only through fantasy, made possible by separation, that the subject can procure him or herself some modicum of what Lacan calls "being." While existence is granted only through the symbolic order (the alienated subject being assigned a place therein), being is supplied only by cleaving to the real.

Thus we see how it is that separation, a neither/nor involving the subject and the Other, brings forth being: creating a rift in the subject-Other whole, the Other's desire escapes the subject—ever seeking, as it does, something else— yet the subject is able to recover a rem(a)inder thereof by which to sustain him or herself in being, as a *being of desire, a desiring being*. Object *a* is the subject's complement, a phantasmatic partner that ever arouses the subject's desire.[14] Separation results in the splitting of the subject into ego and unconscious, and in a corresponding splitting of the Other into lacking Other (Ⱥ) and object *a*. None of these "parties" were there at the outset, and yet separation results in a kind of intersection whereby something of the Other (the Other's desire in this account) that the subject considers his or her own, essential to his or her existence, is ripped away from the Other and retained by the now divided subject in fantasy (figure 5.4).

Figure 5.4

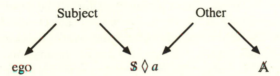

A Further Separation: The Traversing of Fantasy

## A Further Separation: The Traversing of Fantasy

The notion of separation largely disappears from Lacan's work after 1964, giving way in the later 1960s to a more elaborate theory of the effect of analysis. By Seminars XIV and XV, the term "alienation" comes to signify both alienation and separation as elaborated in 1960–64, and a new dynamic notion is added: *la traversée du fantasme*, the crossing over, traversal, or traversing of the fundamental fantasy.

This reformulation begins, in a sense, with Lacan's elaboration of the notion that the analyst must play the role of object *a*, the Other as desire, not as language. The analyst must steer clear of the role in which analysands often cast him or her, that of an all-knowing and all-seeing Other who is the ultimate judge of their value as human beings and the final authority on all questions of truth. The analyst must maneuver away from serving the analysand as an Other to imitate, to try to be like, to desire like (desire's tendency being to model itself on the Other's desire), in short, an Other with whom to identify, whose ideals one can adopt, whose views one can make one's own. Instead, the analyst must endeavor to embody desirousness, revealing as few personal

likes and dislikes, ideals and opinions as possible, providing the analysand
as little concrete information about his or her character, aspirations, and tastes
as possible, as they all furnish such fertile ground in which identification can
take root.

Identification with the analyst's ideals and desires is a solution to neurosis
advanced by certain analysts of the Anglo-American tradition: the analysand
is to take the analyst's strong ego as a model by which to shore up his or her
own weak ego, an analysis coming to a successful end if the analysand is able
to sufficiently identity with the analyst. In Lacanian psychoanalysis, identification with the analyst is considered a trap, leading the analysand, as it does,
to still more alienation within the Other as language and as desire. Maintaining
his or her constant enigmatic desire for something else, the Lacanian analyst
aims, not at modeling the analysand's desire on his or her own, but rather at
shaking up the configuration of the analysand's fantasy, changing the subject's
relation to the cause of desire: object *a*.

This reconfiguration of fantasy implies a number of different things: the
construction in the course of analysis of a new "fundamental fantasy" (the
latter being that which underlies an analysand's various individual fantasies
and constitutes the subject's most profound relation to the Other's desire); the
traversing of the square, in the schema of the split subject provided in chapter
4, to the lower left-hand corner; and a "crossing over" of positions within the
fundamental fantasy whereby the divided subject assumes the place of the
cause, in other words, subjectifies the traumatic cause of his or her own advent
as subject, coming to be in that place where the Other's desire—a foreign,
alien desire—had been (figure 5.5).

Figure 5.5

The traversing of fantasy involves the subject's assumption of a new position with respect to the Other as language and the Other as desire. A move is
made to invest or inhabit that which brought him or her into existence as split
subject, to become that which *caused* him or her. There where it—the Other's
discourse, ridden with the Other's desire—was, the subject is able to say "I."
Not "It happened to me," or "They did this to me," or "Fate had it in store for
me," but "I was," "I did," "I saw," "I cried out."

This "further" separation consists in the temporally paradoxical move by the
alienated subject to become his or her own cause, to come to be as subject in
the place of the cause. The foreign cause, that Other desire that brought one
into the world, is internalized, in a sense, taken responsibility for, assumed (in
the sense of the French word *assomption*), subjectified, made "one's own."[15]

If we think of trauma as the child's encounter with the Other's desire—and
so many of Freud's cases support this view (consider, to cite but one example,

Little Hans' traumatic encounter with his mother's desire)—trauma functions as the child's cause: the cause of his or her advent as subject and of the position the child adopts as subject in relation to the Other's desire. The encounter with the Other's desire constitutes a traumatic experience of pleasure/pain or jouissance, which Freud describes as a *sexual über*, a sexual overload, the subject coming to be as a defense against that traumatic experience.[16]

The traversing of fantasy is the process by which the subject subjectifies trauma, takes the traumatic event upon him or herself, and assumes responsibility for that jouissance.

### Subjectifying the Cause: A Temporal Conundrum

Temporally speaking, this operation of *putting the I back in the traumatic cause* is paradoxical. Was there subjective involvement at the moment(s) of trauma that the subject must come to recognize and take responsibility for? Yes, in some sense. And yet subjective involvement seems to be brought about after the fact. Such a view necessarily contradicts the timeline of classical logic, whereby effect follows cause in a nice, orderly fashion. Separation nevertheless obeys the workings of the signifier, whereby the effect of the first word in a sentence can be brought out only after the last has been heard or read, and whereby its meaning is only constituted retroactively by a semantic context provided after its utterance, its "full" meaning being an historical product. Just as Plato's dialogues take on a first meaning for students new to philosophy, acquiring multiple meanings as they deepen their study of them, Plato's *Symposium* has been shown to mean something else since Lacan's reading of it in Seminar VIII, and will continue to take on new meanings as it is interpreted and reinterpreted in the centuries and millennia to come. Meaning is not created instantaneously, but only ex post facto: after the event in question. Such is the temporal logic—anathema to classical logic—at work in psychoanalytic processes and theory.

Lacan never pinpoints the subject's chronological appearance on the scene: he or she is always either *about to arrive*—is on the verge of arriving—or *will have already arrived* by some later moment in time. Lacan uses the equivocal French imperfect tense to illustrate the subject's temporal status. He gives as an example the sentence *"Deux secondes plus tard, la bombe éclatait,"* which can either mean "Two seconds later, the bomb exploded," or "The bomb would have gone off two seconds later," there being an implicit "if, and, or but": it would have gone off two seconds later if the fuse had not been cut. A similar ambiguity is suggested by the following English wording: "The bomb was to go off two seconds later."

Applied to the subject, the French imperfect tense leaves us uncertain as to whether the subject has emerged or not.[17] His or her ever-so-fleeting existence remains in suspense or in abeyance. Here there seems to be no way of really determining whether the subject has been or not.

Lacan more commonly uses the future anterior (also known as the future perfect) in discussing the subject's temporal status. "By the time you get back, I will have already left": such a statement tells us that at a certain future moment, something will have already taken place, without specifying exactly when. This grammatical tense is related to Freud's *Nachträglichkeit*, deferred action, retroaction, or ex post facto action: a first event ($E_1$) occurs, but does not bear fruit until a second event ($E_2$) occurs. Retroactively, $E_1$ is constituted, for example, as a trauma; in other words, it takes on the significance of a trauma (T). It comes to signify something that it in no way signified before; its meaning and efficacy have changed (figure 5.6).

Figure 5.6

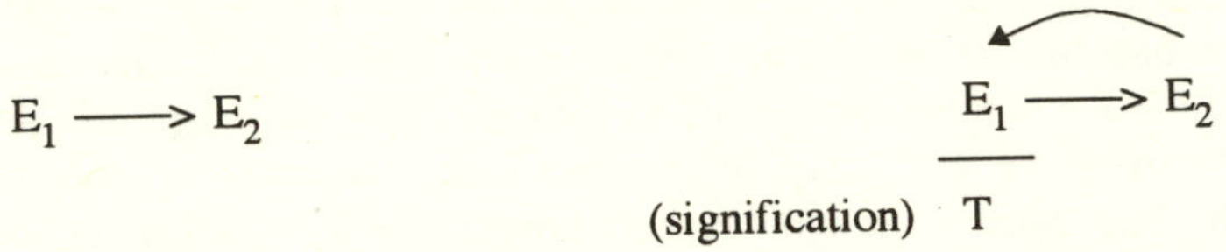

$$E_1 \longrightarrow E_2 \qquad\qquad E_1 \longrightarrow E_2$$

$$\text{(signification)} \quad T$$

In the statement "By the time you get back, I will have already left," my departure is retroactively determined as prior. Without your return, it would have no such status. It takes two moments to create a before and after. The signification of the first moment changes in accordance with what comes afterwards.

Similarly, a first signifier does not, as we shall see below, suffice to create an effect of subjectification until a second signifier has appeared on the scene (figure 5.7). A relation between two signifiers proves to us that a subject has passed that way, and yet we can in no sense pinpoint the subject in either time or space (this will be developed further in the next chapter).

Figure 5.7

$$S_1 \longrightarrow S_2 \qquad\qquad S_1 \longrightarrow S_2$$

$$\$$$

Lacan's article "Logical Time and the Assertion of Anticipated Certainty" sets out to pinpoint the emergence of the subject in a very precise situation with a series of explicit constraints.[18] The moments elaborated in that paper— the instant of the glance, the time for comprehending, and the moment of concluding—were later referred by Lacan to the moments of the analytic process itself.

Just as the time for comprehending is indeterminate for an outsider in the three prisoner problem expounded in that article, the time necessary for comprehending in analysis is indeterminate; in other words, it is not calculable a priori. Yet in associating the end of analysis with the prisoners' moment of concluding (Seminar XX), Lacan suggests a final moment of subjectification that can be forced to occur through a propitious combination of logical and/or analytic conditions.

Thus, while seemingly forever suspended in a future anterior, Lacan nevertheless holds out for us the prospect of a subjectification of the cause at a logically specific, but chronometrically incalculable, moment. We may, in a sense, think of alienation as opening up that possibility, and of this "further separation" as marking the end of the process. Nevertheless, as we shall see, separation can be fostered in certain situations, for example, at the moment of the cut or scansion of an analytic session, a moment which is both logical and chronological.

The traversing of fantasy can, not surprisingly, also be formulated in terms of increasing "signifierization"—a turning into signifiers—of the Other's desire. Insofar as the subject finds, in this further separation, a new position in relation to object $a$ (the Other's desire), the Other's desire is no longer simply named, as it was through the action of the paternal metaphor. When the cause is subjectified, the Other's desire is simultaneously fully brought into the movement of signifiers, and it is at that point, as we can see in Lacan's discussion of Hamlet in Seminar VI, that the subject finally gains access to the *signifier* of the Other's desire, S($\mathbb{A}$).[19] In other words, whereas the Other's desire had simply been named through separation, that name was fixed, static, and thinglike in its unchanging effect, rigid in its limited power of designation.

In neurosis, the name generally remains to be adequately separated from the Other's desire. The name is not the death of the thing—the signifier is. As long as a rigid connection subsists between the Other's desire and $a$ name of the father, the subject is unable to act. Hamlet, according to Lacan, has no access to the phallic *signifier* prior to his duel with Laertes at the end of Shakespeare's play, and that is why he is incapable of taking any action. It is only during the duel that he is able to discern "the phallus behind the king," to realize that the king is but a stand-in for the phallus (the phallus being the signifier of desire,[20] i.e., of the Other's desire) and can be struck without throwing everything into question. Until Hamlet could finally dissociate the king and the phallus ("the king is a thing of nothing"), action was impossible, for to take revenge on the king would have threatened to make Hamlet's whole world collapse. It is only when the king (the object of the Queen's desire) is signifierized that a power can be discerned beyond the king, a legitimacy or authority that is not embodied in the king alone but subsists in the symbolic order beyond the king, above the king.

The name of the Other's desire must be set into motion—from the mother's partner, to teacher, to school, to police officer, to civil law, to religion, to moral law, and so on—and give way before the *signifier* of the Other's desire if subjectification is to take place, that is, if the subject is to become the Other's desire, leaving the signifier to its own devices. In that sense, traversing fantasy entails a separation from language itself, a separation of the subject—who will have become the cause—from his or her own discourse about his or her problem with the Other's desire, inability to deal with the lack detected in the Other, lack of success in maintaining the right distance from and relation to the Other, and so on.

Neurosis is maintained in discourse, and we see in Lacan's notion of traversing fantasy the suggestion of a kind of beyond of neurosis[21] in which the subject is able to act (as cause, as desirousness), and is at least momentarily out of discourse, split off from discourse: free from the weight of the Other. This is not the freedom of the psychotic Lacan mentions in his early paper "Aggressivity in Psychoanalysis" (*Écrits*); it is not a freedom "before" the letter but "after" it.

## Alienation, Separation, and the Traversing of Fantasy in the Analytic Setting

Imagine, for a moment, an analysand—ensconced upon the analyst's couch, talking about his or her dream from the night before, filling the room with his or her discourse, hoping that it will be interesting and satisfying to the analyst, thus in a fantasy mode ($S \lozenge a$)—being suddenly interrupted with a word uttered by the analyst (not by the Other of knowledge to whom that discourse was in some sense addressed), a word which the analysand may have hurriedly glossed over or thought of no importance or interest either to him or herself or to the analyst. Analysands often tailor their discourse, due to transference love, hoping to say what their analysts want them to say, what they think their analysts want to hear, and until such an interruption comes—whether with a cough, a grunt, a word, or the termination of the session—they can go on believing that they are achieving their purpose. Such interruptions often serve to jolt analysands, suddenly bringing them back to the realization that they know not what their analysts want or mean, that the latter are looking for *something else* in their discourse than what the analysands intended, that they want something else from it, something more.

It is in that sense that the Lacanian practice of "punctuating" and "scanding"[22] the analysand's discourse serves to disconnect the analysand therefrom, confronting the analysand with the enigma of the analyst's desire. It is insofar as that desire remains enigmatic, never being precisely where the analysand believes it is—and analysands devote considerable effort to divining that desire—that the analysand's fantasy is repeatedly shaken up in the analytic situation.[23] The Other's desire, in the guise of object *a*, is never precisely where the analysand thinks it is, or wants it to be in his or her fantasy. The analyst, serving as a sham or make-believe object *a*, as a stand-in for or semblance of object *a*, introduces a further gap between $ and *a*, disrupting the fantasized relationship, ◊. The analyst makes *that* relationship untenable, inducing a change therein.

Alienation and separation are involved at all times in the analytic situation, the analysand alienating him or herself as he or she tries to speak coherently, in other words, in a way which will "make sense" to the analyst, the analyst taken here by the analysand to be the locus of all meaning, the Other that knows the meaning of all utterances. In the attempt to make sense, the analysand slips away or fades behind the words he or she says. Because of the very nature of language, those words always and inescapably say more or less than the analysand consciously intends to say in selecting them. Meaning is always ambiguous, polyvalent, betraying something one wanted to remain hidden, hiding something one intended to express.

This attempt to make sense situates the analysand in the register of the Other as meaning: the analysand fades behind a discourse whose "true meaning" can only be determined and judged by the Other (whether parent, analyst, or god). That kind of alienation is unavoidable and is not (unlike alienation as understood by Marxists and critical theorists) condemned in Lacanian analysis.

Nevertheless, the analyst is enjoined not to indefinitely foster this kind of alienation. Though the analyst, in his or her work with neurotics, attempts to bring into focus the analysand's relation to the Other, clearing away in the process the "interference" stemming from the analysand's imaginary relations with others like him or herself (see chapter 7 below), that is by no means the end of the process and could lead, if left at that, to a kind of solution à la American ego psychology, the analysand identifying with the analyst as Other.

The Lacanian analyst adopts a discourse radically different from that of the analysand: a discourse of separation. If the analyst offers up something along the lines of meaning to the analysand, he or she nevertheless aims at something capable of exploding the "analyst-provides-the-meaning-of-the-analysand's-discourse" matrix by speaking equivocally, at several levels at once, using terms which lead in a number of different directions. By intimating several, if not a never-ending panorama of, successive meanings, the register of meaning is itself problematized. As the analysand attempts to fathom the import of the analyst's oracular speech,[24] his or her polyvalent words, or the reason why he or she terminated the session at that precise moment, the analysand is separated from meaning and confronted with the enigma of the analyst's desire. That enigma has an effect on the analysand's deep-rooted fantasy relation to the Other's desire. While the fundamental rule of free association requires the analysand to try to ever further articulate, put into words, symbolize, signifier-ize that relation to the Other's desire, the analyst's action serves to separate the subject to an ever greater extent from the very discourse he or she is required to forge about it.

One is the subject of a particular fate, a fate one has not chosen but which, however random or accidental it may seem at the outset, one must nevertheless subjectify; one must, in Freud's view, become its subject. Primal repression is, in a sense, the roll of the dice at the beginning of one's universe that creates a split and sets the structure in motion. An individual has to come to grips with that random toss—that particular configuration of his or her parents' desire—and somehow become its subject. *"Wo Es war, soll Ich werden."* I must come to be where foreign forces—the Other as language and the Other as desire—once dominated. I must subjectify that otherness.

It is for this reason that we can say that the Lacanian subject is ethically motivated, based as it is on this Freudian injunction so often repeated in Lacan's work. Freud's injunction is inherently paradoxical, enjoining us as it does to put the I (back) in the cause, to become our own cause; but instead of dismissing this paradox, Lacan attempts to theorize the movement implied therein and find techniques by which to induce it. The I is not already in the unconscious. It may be everywhere presupposed there, but it has to be made to appear. It may always already be there, in some sense, but the essential clinical task is to make it appear there where *it* was.

# 6

## Metaphor and the Precipitation of Subjectivity

THE THREE moments constitutive of subjectivity described in the last chapter can be schematized as three substitutions or substitutional metaphors. In alienation, the Other dominates or takes the place of the subject; in separation, object *a* as the Other's desire comes to the fore and takes precedence over or subjugates the subject; and in the traversing of fantasy, the subject subjectifies the *cause* of his or her existence (the Other's desire: object *a*) and is characterized by a kind of pure desiring without an object: desirousness.

$$\frac{\text{Other}}{\text{\$}} \qquad \frac{\text{object } a}{\text{\$}} \qquad \frac{\text{\$}}{\text{object } a}$$

Stated in this way, we can see these three fundamental moments of the constitution of the subject as three moments of metaphorization; the canceling out of one thing by another in Lacan's substitutional metaphors is at the root of Lacanian metapsychology. The subject here can be understood as resulting from a metaphor (or series of metaphors).

But metaphor is generally understood as giving rise to new meaning, in other words, to a new signification, not to a new or radically different subject. One of my principal theses in this book is that the psychoanalytic subject essentially has two faces: the subject as *precipitate* and the subject as *breach*. In the first case, the subject is but a sedimentation of meanings determined by the substitution of one signifier for another or the retroactive effect of one signifier upon another (or of one symbolized event upon another), corresponding to Lacan's "definition" of the subject as "that which one signifier represents to another signifier."[1] In the second, the subject is that which creates a breach in the real as it establishes a link between two signifiers, the subject (as precipitation this time, not as precipitate) being nothing but that very breach.

There is thus one face of the subject that is almost exclusively a signified or signification—the subject of castration (a subject alienated in, taken up into, absorbed by meaning, "dead" meaning)—and another that constitutes a breach between two signifiers (as a spark flying from one signifier to another, creating a connection between them). This twofold notion of the subject is nicely embodied in the expression "precipitation of subjectivity," found in as early a work as "Logical Time and the Assertion of Anticipated Certainty" (1946), where we find the subject as both precipitate and "headlong movement."[2]

As headlong movement or precipitation, the subject surges forth between two signifiers just as "metaphor's creative spark . . . flashes between two signifiers" in the process of metaphorization.[3] In other words, metaphor's creative spark *is* the subject; metaphor creates the subject. Every metaphorical effect is then an effect of subjectivity (and vice versa). There is no such thing as a metaphor without subjective participation, and there is no subjectification without metaphorization.

As metaphor's creative spark, the subject has no permanence or persistence; it comes into being as a spark flashing between two signifiers. As the result of new meaning brought into the world, however, the subject—the split subject found under the bar in the first two metaphors shown above—remains fixated or subjugated, and acquires a kind of permanence as such. The subject's symptomatic fixation has a metaphorical structure, that of a nonsensical signifier standing in for, or over against, the subject: $S_1/\$$.

We can provisionally view symptoms as having such a substitutional structure, wherein the subject as meaning persists indefinitely in its subjugated state unless a new metaphor is achieved. In that sense, analysis can be viewed, in Lacan's theory, as requiring that new metaphors be forged. For each new metaphor brings with it a precipitation of subjectivity which can alter the subject's position. Given that the symptom itself is a metaphor, the creation of a new metaphor in the course of analysis brings about, not the dissolution of all symptoms, but rather the reconfiguration of the symptom, the creation of a new symptom, or a modified subjective position with respect to the symptom. The end of analysis can be viewed as the effectuation of the substitution shown in the third metaphor above, $\$/a$, whereby the subject assumes the place of the Other and of the Other's desire (object $a$), no longer being subjugated thereby or fixated thereupon.

## The Signified

> [You] must not rack your brains to try and understand
> this by seeking to compare it with something similar
> that is already familiar to you; you must recognize in
> it a fundamentally new fact.
> —Freud, *Introductory Lectures on Psychoanalysis*

A new metaphor brings new meaning into the world. It alters the subject as meaning. But what is meaning in the Lacanian scheme of things? What exactly is it that metaphor creates, that metaphor affects or modifies?

What is the signified if not what we commonly refer to as thoughts or ideas? And what are thoughts but specific combinations of signifiers, that is signifiers

strung together in a particular way? When you "grasp" the meaning of something someone says, what goes on other than a situating of the statement in the
context of other statements, thoughts, terms? To understand means to locate or
embed one configuration of signifiers within another. In most cases it is as
nonconscious a process as one could desire, requiring no action on the part of
a subject: things fall into place within the web of multifarious connections
among thoughts already "assimilated."

According to Lacan, something makes sense when it fits into the pre-existing chain. It may add something to the chain without fundamentally altering it
or rocking the boat.

Metaphor, on the other hand, brings about a new configuration of thoughts,
establishing a new combination or permutation, a new *order* in the signifying
chain, a shakedown of the old order. Connections between signifiers are defin-
itively changed. That kind of modification cannot occur without implicating
the subject.

As I said above, it is precisely insofar as understanding involves nothing
more than situating one configuration of signifiers within another that Lacan is
so adamant about refusing to understand, about striving to defer understanding, because in the process of understanding, everything is brought back to
the level of the status quo, to the level of what is already known. Lacan's
writing itself overflows with extravagant, preposterous, and mixed metaphors,
precisely to jolt one out of the easy reductionism inherent in the very process
of understanding. As opposed to the considerable attention that has been devoted to the process by certain German thinkers,[4] in Lacan's framework, *verstehen* might as well be translated as "to assimilate." Thus the gist of Lacan's
claim that meaning (meaning as what you imagine you have understood) is
imaginary. By assimilating something, you have the sense of being someone,
or you imagine yourself as someone (an ego or self), who has accomplished a
certain difficult task; you picture yourself as a thinker. "True understanding,"
on the other hand—which could perhaps be rendered in French using the expression *se saisir de quelque chose*, the emphasis being on the reflexive—is
actually a process which goes beyond the automatic functioning of the symbolic order and involves an incursion of the symbolic into the real: the signifier
brings forth something new in the real or drains off more of the real into
the symbolic.

"True understanding" is, of course, a misnomer, in that understanding is
precisely short-circuited, unnecessary, irrelevant to the process. What is really
implied is that something changes, and that is the point of Lacanian analysis as
well: something takes place at the border of the symbolic and the real which
has nothing to do with understanding, as it is commonly understood. Hence the
irrelevance of the term "insight" in the analytic process: the analysand's subjective frustration at not *understanding* what is going on, how the analytic

process is supposed to work, what is really at the bottom of his or her neurosis, and so on in no way hinders the efficacy of psychoanalysis. Freud occasionally remarks that the analysand who achieves the most in the course of his or her analysis often remembers little, if anything, of it and has no understanding of what occurred in the process.

## Two Faces of the Psychoanalytic Subject

The two faces of the psychoanalytic subject (precipitate of meanings and breach) correspond, in certain respects, to the split discussed in chapter 4 between meaning and being. Here, however, the split is not between unconscious meaning and the false being of the ego, but rather between unconscious meaning and a kind of "being-in-the-breach," or, as Lacan says at one point, a "subject in the real."[5]

### The Subject as Signified

The subject in the real is not the person talked about by the analysand as limited in his or her abilities, incapable of deciding between different courses of action, subjected to the whims of the Other, at the mercy of his or her friends, lovers, institutional setting, cultural-religious upbringing, and so on. That person is what we might call, to borrow a highly ambiguous concept from both Freud and Lacan (to be explained in detail in chapter 8), the "castrated" subject. The concept of castration covers an enormous amount of ground in psychoanalysis and current usage, and I will use it here only in a very precise way: as referring to the subject's alienation by and in the Other and separation from the Other.

The castrated subject is a subject who has come to be within language. The "inadequately" or "insufficiently" castrated subject corresponds to a subject whose separation is not complete—in Lacan's terms from the early 1960s, a subject who "mistakes" the Other's demand (D) for the Other's desire ($a$) in fantasy (his or her fantasy corresponding to $ \$ \lozenge D$ instead of $ \$ \lozenge a$).[6] The subject who refuses to "sacrifice his or her castration to the Other's jouissance" (*Écrits*, p. 323) is the subject who has not undergone the further separation known as traversing fantasy; for castration must be sacrificed, given up, or surrendered if subjectification of the cause is to occur. The subject must renounce his or her more or less comfortable, complacently miserable position as subjected by the Other—as castrated—in order to take the Other's desire as cause upon him or herself. The traversing of fantasy thus involves a going beyond of castration and a utopian moment beyond neurosis.

The castrated subject is thus a subject who has not subjectified the Other's desire and who remains plagued by, and yet obtains a "secondary gain" from, his or her symptomatic submission to the Other. That subject can be characterized by the first two metaphors presented at the beginning of this chapter, but not by the third. Symptoms can be understood as messages about the subject that are designed for the Other, and until the subject can separate from that locus/destination in which his or her message and being takes on meaning, he or she remains castrated.

Castration, in this Lacanian context, clearly has nothing to do with biological organs or threats thereto. Such threats may, nevertheless, serve in specific contexts to separate a male child from his attachment to his mOther as preferred object of pleasure, but seem incapable of bringing on the further separation required to surmount castration.[7]

A kind of being is achieved through the first kind of separation: that provided by fantasy. Nevertheless, Lacan once again generally speaks rather of the "aphanisis" or fading of the neurotic subject in his or her fantasy as the object-cause steals the limelight. Object $a$ comes to the fore and is cast in the leading role in fantasy, the subject being eclipsed or overshadowed thereby.

Thus the false being of the ego and the elusive being provided in fantasy are rejected, one after the other, by Lacan as lacking: neither can take the subject beyond neurosis. In both cases, the subject remains castrated, subjected to the Other. Lacan nevertheless maintains the notion of a being beyond neurosis.[8]

The castrated subject is the subject that is represented. The castrated subject is always presenting itself to the Other, looking to win attention and recognition from the Other, and the more it presents itself, the more inescapably castrated it becomes as it is represented by and in the Other. The castrated subject is the barred subject, the subject under the bar: it is a product of every attempt and intent to signify to the Other. This "subject is constituted by the message" (*Écrits*, p. 305) received by the subject in an inverted form from the Other.

To understand this barred subject, we need to examine more closely the process of the creation of meaning through the effect of one signifier ($S_2$) on another ($S_1$).

OF SIGNIFIERS, UNARY AND BINARY

The inauguration of the subject through separation is related to Freud's notion of primal repression. According to Freud, the unconscious contains *Vorstellungsrepräsentanzen*, literally "representatives of the (re)presentation or idea," but usually rendered in English as "ideational representatives." They are the psychical representatives of *Triebe*, drives. In Freud's view, it is such representatives (and not perceptions or affects)[9] which are repressed. But Freud never really precisely determines the status of those representatives. The unconscious, he writes, is constituted through "a *primal repression*, a first phase of repression, which consists in the psychical (ideational) representative of the drive [*Trieb*] being denied entrance into consciousness. With this a *fixation* is established; the representative in question persists unaltered from then onwards and the drive [*Trieb*] remains attached to it."[10] Primal repression creates the *nucleus* of the unconscious, with which other representatives (of representations) establish connections that may eventually lead to their being drawn into the unconscious.

Lacan proposes that we equate these representatives with signifiers, words standing in for drives (i.e., acting as the representatives of drives) at the ideational level: the level of representation or thought. Signifiers are what allow drives to be represented: *presented to us* as beings of language. Starting from this equation of *Vorstellungsrepräsentanzen* with signifiers,[11] repression is conceptualized by Lacan as leading to the creation of the unconscious on the basis of a coupled pair of signifiers: the "unary signifier," which Lacan represents as $S_1$, and the "binary signifier" $S_2$ (Seminar XI, p. 219). The binary signifier is what is repressed in primal repression.

## THE SIGNIFIER TO WHICH ALL OTHER SIGNIFIERS
## REPRESENT A SUBJECT

The signifier of the Other's desire, the Name-of-the-Father, is the binary signifier that is primally repressed.

This signifier is quite unique: it is the signifier to which all other signifiers represent a subject. Should this signifier be missing, none of the other signifiers represents anything at all. This idea is expounded very schematically in "Subversion of the Subject and Dialectic of Desire" (*Écrits*), and I will try to lay it out here.

As we saw in the preceding chapter, Lacan postulates a primordial signifier that either is there or is not. If it is not, we speak of foreclosure and thus of psychosis, there being no possibility for the existence of a subject as such— that primordial signifier being the sine qua non of subjectivity.

The Name-of-the-Father is thus our Rock of Gibraltar. Lacan says that it is a signifier, but it is quite clearly different from most, if not all, others. If one word in a language becomes antiquated or goes out of style, other related terms tend to take up the slack; in other words, their meanings broaden to include those of the word that has disappeared. The Name-of-the-Father, on the contrary, is neither fungible nor pronounceable.

In psychosis, the barrier between mother and child offered by that name is not erected in a solid enough fashion. The father figure does not succeed in limiting the child's access to the mother; the signifier is not able to neutralize the child's jouissance, and that jouissance irrupts into his or her life, overwhelming and invading him or her. Different forms of psychosis are related to the different ways in which jouissance breaks in on the patient: jouissance invades the body in schizophrenia, and the locus of the Other as such in paranoia.[12]

The Name-of-the-Father does not hold its own in psychosis.

Returning to the case of neurosis, we see that for the Name-of-the-Father, all other signifiers represent a subject. Every signifier used by a neurotic (S', S", S"', etc.) is in some way, shape, or form linked to the Name-of-the-Father (figure 6.1), and the neurotic is thus implicated, to a greater or lesser degree, in every word he or she pronounces or hears. Nothing is innocent: even his or her so-called "empty speech" implies a subject position with respect to the Other, and every term has somehow contributed to making that position what it is.

Figure 6.1

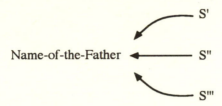

One is continually led back to the case of psychosis in bringing out the essential workings of the signifier in neurosis. Call each of these "other" signifiers an $S_2$, as Lacan often does.[13] In the late 1960s and 1970s, $S_1$ is assigned the role of the "master signifier," the nonsensical signifier devoid of meaning, which is only brought into the movement of language—in other words, "dialectized," a term I shall explain below—through the action of the various $S_2$s.

In accordance with Lacan's later usage, the Name-of-the-Father thus seems to be correlated with $S_1$, the master signifier. If $S_1$ is not in place, every $S_2$ is somehow unbound. The $S_2$s have relations amongst themselves; they may be strung together in perfectly ordinary ways by a psychotic, but they do not seem to affect him or her in any sense; they are somehow independent of him or her. Whereas a neurotic may, upon hearing an unusual term—say, "antidisestablishmentarianism"—be reminded of the first time he heard the word, who it was he learned it from and so on, a psychotic may focus on its strictly phonetic or sonic aspect. He may see meaning in nothing, or find a purely personal meaning in virtually everything. Words are taken as things, as real objects.

For a neurotic, every $S_2$ is individually linked with $S_1$. $S_1$ is not the subject, nor is $S_2$. A subject is that which one signifier represents to or for another. What is representation supposed to consist in here? $S_2$ represents a subject to $S_1$ in the sense that $S_2$ retroactively gives meaning to $S_1$, a meaning it did not have at the outset (figure 6.2). This meaning, written "s" (as a lowercase letter) when Lacan gives his version of the Saussurian sign, is replaced by $ in the fuller version of the signifier's retroactive effect (see, for example, Seminar XVII) that is schematized in figure 6.3. The subject here is but a constellation or conglomeration of *meanings*. If the subject consists in the whole set of meanings generated by the relation between all the $S_2$s and $S_1$, the subject seems to be a sort of sedimentation of meanings furnished by the Other (the subject's statements only taking on meaning in the Other or being granted meaning by the Other).

Figure 6.2

$$S_1 \longrightarrow S_2$$
$$\overline{\phantom{S_1 \longrightarrow S_2}}$$
$$s$$

Figure 6.3

$$S_1 \longrightarrow S_2$$
$$\overline{\phantom{S_1}} \qquad \overline{\phantom{S_2}}$$
$$\$ \qquad a$$

The subject *as* the meaning that settles out, in a sense, from the effect of one signifier upon another corresponds to the subject as eclipsed by meaning, meaning always being in the field of the Other. The subject as meaning—unconscious meaning or meaning in the Other—can be situated on the schema of the split subject (figure 6.4). In the lower right-hand corner unconscious meaning is created, but the subject is deprived of being.

Figure 6.4

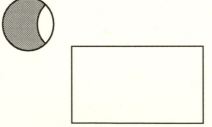

I am not
thinking

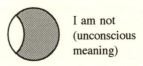

I am not
(unconscious
meaning)

## The Subject as Breach

While there seems to be little, if anything, smacking of subjectivity in such an interpretation, the subject is nevertheless *realized* in forging links between $S_1$ and $S_2$. The subject is not simply the sedimentation of meanings (under the bar in the following matheme),

$$\frac{S_1}{s} \rightarrow S_2$$

but also *the forging of links between signifiers*. Freud's term for the paths forged from neuron to neuron in his physiological sketch of the psyche in his "Project for a Scientific Psychology"[14] is *Bahnung* (lamely rendered in the English translation as "facilitation"), which Lacan translates as *frayage*, a sort of breach or path-breaking. He takes Freud's idea to be that of a breaking-through that establishes a link (or articulation) between so-called conceptual memories, and readily associates these neuronal links with the links between signifiers. The subject is the path forged between signifiers; in other words, the subject is, in a sense, what links them to one another.

By the time Lacan elaborates the four discourses (Seminar XVII), $S_1$ has become a positional notion. There is no single, unique $S_1$; $S_1$ simply designates a signifier which is isolated from the rest of discourse (or, as Freud says in *The Interpretation of Dreams*, which is cut off from the "psychical chain" of the person's conscious thoughts).[15] An $S_1$ is often recognizable in analysis by the fact that the analysand repeatedly butts up against the term; it may be a term like "death," for instance, or any other term that seems opaque to the analysand and that always seems to put an end to associations instead of opening things up. Here the analysand is, in a sense, encountering a total opacity of meaning; he or she may well know what the words *mean* in his or her mother tongue, remaining ignorant, however, of what they mean *to him or her*, their special, personal meaning that has some kind of subjective implication. The subject here is eclipsed by a master signifier without meaning:

$$\frac{S_1}{\cancel{S}}$$

In that sense the master signifier is nonsensical.

### THE PRECIPITATION OF SUBJECTIVITY: DIALECTIZING A MASTER SIGNIFIER

One of the goals of analysis is to "dialectize" such isolated terms, these words that put a stop to the flow of the patient's associations, that freeze the subject— or rather, annihilate him or her. "Dialectize" here is the term Lacan uses to indicate that one tries to introduce an outside, in some sense, of this $S_1$, that is, to establish an opposition between it and another signifier, $S_2$. If we can bring this $S_1$ into some kind of relationship with another signifier, then its status as a master signifier subjugating the subject changes. A bridge is built between it and another linguistic element, and a loss takes place:

$$\frac{S_1}{\$} \quad \rightarrow \quad \frac{S_2}{a}$$

(I won't go into the complexities of the "loss"—object $a$—here; see chapter 7 below). Plainly speaking, the analysand is no longer stuck at that particular point of his or her associations; after running up against the same term off and on for what may have been months on end, it begins to give. A meaning of that master signifier for the subject is created, and the subject is once against split between meaning and being,

$$meaning \ \frac{\overset{\displaystyle S}{S_1}}{\$} \quad \rightarrow \quad \frac{S_2}{a} \ being$$

having come to be momentarily in the forging of a link between $S_1$ and $S_2$. The creation of an opposition between an $S_1$ and another signifying element is what allows for a subjective *position*. Note the opposition here between *the subject who has come to be* in the bridge-building between $S_1$ and $S_2$—along the arrow, in a sense[16]—and *the barred or alienated subject of meaning*, $\$$ (relegated to a site below the bar).

Each isolated $S_1$ is, when it appears, nonsensical. $S_1$, unlike $S(\mathbb{A})$, is not unpronounceable. It is not some mysterious, hidden signifier that finally wells up from the depths one day; it may very well be a word or name the analysand has used every day of his or her life. It insists, however, in the realm of non-meaning when it comes up in a context that seems to involve the analysand, though the analysand does not know how or why. Nonsense may, of course, take other forms as well: it may appear in an incomprehensible slurring of words to which no meaning whatever can be attributed, as the resulting sounds suggest nothing in the way of a play on words.

Lacan's emphasis, in any case, on the importance of nonsense is related to the analytic aim of dialectizing the signifiers that, in the course of analytic treatment, come to the fore as isolated master signifiers. Autism might be seen as a case in which there is one or only a very few master signifiers that are virtually impossible to dialectize. In neurosis, there is generally a whole series of master signifiers that manifest themselves in the course of treatment and that catch our attention as being stopping points or dead ends of some kind. It is those dead ends that analysis sets out to make into through streets. The subject appears in the process of clearing an obstacle out of an impasse, thereby creating an outlet. The subject is, in a sense, the splitting of that obstacle into two separate parts: $S_1$ and $S_2$ (figure 6.5).

Figure 6.5

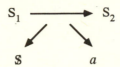

I have, by this point in the discussion, provided at least four separate ways of understanding what psychoanalysis sets out to achieve: the dialectization of master signifiers, the precipitation of subjectivity, the creation of a new metaphor, and the subjectification or "assumption" of the cause. The reader who is by now familiar with Lacan's ever more polyvalent "algebra" is no doubt prepared to hear that they are all one and the same, that is, that they are all partial ways of characterizing the same basic aim. When a master signifier is dialectized, metaphorization occurs, the subject is precipitated, and the subject assumes a new position in relation to the cause. They all come under the process of separation and of that further separation Lacan refers to as the traversing of fantasy.

Separation is ultimately what analysis with neurotics is all about. Apart from all the symptoms neurotics present, whether psychosomatic or "purely" psychical, that stem from identification with parents, relatives, and so on, and that must obviously be worked through, a large part of the work with neurotics revolves around the completion of separation. Whereas Freud suggests that analysis, when pursued far enough, always comes up against the insurmountable "rock of castration,"[17] Lacan suggests that separation can take the subject beyond that point. Subjectifying one's fate, that foreign cause (the Other's desire) that brought one into the world, alienation can be surpassed. A utopian moment of sorts in Lacan's work, this passage beyond castration was, to the best of my knowledge, never recanted in Lacan's later work, unlike other utopian moments (e.g., full speech), which were implicitly critiqued in common instances of "Lacan against Lacan" (the late Lacan against the early Lacan). Thus it stands as a cornerstone of Lacan's rebuttal to, or surpassing of, Freud.[18]

# Part Three

THE LACANIAN OBJECT: LOVE, DESIRE, JOUISSANCE

# 7

## Object (a): Cause of Desire

WITH OBJECT $a$, Lacan felt he had made his most significant contribution to psychoanalysis.[1] Few concepts in the Lacanian opus are elaborated so extensively, revised so significantly from the 1950s to the 1970s, worked over from so many different perspectives, and require so many modifications in our usual ways of thinking about desire, transference, and science. And few concepts have so many avatars in Lacan's work: the other, *agalma*, the golden number, the Freudian Thing, the real, the anomaly, the cause of desire, surplus jouissance, the materiality of language, the analyst's desire, logical consistency, the Other's desire, semblance/sham, the lost object, and so on and so forth. As literally thousands of pages in Lacan's work, most of it as yet unpublished, are devoted to the development of this concept,[2] I cannot possibly hope to provide an account for object $a$ that adequately explains or covers all of Lacan's glosses. Moreover, many of his elaborations involve algebraic, topological, and logical formulations that would require extensive commentary and be of little interest to most readers.[3] While warranting a book-length study,[4] I shall limit myself here to what I consider to be some of the most salient aspects of Lacan's foremost contribution to psychoanalysis.

In earlier chapters of this book, I was obliged to introduce object $a$ in a number of different contexts to explain the advent of the subject and corresponding changes in the Other. As is only to be expected, Lacan's concept of the object and the subject undergo contemporaneous revisions, and one cannot grasp Lacan's theory at any particular moment in time without taking both concepts into account. In chapter 3, I referred to object $a$ as the residue of symbolization—the real ($R_2$) that remains, insists, and ex-sists after or despite symbolization—as the traumatic cause, and as that which interrupts the smooth functioning of law and the automatic unfolding of the signifying chain. In chapter 5, I discussed object $a$ as a last reminder or remainder of the hypothetical mother-child unity to which the subject clings in fantasy to achieve a sense of wholeness, as the Other's desire, as the jouissance object, as that "part" of the mOther the child takes with it in separation, and as the foreign, fateful cause of the subject's existence that he or she must become or subjectify in analysis. In chapter 6, I briefly mentioned object $a$ in the context of Freud's lost object, as the subject's being, and as a product of the dialectization of a master signifier.

The reader's task in "thinking together" all of these ways of talking about object *a* has not been an easy one, and I hope to partially rectify that in the present chapter. Nevertheless, just as in part 2 of this book, it was not always possible to think together all of his formulations concerning the subject, it is not a simple matter to reconcile all of his formulations concerning the object. This is, no doubt, part of what makes the concept so fruitful for further thought, but so infuriating to the systematizer and so bothersome to the "scientifically minded." Can a concept which is so highly polyvalent be of any value to the constitution of psychoanalysis as a significant discourse, much less as a science? I will take up the relation between psychoanalysis and science in chapter 10.

Here let us back up several steps, and consider the concept of the object from the perspective of the imaginary, the symbolic, and the real. This will provide some perspective on the evolution of Lacan's notion of the object from the 1930s on.


## "Object Relations"

### *Imaginary Objects, Imaginary Relations*

The foremost imaginary object is the ego. As I explained in the first subsection of chapter 4, the ego is an imaginary production,[5] a crystallization or sedimentation of images of an individual's own body and of self-images reflected back to him or her by others. In contradistinction to Freud, Lacan maintains that this crystallization does not constitute an agency, but rather an object. That object is cathected or invested with libido like other objects, and thus the infant's "own" ego is not necessarily cathected any more than other objects (or egos) in the infant's environment. The object, as understood at this imaginary level, is one towards which libido is directed or withdrawn, as is the case with love objects as we find them in Freud's work.

Playing off the inherently foreign and objectlike nature of the ego, Lacan refers to it in the early 1950s as an other (*autre* in French), hence his abbreviation *a* for the ego, which is usually italicized, indicating (in accordance with Lacan's general typographical conventions) that it is imaginary. One's own ego is designated as *a* and another's ego as *a'*. Such designations highlight the similarity between them.

"Imaginary relations" are not illusory relationships—relationships that don't *really* exist—but rather relations between egos, wherein everything is played out in terms of but one opposition: same or different. They involve other people who you consider to be *like* yourself for a variety of reasons. It could be because the two of you look very much alike, are similar in size or age, and so on. In the case of an infant, it is generally that child in the family, extended family, or circle of friends who bears the greatest affinity to the infant in terms of size, age, interests, and abilities and who also stands in a similar relation to a parental or authority figure (figure 7.1). The determination of who is similar and who is not thus also involves symbolic components.[6]

Figure 7.1

<table>
<tr><td>

Two siblings in
the same situation
with respect to one and
the same parental figure

</td><td>

Two children in
the same situation
with respect to
two different parental figures

</td></tr>
</table>

SAME (LOVE), DIFFERENT (HATE)

Corresponding to the main imaginary opposition of same and different, imaginary relationships are characterized by two salient features: love (identification) and hate (rivalry). Insofar as the other is like me, I love and identify with him or her, feeling his or her joy and pain as my own. In the case of identical twins, one often finds that one twin cathects the other twin's ego almost as much as his or her own. This is true, though no doubt to a lesser extent, in many close-knit families, there being a great deal of solidarity among the children. In such cases we see the ever so rare implementation of the biblical injunction to love thy neighbor as thyself. Insofar as I love my self, another self like myself is equally worthy of love.

This also explains, in a sense, the flip side of such close identification: the tension generated by *la petite différence*. Difference inevitably creeps between even the most identical of twins, whether due to differential treatment by parents or changes in appearance over time, and the closer the relationship at the outset, the greater the rage over minute differences is likely to be.

Sibling rivalry is the best-known example of imaginary relations involving hatred. Whereas very young children usually do not call into question their subordination to their parents—perceiving a clear difference between the parents and themselves—they do regularly contest, right from a very tender age, their rank and status among their siblings. Children generally consider their siblings as in the same category as themselves, and cannot abide overly preferential treatment by the parents of anyone other than themselves, double standards, and so on. They come to hate their siblings for taking away their special place in the family, stealing the limelight, and performing better than they do in activities valued by the parents. That same kind of rivalry generally extends in time to classmates, cousins, neighborhood friends, and so on. The rivalry in such relationships very often revolves around status symbols and implies all kinds of other symbolic and linguistic elements as well. What distinguishes such relationships is that the two parties see themselves as more or less equals—regardless of slight age differences, grade point averages, social success, and so on—and can very easily imagine themselves as in the other's shoes, rivalry and jealousy arising out of such comparisons.

Those whom we consider like ourselves generally stand in a similar relation to the Other as we do. And since the Other generalizes—from our parents to the academic Other, the law, religion, God, tradition, as so on—imaginary relations are not simply relations characteristic of early childhood that are somehow outgrown in time. They remain important all our lives.

In the early to mid-1950s, the other, *a*, is the Lacanian object, and there is no other object in view in Lacan's work. It is not until Seminar VII, where Lacan explores *das Ding*, Seminar VIII where he isolates *agalma* in Plato's *Symposium*, and Seminar IX that Lacan begins to conceptualize a wholly different kind of object: a real object, cause of desire. From then on, Lacan devotes virtually all of his interest to the latter, but in no sense invalidates the importance of the object situated at the imaginary level. Consider, for example, the analytic situation.

In analysis, the analyst is often taken by the analysand (especially at the outset) as a stand-in for the imaginary other; this is seen in the analysand's attempt to identify with the analyst as *like* the analysand, the same as the analysand in terms of level of culture, interests, psychoanalytic orientation, religion, or what have you. In my own practice, it is quite common for analysands to mention within two or three sessions that we have the same books on our shelves, implying thereby that our concerns and perspectives are the same. This attempt to find similarities, to identify with me as an other, may at first give rise to love, but ultimately leads to rivalry: the analysand may at first cast me as similar to him or herself, but is then led to seek out areas in which he or she is different, that is, superior or inferior.

This level of rivalry is the level at which Lacan situates what most American analysts call "countertransference": it is the level at which the analyst gets caught up in the same game of comparing him or herself with his or her analysands, sizing their discourse up in terms of his or her own. "Are they ahead of me or behind me in their comprehension of what is going on here in the analytic setting or elsewhere? Are they submissive to my wishes? Do I have any control over the situation? Do I have the upper hand? How come this person gets on my nerves and makes me feel so lousy about myself?" Lacan's perspective is not that countertransferential feelings do not exist, but that they are always and inescapably situated at the imaginary level and thus must be set aside by the analyst. They must not be revealed to the analysand, as that positions the analyst and analysand at the same level, as imaginary others for each other, capable of having similar feelings, hang-ups, insecurities, and so on. Such positioning prevents the analysand from casting the analyst in some Other role.

## *The Other as Object, Symbolic Relations*

> [A]ll of these are aimed at *some other person*—but
> most of all at the prehistoric, unforgettable other per-
> son who is never equaled by anyone later.
>    —Freud, SE I, p. 239

Symbolic relations are those with the Other as language, knowledge, law, career, academia, authority, morality, ideals, and so on, and with the objects
designated (or, more strongly stated, demanded) by the Other: grades, diplomas, success, marriage, children—all the things usually associated with anxiety in neurosis. Nevertheless, the only truly important "object" (if it may
loosely be called one) at the level of symbolic relations in the analytic situation
is the analyst as Other, as avatar or representative of the Other.[7]

In Lacan's two-tiered model of the analytic setting (imaginary and symbolic), characteristic of his work in the early to mid-1950s, the goal in analyzing neurotics is to eliminate the interference in symbolic relations created by
imaginary relations, in other words, to get imaginary interests out of the way
so as to confront the analysand with his or her problems with the Other as such.
In the case of heterosexual neurotics, for example, this generally involves,
among other things, working through and thus dissipating imaginary identifications with members of the same sex (figure 7.2).

Figure 7.2

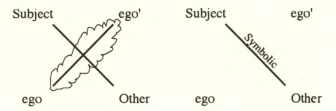

At this early stage of Lacan's work, *the subject consists in a stance adopted
with respect to this Other*, a symptomatic stance in which the subject tries to
maintain the "right" distance from the Other, never fully meeting the Other's
demands but never frustrating them altogether either, never getting too close
to achieving those goals promulgated by the Other but never too far away from
achieving them either.

Analysts are often cast in the position of the Other by their analysands.
Lacan formulates this by saying that the analyst is viewed by the analysand as
the subject supposed to know: to know what is the matter when psychological
difficulties arise, when symptoms appear, and so on. In Western societies,
analysts are often presumed to have such knowledge, even by people who

never consult an analyst in their lifetimes. This presumption has to do with the social function of psychoanalysis in certain parts of the world today.

A problem arises, however, if the analyst agrees to play the role of the subject supposed to know, and falls into the trap of believing he or she really does know that which can never be known in advance, but only constructed in the course of analysis. The analyst thereby slips into a false sense of mastery—which generates an imaginary relationship with the analysand. Analysis has taken over the former role of confession for many and prayer/atonement for others, situating the analyst in the God-like position of the all-knowing Other, fit to deliberate on all questions of normal and abnormal, right and wrong, good and bad. Lacan, at one point, identifies the analysand's assumption that the analyst has a certain stock of knowledge about his or her symptom, desire, fantasy, and pleasure as the mainspring of transference (the projection of knowledge onto another elicits love, transference love).[8] But while all of these factors predestine the analyst for the role of Other, he or she must not fall into the trap of interpreting from that position.

Freud, of course, did just that at the outset: for years he explained to his analysands his theories about the unconscious, repression, symptom formation, and so on, interpreting what they told him on the basis thereof and attempting to elicit from them an expression of agreement or belief.[9] Fortunately he did not worry too much if that expression was not forthcoming, and gradually abandoned the approach of explaining everything he thought—his whole way of understanding the situation—to his analysands. For espousing a theory in the analytic situation is very likely to lead analysands to seek ways of disproving it (as did the butcher's wife discussed by Freud in *The Interpretation of Dreams*, who claimed to have had a dream which disproved Freud's theory that every dream is the fulfillment of a wish),[10] of coming up with a better theory than the analyst's, thereby removing the analyst from the position of the subject supposed to know, casting him or her instead as an ordinary person like the analysand, who is not always right and who may even turn out to be dumber than the analysand.

It is not that the analyst must, at all costs, remain in the position of the subject supposed to know—quite the contrary. But explicitly acting as if one were such a subject tends to elicit imaginary relations of rivalry on the analysand's part, the worst possible relations between analyst and analysand. That is Pitfall 1. Pitfall 2: if analysts believe they really do have that presumed knowledge, they are bound to hand down interpretations as if they were lecturing from a pulpit, providing interpretations which can have little if any beneficial effect on their analysands, and serve only to make the latter more dependent on their analysts. For by responding to the analysand's demand for advice and interpretation, for "understanding" of his or her symptoms, the analyst gives what he or she has ("knowledge") instead of what he or she does not have (lack, in other words, desire), and encourages the analysand to demand rather than desire, to remain alienated rather than separate.

The analyst, rather than considering him or herself to be the representative of knowledge in the analytic situation, must take the analysand's unconscious as the representative of knowledge. The unconscious—when it speaks or manifests itself through interruptions, slips, and slurs of the analysand's speech, bungled actions, forgotten appointments, mistaken dollar amounts—must be taken by the analyst to be the ultimate authority, the Other, the subject supposed to know.

Nevertheless, at the outset, the analysand casts the analyst as the Other of demand,[11] in other words, the (usually parental) Other to whom the analysand has always addressed his or her demands for knowledge, help, nourishment, recognition, attention, affection, approval, and disapproval. All such demands boil down, according to Lacan, to one and the same thing: the demand for love.[12] Above and beyond all the specific demands one formulates, it is always love that one is seeking.

Certain analysts (including, for example, Winnicott) believe that it is the analyst's duty to play mother to the analysand, as the analysand's neurosis is indicative of "inadequate mothering." According to them, the analyst has to attempt to be a "good enough mother," making up for the inadequate attention, approval, disapproval, love, and discipline the analysand received growing up. The analyst has to be the perfect love object, neither smothering, nor absent. The problem, according to Lacan, is that this makes the analysand ever more dependent on the analyst, and the analysand's desire (as expressed in his or her fantasy) comes to revolve entirely around the analyst's demand ($ ◊ D)—that the analysand get better, dream, daydream, reflect, or whatever else it is the analyst demands or the analysand thinks the analyst is demanding.

Analysts always make some demands on their analysands regarding appointment times, frequency of sessions, payment, and speech (requiring the analysand to say whatever comes to mind, for instance), but when the analyst is cast as parental Other, such demands are read as signs of love, which in turn fuel the analysand's demands, fixating him or her on one love object. For love (correlated with demand) *has* an object.[13] When Freud speaks of "object choice," it has to do with the subject's repetitive demand for the same kind of love object, or the same kind of relationship with a love object. And when Lacan, in his early work, speaks of objects "of desire" or "in desire" (see in particular Seminar VI), such objects are clearly love objects, in other words, objects to which the subject addresses his or her demand for love.

demand → object

In the early to mid-1950s, Lacan conceives of analysis as involving a progressive dissipation of the analysand's imaginary relations and a progressive bringing into focus of his or her symbolic relations, that is, his or her relationship to the Other. At this point in his theory, analysis consists ultimately in a "rectification" of the subject's position with respect to the Other, an Other *not* embodied by the analyst. Lacan believes, at this time, that such repositioning brings about a kind of full-fledged desire, free from the Other's dominion. Later, however, Lacan comes to see that an analysis carried out at that level does not go far enough in constituting the subject as desire and leaves him or her stuck at the level of demand, dependent upon the Other's demand. In Seminar I, Lacan already situates the Other (as language, tradition, etc.) *between* the analyst and analysand,[14] but the analyst's ex-centric role is nowhere specified there. All Lacan stresses at that point is the analysand's relation to the Other, and, as we have seen, if the analyst does not truly relinquish or renounce the role of Other by assuming some *other* position, the analysand remains stuck or stranded at the level of demand, hung up on the Other's demand, unable to truly desire.

In examining the various roles of the analyst as the analysand's object— other ($a'$) or Other (A)—we have seen that the analyst must avoid the pitfalls of the imaginary (thinking of him or herself as like the analysand, however true this may be in many respects) and must not interpret from the position of the omniscient Other. Where then is the analyst to situate him or herself? If the analyst is to be neither imaginary rival nor representative of the Other, what kind of object is there left to be? What role then is left the analyst? What part does the analyst play in the analysand's psychic economy? It is Lacan's elaboration of the nature of desire that allows him to answer those questions. Let us jump right to his conclusions regarding desire.

### Real Objects, Encounters with the Real

> [D]esire is neither the appetite for satisfaction nor the
> demand for love, but the difference which results
> from the subtraction of the first from the second—the
> very phenomenon of their splitting.
> —Lacan, *Écrits*, p. 287

> Je te demande de refuser ce que je t'offre parce que ce
> n'est pas ça![15]
> —Lacan

> Just because people ask you for something doesn't
> mean that's what they really want you to give them.[16]
> —Lacan, Seminar XIII, March 23, 1966

*Desire, strictly speaking, has no object.* In its essence, desire is a constant search for something else, and there is no specifiable object that is capable of satisfying it, in other words, extinguishing it. Desire is fundamentally caught up in the dialectical *movement* of one signifier to the next, and is diametrically opposed to fixation. It does not seek satisfaction, but rather its own continuation and furtherance: more desire, greater desire! It wishes merely to go on desiring. Thus desire, according to Lacan, is not all that goes by that name in common parlance, for it is rigorously distinct from demand.

The only object involved in desire is that "object" (if we can still refer to it as an object) that *causes* desire. Desire has no "object" as such.[17] It has a cause, a cause that brings it into being, that Lacan dubs object (a), cause of desire. The bracketing or placing in parentheses of the object—seen most clearly in Lacan's 1966 postface (simply called "Suite") to the "Seminar on 'The Purloined Letter'" (*Écrits* 1966)—is a sign of the object's transposition from the imaginary register to the real: Lacan no longer writes object *a* (the "a" being in italics), but rather object (a). It is, no doubt, misleading in many ways to even retain the term "object" in speaking of the cause, but by maintaining the term while changing its meaning Lacan in a sense is seeking to preempt discussion of what more commonly, in psychoanalytic theory, goes by the name "object," implicitly suggesting that it is of only secondary importance.[18]

Object (a) as the cause of desire is that which elicits desire: it is responsible for the advent of desire, for the particular form the desire in question takes, and for its intensity. Drawn schematically, we have:

cause $\rightarrow$ desire $\rightarrow$ metonymic slippage from one object to the next[19]

Let us now back up for a moment. What arouses desire in a child is the Other's desire, not the Other's demand, nor even the Other's desire for this or that particular thing or person. The Other's desire, as it alights upon specific objects and people, directs the child's desire but does not cause it. It is the Other's desire as pure desirousness—manifested in the Other's gaze at something or someone, but distinct from that something or someone—that elicits desire in the child. It is not so much the object looked at as the looking itself, the desire manifested in the very act of looking, for example, that arouses the child's desire.

Apart from the various qualities or attributes analysands mention to their analysts as playing a role in their "object choice"—hair color, eye color, and so on—analysands often recount something far more difficult to get a handle on or put into words: a certain way a man has of looking at a woman may sum up for that woman everything she really wants in a man. (Not what she *says* she wants in a man, appealing to typical American discourse about needs: "I need affection, support, and encouragement." For that is all conscious ego discourse: verily and truly the discourse of the Other, the social American Other.) That particular way of looking, that—to use an example—impertinent, unblinking way of looking, may be what really causes her to desire, stimulating in her a desire which cannot be extinguished by all the fine qualities revindicated by the ego: a man who is caring, a good father, a good provider, and so on and so forth. It is the desire-causing look that determines for her what Freud called "object choice" and what I will call *the choice of companions*. For that look, as found in the world, is associated with someone: an "individual."

That individual is adopted as the subject's companion in the hope of remaining in close proximity to the desire-inspiring look.

object as cause $\rightarrow$ desire $\rightarrow$ companion
gaze/look (a)            $\math$
voice (a)

But the fact of the matter is that the companion (with all his individual characteristics, foibles, distinguishing qualities, etc.) has little or no value to desire compared with the cause. The woman may be interested in little else in her companion than his ability to give her that look; should he no longer be able to, due to a turnaround in their relationship, she may well move on, searching to situate herself anew in that desire-eliciting relation to a certain kind of look.

In the case of certain men it is a woman's voice that is of primary importance; it is not so much what she says as the way in which she says it, the tone and timber of her voice, that arouses their desire. When a man has found someone whose voice expresses desire in much the same way as did his mother's voice, for example, he may fly in the face of public opinion, social pressure, and conventional morality, abandoning his search for a woman with all the qualities he was taught to seek out.

Not necessarily for love, as is commonly thought, but for desire—in order to be able to maintain a position as desiring subject.

Note that the two examples I have thus far given of object (a) are the Other's desire as manifested in the voice and in the gaze, both of which are unspecularizable: you cannot see them per se, they have no mirror images, and they are extremely difficult to symbolize or formalize. They belong to the register of what Lacan calls the real, and resist imaginarization and symbolization. They are nevertheless closely related to the subject's most crucial experiences of pleasure and pain, excitement and disappointment, thrill and horror. They resist analytic action—which involves speech, putting things into words, trying to say what the problem is, to speak it—and are related to a jouissance that defines the subject's very being.

The real is essentially that which resists symbolization and thus resists the dialectization characteristic of the symbolic order, in which one thing can be substituted for another. Not everything is fungible; certain things are not interchangeable for the simple reason that they cannot be "signifierized." They cannot be found elsewhere, as they have a Thing-like quality, requiring the subject to come back to them over and over again.

The challenge Lacanian psychoanalysis accepts is that of inventing ways in which to hit the real, upset the repetition it engenders, dialectize the isolated Thing, and shake up the fundamental fantasy in which the subject constitutes him or herself in relation to the cause.

## Lost Objects

Lacan explicitly acknowledges his debt to a number of psychoanalysts who helped him on his way to the concept object (a): Karl Abraham, Melanie Klein ("part-objects"), and Donald Winnicott ("transitional objects").[20] Neverthe-less, it is clearly to Freud that he is most indebted for his formulation of the notion of the "lost object." As is so often the case, however, Lacan's "lost object" goes far beyond anything "found" in Freud's work. Examined in con-text, Freud never claims that objects are inexorably or irremediably lost, or that the "rediscovery" or "refinding" of an object implies an object that is always already lost.

Consider, for example, what Freud says in "Negation":

> Experience has taught that it is important not only for a thing [*ein Ding*] (an object which affords satisfaction) to possess the property of being "good"—thus deserving to be taken into the ego—but also for it to be there in the outside world, ready to be seized when needed. In order to understand this step forward [from the simple judg-ment of attribution of the quality "good" or "bad" to the judgment of existence], we must recall that all representations [mental images] come from perceptions and are repetitions thereof. At the outset, the very existence of a representation thus guaran-tees the reality [the existence in the outside world] of that which is represented [imagined or pictured in the mind]. The opposition between subjective and objective does not exist from the first. It is only constituted by the fact that thought has the ability to make present a second time something that was once perceived, by reproducing it in a representation, the outside object no longer having to be present. Thus the first and most immediate aim of reality testing is not to find an object in real perception corresponding to what is represented [in the mind], but to refind such an object—to convince oneself that it is still out there. . . . [A]n essential precondi-tion for the institution of reality testing is clearly that objects shall have been lost which formerly afforded real satisfaction. (SE XIX, pp. 237–38, translation modified)

Freud does not claim here that the object is, of its very nature, lost in any absolute sense. An object is *encountered* at the outset, not actively sought out by the child, because the child is not able to seek out an object until *after* such an encounter. Afterwards, the memory of the experience of satisfaction is recalled to mind (reactivated, so to speak, or recathected), and satisfaction may be either hallucinated (primary process) or sought out in the "external" world (secondary process). Thus there is no initial *Objektfindung* but only a *Wiederzufindung*, no deliberate *finding* of an object, only a *refinding* of an object in the "outside" world that corresponds to one's memory of an experi-ence of satisfaction once *happened upon* (τυχή). Animals, by contrast, are led to *find* what instinct (as a sort of imprinted, pre-inscribed, encrypted knowledge) instructs them to look for.[21] Humans, lacking such innate knowledge of what will provide satisfaction, must first encounter it through the good graces of fortune, and only then can initiate action to repeat the satisfying experience.

Similarly, when Freud says in the *Three Essays on the Theory of Sexuality* that "[t]he finding of an object is in fact a refinding of it" (SE VII, p. 222), he is referring to the fact that object-choice after the latency period repeats the child's first object-choice: the breast. Here too, an initially encountered object is found anew at some later point in time.

Freud's language is, nevertheless, highly suggestive, and Lacan provides a sort of Talmudic reading (as he himself says in Seminar VII, p. 58) of Freud's texts, attaching more importance to the letter of the text than to its fairly obvious meaning. If the object was never found, strictly speaking, that is perhaps because it is essentially phantasmatic in nature, not corresponding to a *remembered* experience of satisfaction. There never was such an object in the first place: the "lost object" never *was*; it is only constituted as lost after the fact, in that the subject is unable to find it anywhere other than in fantasy or dream life. Using Freud's text as a springboard, the object can be viewed as always already lost.[22]

We could account for the lost object in yet another way. The breast is not, during the first experience of satisfaction, constituted as an object at all, much less as an object that is not part of the infant's body and that is largely beyond the infant's control. It is only constituted after the fact, after numerous vain attempts by the infant to repeat that first experience of satisfaction when the mother is not present or refuses to nurse the child. It is the absence of the breast, and thus the failure to achieve satisfaction, that leads to its constitution as an object as such, an object separate from and not controlled by the child. Once constituted (i.e., symbolized, though the child may as yet still be unable to speak in any way intelligible to others), the child can never again refind the breast as experienced the first time around: as *not separate* from his or her lips, tongue, and mouth, or from his or her self. Once the object is constituted, the "primal state" wherein there is no distinction between infant and breast, or between subject and object (for the subject only comes into being when the lacking breast is constituted as object, and qua relation to that object), can never be re-experienced, and thus the satisfaction provided the first time can never be repeated.[23] A kind of innocence is lost forever, and the actual breasts found thereafter are never quite *it*. *Object (a) is the leftover of that process of constituting an object, the scrap that evades the grasp of symbolization*.[24] It is a reminder that there is something else, something perhaps lost, perhaps yet to be found.

That is precisely what I said of object (a) in chapter 5: it is the rem(a)inder of the lost hypothetical mother-child unity.

## The Freudian Thing

Other aspects of the Lacanian object are "derived" from Freud's work in a similar fashion. *Das Ding* (the Thing), already encountered in the passage from "Negation" quoted above, is extensively discussed by Lacan in Seminar VII on the basis of Freud's "Project for a Scientific Psychology." There Freud describes the Thing in neuronal terms as that which is invariable in, say, the infant's various perceptions of the breast: the one neuron ("neuron $a$," as it is felicitously referred to in Freud's manuscript) in the "neuronal complex" corresponding to the "constant portion of the perceptual complex" (SE I, p. 328). That which is variable ("neuron $b$") comes into association with other neurons (the seat of memories of other specific perceptions), establishing links with them. In Lacan's "translation" of Freud's neurons as signifiers, and of the so-called facilitations (*Bahnungen*, breaches) among them as the articulations or links between signifiers (Seminar VII, p. 39), we find something (neuron $a$) which remains isolated or cut off from the rest of the signifying chain, though the chain necessarily circles around it: the Thing, alias object (a).

Freud extends his description to the other: the fellow human being, fellow creature, or neighbor (*Nebenmensch*) who first cares for the infant in its helpless state. "[T]he complex of a fellow creature falls into two portions. One of these gives the impression of being a constant structure and remains as a coherent 'thing'" (SE I, p. 331). Insofar as that constant portion remains cut off from associative links with the other neurons—in other words, signifiers—Lacan can continue his "translation" as follows: "*Das Ding* is from the outset what I call the nonsignified [or beyond-of-the-signified: *hors-signifié*]. The subject keeps his distance from this nonsignified and from an affective relation to it, constituting himself in a type of relation, characterized by primal affect, that is prior to any and all repression" (Seminar VII, p. 54).

Here *das Ding* appears as the unsignified and unsignifiable object within the Other (or "Other-complex")—*in* the Other yet more than or beyond the Other.[25] It is that object from which the subject keeps his or her distance, not getting too close or too far away either. *The subject comes into being as a defense against it, against the primal experience of pleasure/pain associated with it.* The subject's relation to it is characterized by a primal affect, whether this be revulsion, disgust, or aversion, as in hysteria, or a sense of being overwhelmed[26] or overcome, leading to avoidance, as in obsession. Indeed, these differing "primal affects," primal stances adopted with respect to the "thing" (object $a$) encountered by the infant in its relations with a fellow creature (parental Other), constitute structural diagnostic criteria by which to distinguish hysteria from obsession. In Freud's letters to Fliess, in particular, we see that hysteria is defined as a particular kind of affective response to a sexually charged "primordial" encounter with an other person, one of unpleasure or disgust; whereas obsession is variously defined in terms of a different response: pleasure, a sense of being overwhelmed, and guilt.[27]

Here we see that what Lacan calls the "Freudian Thing" is an early version of object (a), and that the primal relation to it described by Freud is the same as that constituted by the fundamental fantasy, as described above in chapters 5 and 6.

## Surplus Value, Surplus Jouissance

In Seminar XVI, Lacan equates object (a) with Marx's concept of surplus value.[28] As that which is most highly prized or valued by the subject, object (a) is related to the former gold standard, the value against which all other values (e.g., currencies, precious metals, gems, etc.) were measured. For the subject, it is that value he or she is seeking in all of his or her activities and relations.

Surplus value corresponds in quantity to what, in capitalism, is called "interest" or "profit": it is that which the capitalist skims off the top for him or herself, instead of paying it to the employees. (It also goes by the name of "reinvestment capital," and by many other euphemisms as well.) It is, loosely speaking, the *fruit* of the employees' labor. When, in legal documents written in American English, someone is said to have the right to the fruit or "usufruct" of a particular piece of property or sum of money held in trust, it means that that person has a right to the profit generated by it, though not necessarily to the property or money itself. In other words, it is a right, not of ownership, but rather of "enjoyment." In everyday French, you could say that that person has *la jouissance* of said property or money. In the more precise terms of French finance, that would mean that he or she enjoys, not the land, buildings, or capital itself (*la nue-propriété*; literally, "naked property"), but merely its excess fruits, its product above and beyond that required to reimburse its upkeep, cultivation, and so on—in a word, its operating expenses. (Note that in French legal jargon, *jouissance* is more closely related to possession.)[29]

The employee never enjoys that surplus product: he or she "loses" it. The work process produces him or her as an "alienated" subject ($), simultaneously producing a loss, (a). The capitalist, as Other, enjoys that excess product, and thus the subject finds him or herself in the unenviable situation of working for the Other's enjoyment, sacrificing him or herself for the Other's jouissance— precisely what the neurotic most abhors!

Like surplus value, this surplus jouissance may be viewed as circulating "outside" of the subject in the Other. It is a part of the libido that circulates *hors corps*. (See the section on "Castration" in chapter 8 for further discussion of this point.)

The distinction between an object *of* desire and an object which *causes* desire is truly a crucial one. Unfortunately, explanations of object (a) in the literature are often cast in the same basic language as that used in discussing Freudian objects: the mother is the child's first object; a boy must go on to find another love object of the same sex as his mother; a young girl must go on to find a love object of the opposite sex from that of her first main object; and so on. This merely compounds the difficulty of grasping an already highly complex part of Lacan's theory.

The discussion I have provided here is by no means exhaustive, and further facets of object (a) are taken up in the chapters to come, as well as in the appendices.

# 8

## There's No Such Thing as a Sexual Relationship

THE DIALECTIC of part and whole is crucial to Lacan's formulation of sexual difference or "sexuation," as he calls it. In both the French- and English-language literature on the subject, Lacan's discussion is often mistakenly understood to center around the dialectic of all and some; this misunderstanding is especially egregious in the translated chapters of *Encore* (Seminar XX) that appear in *Feminine Sexuality*.

The dialectic of all and some is, rightly or wrongly, generally traced back to Aristotle, whereas the dialectic of part and whole is usually credited to the Presocratics and Hegel. Nevertheless, Lacan's is a dialectic of part and whole with a twist: the whole is never whole (the Other does not exist), and the part is undefinable, unsituable, unspecifiable,[1] and "has nothing to do with the whole."[2] His dialectic is thus likely to be more comprehensible to mathematicians familiar with modern developments in set theory and to poststructuralists than to those with more traditional philosophical backgrounds.  ·

There are many hurdles to be overcome in the presentation of Lacan's view of sexual difference. A number of authors writing in English (or whose work has been translated into English) have discussed Lacan's work on sexuation without having a firm grasp of other aspects of his thought; they have thus provided the reading public with patently or partially false interpretations, and have critiqued views Lacan never espoused.[3] It is no difficult task to latch onto one of Lacan's more metaphysical-sounding claims ("A letter always reaches its destination"), take it out of context, and attack it for what it does not mean (as Derrida does in "The Purveyor of Truth"); and anyone can locate the word "phallus" in Lacan's texts and tax him with phallocentrism. It is a far more difficult matter to sift through his voluminous explanations of sexual difference (Seminars XVIII–XXI and elsewhere), discern his central concerns, and isolate his main theses.

What I propose to do here is (1) explain what Lacan means by castration, the phallus, and the phallic function; (2) indicate what Lacan is getting at with the notion that there is no such thing as a sexual relationship; (3) lay out his "formulas of sexuation" in some, though by no means all, of their complexity so as to recenter the debate over sexual difference around what he actually says;[4] and (4) address certain broader issues raised by his account. Lacan clearly provides us with the wherewithal to look beyond the Freudian terms of some of his own formulations: we can, by viewing castration as alienation, the phallus as the signifier of desire, and the Name-of-the-Father as S(Å), adumbrate a theory of sexuation that goes beyond Freud's largely culture-specific terms.

## Castration

In Seminar XIV, Lacan asks,

> What is castration? It is certainly not like the formulations Little Hans puts forward, that someone unscrews the little faucet, for it nevertheless remains in place. What is at stake is that he cannot take his jouissance inside himself. (April 12, 1967)

Castration has to do with the fact that, at a certain point, we are required to give up some jouissance. The immediate implication of this is that Lacan's notion of castration focuses essentially on the renunciation of jouissance and not on the penis, and therefore that it applies to both men and women insofar as they "alienate" (in the Marxist sense of the term) a part of their jouissance.

Castration, in Lacan's work, is very closely related to alienation and separation. As we have seen, in alienation the speaking being emerges and is forced to give up something as he or she comes to be in language.[5] Separation requires a second renunciation: the pleasure derived from the Other as demand, from casting the Other's demand as the object in fantasy ($ ◊ D instead of $ ◊ a), that is, the pleasure obtained from the drives.

What happens to the jouissance that is sacrificed? Where does it go? Is it simply annihilated? Does it simply vanish? Or does it shift to a different level or locus? The answer seems clear: it shifts to the Other; it is, in a sense, transferred to the Other's account.[6] Now what could that possibly mean? A certain jouissance that is "squeezed" out of the body is refound in speech. The Other as language enjoys in our stead. Stated differently, it is only insofar as we alienate ourselves in the Other and enlist ourselves in support of the Other's discourse that we can share some of the jouissance circulating in the Other.

When one reads *Finnegans Wake*, one has the sense of the jouissance packed in the signifier, in the Other as language. The concatenations of letters, and the linguistic "finds," seemingly just waiting in the language to be exploited, suggest a life of language independent of our own. Strictly speaking, language obviously does not get off on itself, but it is insofar as the Other as language is "in" us that we can derive a certain jouissance therefrom.

The sacrifice involved in castration is to hand over a certain jouissance to the Other and let it circulate in the Other, that is, let it circulate in some sense "outside" of ourselves. That may take the form of writing, for example, or of the establishment of a "body of knowledge," knowledge that takes on "a life of its own," independent of its creator, as it may be added to or modified by others.

Castration can thus be associated with other processes in other domains: in the economic register, capitalism requires the extraction or subtraction from the worker of a certain quantum of value, "surplus value." That value (which is not so much a plus or surplus as a minus from the worker's point of view) is taken away from the worker—the worker is subjected to an experience of loss—and transferred to the Other qua "free" market. Surplus value, equated in the last chapter with surplus jouissance (Lacan's *plus-de-jouir*), circulates in an "alien" world of "abstract market forces." Capitalism creates a loss in its field, which allows an enormous market mechanism to develop. Similarly, our advent as speaking beings creates a loss, and that loss is at the center of civilization and culture.

Freud talked about that loss in terms of "instinctual renunciation" that he considered necessary for all cultural achievement. He generally associated it with the Oedipus complex and its resolution (giving up one love object and having to seek another elsewhere), and believed that the renunciation required of girls is less than that required of boys—hence the supposedly lesser contribution of females to culture as a whole.

In Lacan's work, the sacrifice of jouissance—and the extent of the sacrifice should not be underestimated, for it leaves behind a "mere pittance of pleasure"—is necessitated by the Other's demand that we speak, and is foiled only by the autist. That demand is obviously tied to all of culture, all bodies of knowledge, for without language we could have no access to any of them.

Claude Lévi-Strauss may be understood as suggesting that a similar structure is at work in kinship rules: the exchange or circulation of women is based on a fundamental loss engendered by the incest taboo.[7] Consider what he says in *Structural Anthropology*:

> Without reducing society or culture to language, we can initiate this "Copernican revolution" . . . which will consist of interpreting society as a whole in terms of a theory of communication. This endeavor is possible on three levels, since the rules of kinship and marriage serve to insure the circulation of women between groups, just as economic rules serve to insure the circulation of goods and services, and linguistic rules serve to insure the circulation of messages.[8]

If we modify this quote slightly, changing the theory of communication into a theory of the signifier, the circulation of women into the circulation of the signifier of desire, the circulation of goods and services into the circulation of surplus value, and the circulation of messages into the circulation of lack of jouissance (and a corresponding surplus jouissance), we find the same structure in all three "systems": a lack or loss is generated which then circulates in the Other.

Lacan himself provides an example from the political register:

[N]o jouissance is given to me or could be given to me other than that of my own body. That is not clear immediately, but is suspected, and people institute around this jouissance, which is good, which is thus my only asset, the protective fence of a so-called universal law called the rights of man: no one can stop me from using my body as I see fit. The result of the limit . . . is that jouissance dries up for everybody. (Seminar XIV, February 22, 1967)

A limitation is created in the form of a law, which is initially designed to give me the right to exclusive jouissance of my own body (prohibiting others from using it as *they* see fit), yet that very same limitation nevertheless results in the destruction of my own jouissance.

Such a notion is central to Lacan's reading of Freud in Seminar VII, for example. The reality principle places limits on the pleasure principle that are in the ultimate interest of the pleasure principle, but goes too far. The renunciation imposed by the reality principle is *incommensurate* with the function the reality principle is supposed to serve: circuitous or deferred maintenance of the pleasure principle. Just as Freud's superego oversteps its boundaries— in a sense, inflicting the most severe punishment precisely on those who act the most ethically[9]—the law inevitably exceeds its authority: the symbolic order kills the living being or organism in us, rewriting it or overwriting it with signifiers, such that being dies ("the letter kills") and only the signifier lives on.

Limit, lack, loss: these are central to Lacanian logic, and they constitute what Lacan refers to as castration. They may, in particular case histories and particular sectors and phases of Western culture, often be associated with genitalia, the male organ's tumescence and detumescence, and children's theories of sex and where babies come from. *Such particulars are, nevertheless, contingent compared to the structure of lack/loss itself.*

## The Phallus and the Phallic Function

In its quest for love and attention, a child is sooner or later confronted with the fact that it is not its parents' sole object of interest. Their multiple, and no doubt multifarious, objects of interest all have one thing in common: they divert the parents' attention away from the child. The parents' attention is what has the highest value in the child's universe: it is the gold standard, so to speak, that value against which all other values are measured. All objects or activities which attract their attention away from the child take on an importance they might otherwise never have had. Not surprisingly, one signifier comes to signify that part of the parents' desire which goes beyond the child (and by extension, their desire in general). Lacan refers to it as the "signifier of desire," and—as "man's desire is the Other's desire"—it can also be referred to as the "signifier of the Other's desire." It is the signifier of that which is worthy of desire, of that which is desirable.

Psychoanalytic practice suggests, as do other practices, that in Western cultures in general, that signifier is the phallus. Though many claim that that is no more than a preconceived notion, psychoanalysis claims that it is a clinical observation, and as such contingent.[10] It is verified time and again in clinical practice, and thus constitutes a generalization, not a necessary, universal rule. There is no theoretical reason why it could not be something else, and there perhaps are (and have been) societies in which some other signifier plays (or played) the role of the signifier of desire.

Why has the phallus come to play that role in our society? Lacan provides various possible reasons:

> One might say that this signifier is chosen as that which is most salient (or protruding [*saillant* means both]) of what can be grabbed in sexual intercourse as real [as a real, not imaginary or symbolic, activity], and also as that which is the most symbolic, in the literal (typographical) sense of the term, since it is equivalent in intercourse to the (logical) copula. One might also say that, by virtue of its turgidity (tumescence), it is the image of the vital flow as it is transmitted in generation. (*Écrits*, p. 287; *Feminine Sexuality*, p. 83)

Whatever the reasons proposed for the de facto status of the phallus—and all such reasons are "anthropological" or imaginary in nature, not structural—the fact remains that, in our culture, the phallus generally serves as desire's signifier.[11]

Now the signifier of desire is not the same as the cause of desire. Desire's cause remains beyond signification, unsignifiable. Within Lacanian psychoanalytic theory, the term "object (a)" is obviously a signifier which signifies the Other's desire insofar as it serves as cause of the subject's desire; but object (a), considered to play a role "outside of theory," that is, as real, does not signify anything: it *is* the Other's desire, it is desirousness as real, not signified.

The phallus, on the other hand, is never anything but a signifier: in theory, just as in everyday language, it is the signifier of desire. Object (a) is thus the real, unspeakable cause of desire, while the phallus is "the name of desire" and thus pronounceable.

Insofar as desire is always correlated with lack, the phallus is *the signifier of lack*. Its displacements and shifts indicate the movement of lack within the structure as a whole. Whereas castration refers to a primordial loss which sets the structure in motion, the phallus is the signifier of that loss. As Lacan says in his 1959 paper "On Ernest Jones' Theory of Symbolism," "the phallus . . . is the signifier of the very loss the subject undergoes due to the breaking into pieces brought on by the signifier [*morcellement du signifiant*]" (*Écrits* 1966, p. 715). Elsewhere in the same article, Lacan says that "the phallus functions as the signifier of the lack of being [want in being or want to be (*manque à être* without the usual dashes)] that determines the subject in his relation to the signifier." It is thus the signifier of that loss or absence of being which is behind the subject's very relation to the signifier: there is no subject at the outset, and the signifier names the as yet empty space in which the subject will come to be. In his 1966 afterword to that article, Lacan writes, "[A] symbol comes to the place of the lack constituted by the 'not in its place' [or missing from its place: *manque à sa place*] that is necessary for the initiation of the dimension of displacement from which the play of the symbol in its entirety derives" (*Écrits* 1966, p. 722; he uses the word "symbol" here instead of "signifier" as he is commenting on Jones' theory of symbolism). It is clear here that a lack or loss of something is required to set the symbolic in motion.[12]

Perhaps the simplest way of putting this is as follows: Why would a child ever bother to learn to speak if all of its needs were anticipated, if its caretakers fed it, changed it, adjusted the temperature, and so on before it even had a chance to feel hunger, wetness, cold, or any other discomfort? Or if the breast or bottle were always immediately placed in its mouth as soon as it began to cry? If nourishment is never missing, if the desired warmth is never lacking, why would the child take the trouble to speak? As Lacan says in the context of his discussion of anxiety, "What is most anxiety producing for the child is when the relationship through which it comes to be—on the basis of lack, which makes it desire—is most perturbed: when there is no possibility of lack, when its mother is constantly on its back" (Seminar X, December 5, 1962). Without lack, the subject can never come into being, and the whole efflorescence of the dialectic of desire is squashed.[13]

The lack in question in the case of the phallus is the "lack of having [failure to have or possess: *manque à avoir*] engendered by any particular or global *frustration of demand*" (*Écrits* 1966, p. 730; *Feminine Sexuality*, p. 91; my emphasis)—that is, precisely that lack which causes the subject to desire, not simply demand.

*Now the "phallic function,"* as Lacan terms it, *is the function that institutes lack*, that is, the alienating function of language. As we shall see, the phallic function plays a crucial role in Lacan's definition of masculine and feminine structure, for the latter are defined differently in terms of that loss, that lack instituted by alienation, by the splitting brought on by our use of—or rather use by—language.[14]

As we shall also see, lack (as introduced by the phallic function) and its circulation are by no means the whole story: Lacan's economy of jouissance is not a closed economy governed by the law of the "Conservation of Jouissance," whereby what is sacrificed at one point is refound at another, no more, no less. Just as in Freud's economy, libido seems to be conserved *except* when Freud talks about repetition and the excessive, incommensurate nature of the superego, in Lacan's economy, there seems to be a smooth displacement of lack and desire *only* as long as we confine our attention to the symbolic universe defined by the signifier qua signifying. Everything changes when we broaden our perspective to include the real and the signifierness of the signifier.[15]

## "There's no Such Thing as a Sexual Relationship"

*L'être sexué ne s'autorise que de lui-même.*
   —Lacan, Seminar XXI, April 9, 1974[16]

Having devoted half a century to the study of love, sex, and language, Lacan came out, in the late 1960s, with one of those bombshell expressions for which he was so well known: "there's no such thing as a sexual relationship" (*"il n'y a pas de rapport sexuel"*).[17]

The French wording is ambiguous in that *rapports sexuels* can be used to refer simply to sexual intercourse. Nevertheless, Lacan was not asserting that people are not having sex—a ridiculous claim, to say the least; his use of the word *rapport* here suggests a more "abstract" realm of ideas: relation, relationship, proportion, ratio, fraction, and so on.

There is, according to Lacan, *no direct relationship* between men and women insofar as they are men and women. In other words, they do not "interact" with each other as man to woman and woman to man. Something gets in the way of their having any such relationship; something skews their interactions.

There are many different ways of thinking about what such a relationship—if it existed—might involve. We might think that we would have something along the lines of a relationship between men and women if we could define them in terms of one another, say, as opposites, yin and yang, or in terms of a simple complementary inversion like activity/passivity (Freud's model, albeit unsatisfactory even to his mind). We might even imagine associating masculinity with a sine curve and femininity with a cosine curve, for that would allow us to formulate something we might take to be a sexual relationship as follows: $\sin^2 x + \cos^2 x = 1$ (figure 8.1).

Figure 8.1

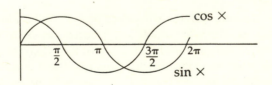

The advantage of this particular formula is that it seems to account, in a very graphic way, for what Freud says in describing the different kinds of things men and women are looking for from each other: "One forms the impression that the love of man and the love of woman are separated by a psychological phase-difference" (SE XXII, p. 134). Here, despite the apparent heterogeneity of the masculine and feminine curves, despite their phase-lag, we would be able to combine them in such a way as to make them add up to one.

But according to Lacan, no such equation is possible: nothing that would qualify as a true relationship between the sexes can be either spoken or written. There is nothing complementary about their relationship, nor is there a simple inverse relationship or some kind of parallelism between them. Rather, *each sex is defined separately with respect to a third term*. Thus there is only a nonrelationship, an absence of any conceivable direct relationship between the sexes.

Lacan sets out to show (1) that the sexes are defined separately and differently, and (2) that their "partners" are neither symmetrical nor overlapping. Analysands demonstrate day in and day out that their biomedically/genetically determined sex (genitalia, chromosomes, etc.) can be at odds with both socially defined notions of masculinity and femininity and their own choice of sexual partners (still assumed by many people to be based on reproductive instincts). Analysts are thus daily confronted with the inadequacy of defining sexual difference in biological terms. Lacan begins to explore a strictly psychoanalytic approach to defining men and women in Seminar XVIII, and continues doing so into the mid-1970s.

His attempt may at first seem needlessly complex and to include a great deal of "extraneous material" of Freudian origin; one must keep in mind, however, that Lacan was inventing as he developed this new way of distinguishing between the sexes, and did not necessarily always have a crystal-clear idea of where he was going. I will attempt first to briefly explain the main outlines of his theory, only then proceeding to a discussion of the mathemes which pose a serious obstacle to certain readers at the outset.[18]

### Distinguishing between the Sexes

> [P]ure masculinity and femininity remain theoretical
> constructions of uncertain content.
>   —Freud, SE XIX, p. 258

According to Lacan, men and women are defined differently with respect to language, that is, with respect to the symbolic order. Just as Lacan's contribution to the understanding of neurosis and psychosis suggests that the latter involves a part of the symbolic that is foreclosed and returns in the real whereas the former does not, masculinity and femininity are defined as different kinds of relations to the symbolic order, different ways of being split by language. His formulas of sexuation thus concern only speaking subjects, and, I would suggest, only neurotic subjects: the men and women defined in these formulas are neurotic, clinically speaking; neurotic men differ from neurotic women in the way in which they are alienated by/within the symbolic order.

MEN

Those who, from a psychoanalytic perspective, are considered to be men—regardless of their biological/genetic makeup—are wholly determined by the "phallic function." Since the phallic function refers to the alienation brought about by language, Lacan's major point about men can be expressed in a variety of ways:

- Men are wholly alienated within language.
- Men are altogether subject to symbolic castration.
- Men are completely determined by the phallic function.

Despite the infinite permutations allowed by language in the constitution of desire, man can be seen as bounded or finite with respect to the symbolic register. Translated in terms of desire, the boundary is the father and his incest taboo: man's desire never goes beyond the incestuous wish, impossible to realize, as that would involve overstepping the father's boundaries, and thus uprooting the very "anchoring point" of neurosis: *le nom du père*, the father's name, but also *le non du père*, the father's "No!" (*nom* and *non* being homonyms in French). This is where it appears quite clear that masculine structure is in certain respects synonymous in Lacan's work with obsessive neurosis.

Linguistically speaking, man's limit is that which institutes the symbolic order itself, that first signifier $(S_1)$—the father's "No!"—which is the point of origin of the signifying chain and which is involved in primal repression: the institution of the unconscious and of a place for the neurotic subject.[19]

Man's pleasure is similarly limited, its boundaries being determined by the phallic function. Man's pleasures are limited to those allowed by the play of the signifier itself—to what Lacan calls phallic jouissance, and to what might similarly be called symbolic jouissance.[20] Here thought itself is jouissance-laden (see Seminar XX, p. 66), a conclusion amply borne out by Freud's work on obsessive doubt (consider the case of the "Rat Man") and felicitously reflected in the expression "mental masturbation." Insofar as it is related to the body, phallic or symbolic jouissance involves only the organ designated by the signifier, which thus serves as a mere extension or instrument of the signifier. That is why Lacan occasionally refers to phallic jouissance as "organ pleasure" (cf. SE XVI, p. 324).

Men's fantasies are tied to that aspect of the real that under-writes, as it were, the symbolic order: object (a). Object (a) keeps the symbolic moving in the same circuitous paths, in constant *avoidance* of the real.[21] There is, for those who come under the category "Men," a kind of symbiosis between subject and object, symbolic and real, as long as the proper distance is maintained between them. The object here is only peripherally related to another person, and Lacan thus refers to the jouissance derived therefrom as masturbatory in nature (Seminar XX, p. 75).

## WOMEN

While men are defined as being wholly hemmed in by the phallic function, wholly under the sway of the signifier, women (i.e., those who, from a psychoanalytic perspective, are considered to be women, regardless of their biological/genetic makeup) are defined as *not* being wholly hemmed in. A woman is not split in the same way as a man: though alienated, she is not altogether subject to the symbolic order.[22] The phallic function, while operative in her case, does not reign absolutely. With respect to the symbolic order, a woman is not whole, bounded, or limited.

Whereas men's pleasure is altogether determined by the signifier, women's is partially determined by the signifier, but not wholly. While men are limited to what Lacan calls phallic jouissance, women can experience both that *and* another kind of jouissance, which he calls the Other jouissance. Not that every subject who can be situated under "Women" experiences it—far from it, as is so often attested—but it is, according to Lacan, a structural potentiality.

What is that Other jouissance of which those who, psychoanalytically speaking, are to be classified as women are capable? The very fact that Lacan spells "Other" with a capital O here indicates the Other jouissance's connection with the signifier, but it is connected with $S_1$ not $S_2$—not with "just any" signifier, but with the "Other signifier" (to coin a phrase): the unary signifier, the signifier that remains radically Other, radically different from all other signifiers. Whereas $S_1$ (the father's "No!") functions for a man as a limit to his range of motion and pleasures, $S_1$ is an elective "partner" for a woman, her relationship to it allowing her to step beyond the boundaries set by language and beyond the pittance of pleasure language allows. An endpoint for men, $S_1$ serves as an open door for women.[23]

Feminine structure proves that the phallic function has its limits and that the signifier isn't everything. Feminine structure thus bears close affinities to hysteria as defined in the hysteric's discourse (see Seminar XVII and chapter 9 of the present study).

BEYOND BIOLOGY

Lacan's way of defining man and woman has nothing to do with biology, and can be understood as accounting for the existence of (genetically) male hysterics and (genetically) female obsessive-compulsives. A male hysteric is, if my interpretation of Lacan is correct here, characterized by feminine structure: he may potentially experience both phallic and the Other jouissance. A female obsessive-compulsive is characterized by masculine structure, her jouissance being exclusively symbolic in nature.

From a clinical vantage point, a great many biological females turn out to have masculine structure, and a great many biological males prove to have feminine structure.[24] Part of an analyst's training must thus consist in breaking old habits of thought whereby one immediately assumes that a female is an hysteric and thereby can be characterized as having feminine structure. Each person's relation to the signifier and mode of jouissance has to be examined more carefully; one cannot jump to conclusions on the basis of biological sex.[25]

The fact that so many people cross over the hard and fast biological distinctions perhaps explains, in part, the widespread use in America of the category "borderline." It is often precisely those patients who cross those boundaries who are diagnosed by psychiatrists, psychoanalysts, and psychologists as borderline. (Lacan rejects the borderline category outright.)

Lacan's distinctive way of defining masculinity and femininity shows why there is no such thing as a relationship between the sexes, but this point must await clarification until man's partner and woman's partner*s* are articulated in more detail below. Those altogether averse to Lacan's logical excursions would do well to skip to the section entitled "A Dissymmetry of Partners."

### The Formulas of Sexuation

In Seminar XX, Lacan provides a schema (figure 8.2), part of which he had been working on for years, and part of which he claims to have whipped up in a flash the very morning before he first drew it on the blackboard at his seminar.

Figure 8.2

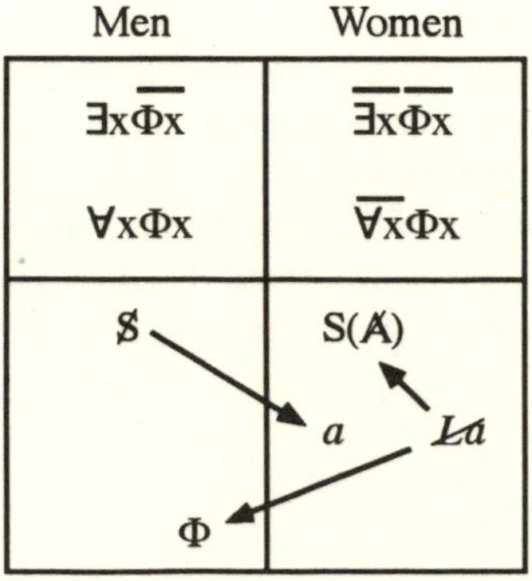

I'll begin my interpretation of this schema by commenting on several passages from Seminar XX.

## MASCULINE STRUCTURE

We'll start with the four propositional formulas at the top of the table, two of which lie to the left, the other two to the right. Every speaking being situates him or herself on one side or the other. On the left, the lower line—$\forall x \Phi x$—indicates that it is through the phallic function that man *as whole* can be situated. (p. 74, my emphasis)

The formula $\forall x \Phi x$ thus means that *the whole of a man falls under the phallic function* (x standing for any given subject or part thereof, $\Phi x$ for the phallic function as applicable to that subject or part, and $\forall x$ for the whole of x).[26] To paraphrase this formula, man is altogether determined by symbolic castration, that is, every bit of him falls under the sway of the signifier. Returning to the quote, we see that there is an exception however:

[M]an *as whole* can be situated [as determined by the phallic function], with the proviso that this function is limited due to the existence of an x by which the function $\Phi x$ is denied: $\exists x \overline{\Phi x}$. That is what is known as the father's function. . . . The whole here is thus based on the exception—the exception posited as the term that altogether negates $\Phi x$. (p. 74, my emphasis)

Man can be considered as a whole, because there is something that delimits him ($\exists x$: there exists some x [some subject or part thereof] such that $\overline{\Phi x}$, the phallic function is foreclosed). He can be taken as a whole because there is a definable boundary to his set (figure 8.3).

Figure 8.3

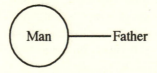

It must be kept in mind that Lacan's work on sexual difference is based on and coextensive with his reworking of traditional logic in terms of his own logic of the signifier. A signifier never stands alone. We would never talk about black if there were nothing but darkness around us, that is, no cases in which black was not found. It is because something other than black shows up on occasion that black takes on meaning. It is in opposition to "white" and all the other color words that the word "black" has meaning.

While Lacan uses the language of the theory of classes in the early sixties, he continues to develop the same idea in the early seventies in terms of his own unique use of the symbols of classical logic. In *L'Étourdit*, for example, he says that "there is no universal statement which can but be controlled through an existence which negates it."[27] In other words, *every universal claim is grounded in the ex-sistence of an exception which proves the rule*, to paraphrase a well-known French maxim.[28]

Man's essence (as wholly, universally defined by the phallic function) thus necessarily implies the existence of the father. Without the father, man would be nothing, without form (*informe*). Now the father as boundary (to pursue the simile) occupies no area: he defines a two-dimensional surface within his boundaries, but fills no space. This father who marks the limit of a man's manhood is not just any old father: Lacan associates him with the primal father presented in Freud's *Totem and Taboo*, the father of the primal horde, who has not succumbed to castration and supposedly controls every single woman in the horde. While all men are marked by symbolic castration, there nonetheless exists or persists one man to whom the phallic function does not apply, one man who was never put in his place by succumbing to symbolic castration. He is not subject to the law: *he is his own law*.

Does this primal father, seemingly asserted to exist in Lacan's upper formula for masculine structure ($\exists x \overline{\Phi x}$), exist in the usual sense? No, he ex-sists: the phallic function is not simply negated in some mild sense in his case; it is foreclosed (Lacan indicates that the bar of negation over the quantifier stands for discordance, whereas the bar of negation over the phallic function stands for foreclosure),[29] and foreclosure implies the utter and complete exclusion of something from the symbolic register. As it is only that which is *not foreclosed* from the symbolic order that can be said to exist, existence going hand in hand with language, the primal father—implying such a foreclosure—must ex-sist, standing outside of symbolic castration. We obviously have a name for him, and thus in a sense he exists within our symbolic order; on the other hand, his very definition implies a rejection of that order, and thus by definition he ex-sists. His status is problematic; he is what Lacan, back in the 1950s, might have qualified as "extimate": excluded from within. He can, however, be said to ex-sist, because, like object (a), the primal father can be written: $\exists x \overline{\overline{\Phi x}}$.

Now the mythical father of the primal horde is said not to have succumbed to castration, and what is symbolic castration but a limit or limitation? He thus knows no limits. According to Lacan, the primal father lumps all women into the same category: accessible. The set of *all* women exists for him and for him alone (figure 8.4). His mother and sisters are just as much fair game as are his neighbors and second cousins. The effect of castration (the incest taboo, in this case) is to divide that mythical set into at least two categories: accessible and inaccessible. Castration brings about an exclusion: mom and sis are off-limits (figure 8.5).

But castration also changes a man's relation to even those women who remain accessible: they become defined in a sense as simply *not* off-limits. In

Figure 8.4

all women

Figure 8.5

all other women   mom

Seminar XX, Lacan says that a man could only really *jouir d'une femme* from the position of noncastration. *Jouir d'une femme* means to get off on a woman, to really enjoy her, to take full advantage of her, the implication being that one's pleasure really comes from her, not from something one imagines her to be, wants her to be, fools oneself into believing she is or has, or what have you. Only the primal father can really get off on women themselves. Ordinary masculine mortals must resign themselves to getting off on their partner, object (a).

Thus only the mythical primal father can have a true sexual relationship *with* a woman. To him there is such a thing as a sexual relationship. Every other man has a "relationship" with object (a)—to wit, fantasy—not with a woman per se.

The fact that every single man is nevertheless defined by both formulas— one stipulating that he is altogether castrated and the other that some instance (*Instanz*) negates or refuses castration—shows that incestuous wishes live on indefinitely in the unconscious. Every man, despite castration (that splitting up of the category of women into two distinct groups), continues to have incestu- ous dreams in which he grants himself the privileges of the imagined pleasure- finding father who knows no bounds.

Speaking in *quantitative* terms for a moment, Lacan can also be seen to be saying here that while there was, once upon a time, an exception to the rule of castration, you can be absolutely sure now, whenever you meet a man, that he is castrated. So you can safely say that all people who are men, not in biologi- cal but rather in psychoanalytic terms, are castrated. But while men are wholly castrated, there is nevertheless a contradiction: that ideal of noncastration—of knowing no boundaries, no limitations—lives on somewhere, somehow, in each and every man.

Figure 8.6

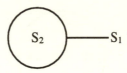

Masculine structure can, to modify figure 8.3, be depicted as in figure 8.6. $S_2$ corresponds to $\forall x \Phi x$ and stands for the son here, while $S_1$ corresponds to $\exists x \overline{\Phi x}$ and stands for the father.

$$
\begin{array}{lll}
\text{Father} & \exists x \overline{\Phi x} & S_1 \\
\text{Son} & \forall x \Phi x & S_2
\end{array}
$$

This partial presentation of the formulas of sexuation should already make it clear to what extent Lacan's discussion of them is multilayered, involving material from logic and linguistics, as well as from Freud.

### FEMININE STRUCTURE

As for the two formulas defining femininity, we find firstly that *not all* of a person who, regardless of anatomy, falls under the psychoanalytic category of "Women" is defined by the phallic function ($\overline{\forall x \Phi x}$): not all of a woman comes[30] under the law of the signifier ($\overline{\forall} x$, not the whole of x [a given subject], or not every part of x, such that $\Phi x$, i.e., such that the phallic function applies to x). Lacan does not cast this idea in positive terms, by stating, for example, that *some part of every woman* escapes the reign of the phallus. He leaves it as a possibility, not a necessity; but that possibility is nevertheless decisive in the determination of sexual structure.

The second formula ($\overline{\exists x\, \overline{\Phi x}}$ ) states that you cannot find even one woman for whom the phallic function is totally inoperative: every woman is *at least in part* determined by the phallic function ($\overline{\exists} x$, there does not exist even one x [a subject or part thereof] such that $\overline{\Phi x}$, i.e., such that the phallic function is inapplicable to it). Were the phallic function to be *totally* inoperative for a subject, he or she would be psychotic, the bar over the phallic function designating foreclosure.[31]

The kind of image I find useful as a preliminary illustration of the two formulas for feminine structure is the tangent curve (figure 8.7), where, at $\pi/2$, the curve goes right off the map and then mysteriously reappears on the other side. We can attribute no real value to it at $\pi/2$, and are forced to resort to expressions like "The value of y approaches positive infinity as x goes to $\pi/2$ from 0 and approaches negative infinity as x goes from $\pi$ to $\pi/2$." No one really knows how the two sides of the curve meet up, but we adopt a system of symbols with which to talk about its value at that point. The status of the Other jouissance associated with the lower formula of feminine structure

Figure 8.7

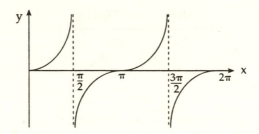

($\overline{\forall}$x $\Phi$x; see figure 8.2), potentially experienceable by those who come under the category "Women," is akin to that of the value of the tangent curve at $\pi/2$. It goes right off the scale, right off the map of representation. Its status is akin to that of a logical exception, a case which throws into question the whole.

The formula $\overline{\exists}$x $\overline{\Phi}$x summarizes, in a sense, the fact that while not all of a woman is determined by the phallic function, to assert the *existence* of some part of her that rejects the phallic function would amount to claiming that something that says no to the phallic function is nevertheless subject to it, situated within the symbolic order—for to exist is to have a place within the symbolic register. Which is why Lacan never claims that the feminine instance posited to go beyond the phallus *exists*: he maintains its radical alterity in relation to logos, to the symbolic order as structured by the signifier of desire. While denying the *existence* of this "realm beyond the phallus," $\overline{\exists}$x $\overline{\Phi}$x does not, as we shall see further on, in any way deny its *ex-sistence*.[32]

Woman is thus not somehow less "complete" than man, for *man is whole only with respect to the phallic function*.[33] Women are no less "whole" than men except when considered in terms of the phallic function; women are no more "undefined" or "indefinite" than men except in relation to the phallic function.

### A Dissymmetry of Partners

THE PHALLUS: ONE OF WOMAN'S PARTNERS

Consider now the symbols, or mathemes, as Lacan calls them, located under the formulas of sexuation. In figure 8.8, we see that the crossed-out *La*—symbolizing, in one sense, that woman is not whole—while linked (by arrows indicating Woman's partners) on the one hand to $\Phi$ (phi, the phallus as signifier), is linked on the other to S($\mathbb{A}$), the signifier of the lack in the Other.

I discussed the phallus as signifier of desire in some detail at the beginning of this chapter. What Lacan adds here is the notion that a woman generally gains access to the signifier of desire in our culture via a man or a "masculine instance," that is, someone who comes under the psychoanalytic category "Men."

Figure 8.8

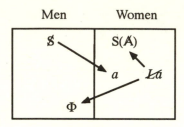

S(Ⱥ): ~~WOMAN~~'S OTHER PARTNER

*Si quelque chose ex-siste à quelque chose, c'est*
*très précisément de n'y être pas couplé, d'en être*
*"troisé," si vous me permettez ce néologisme.*
     —Lacan, Seminar XXI, March 19, 1974[34]

Looking back at our table, we see that women, while "coupled," on the one
hand, to the phallus, are also inextricably "tripled" (*troisées*) to the signifier of
a lack or hole in the Other.

That lack is not simply the lack—directly correlated with desire—that
shows that language is ridden with desire and that one's mother or father, as an
avatar of the Other, is not complete and thus wants (for) something. For the
signifier of that desire-implying lack (or lack-implying desire) is the phallic
signifier itself. Lacan is not terribly loquacious in the 1970s regarding S(Ⱥ),
and thus I will offer my own interpretation of its function here.[35]

In chapter 5, I spoke of S(Ⱥ) as "the signifier of the Other's desire," in the
context of Lacan's discussion of Hamlet in Seminar VI. At that stage in
Lacan's work, S(Ⱥ) seems to be Lacan's term for the phallus as signifier, and
thus in a sense it is what allows Lacan to first separate the phallus as imaginary
($-\phi$) from the phallus as symbolic ($\Phi$). Symbols' meanings often evolve very
significantly over time in Lacan's texts, and I would suggest that S(Ⱥ) shifts
between Seminars VI and XX from designating the signifier of the Other's lack
or desire to designating the signifier of the "first" loss.[36] (That shift corresponds to a change in register, as is so often the case in Lacan's work: from
symbolic to real. Note that all of the elements found under "Men" are related
to the symbolic, whereas all those under "Women" are related to the real.)

That first loss can be understood in quite a variety of ways. It might be
understood at the frontier of the symbolic and the real as the loss of a "first"
signifier ($S_1$, the mOther's desire), when primal repression occurs. The "disappearance" of that first signifier is necessary for the instituting of the signifying
order as such: *an exclusion must occur for something else to come into being.*
The status of that first excluded signifier is obviously quite different from that
of other signifiers—being more of a border phenomenon (between the sym-

bolic and the real)—and bears close affinities to that of a primordial loss or lack at the origin of the subject. I would suggest that the first exclusion or loss somehow *finds* a representative or signifier: S(A̸).

Now what does it mean for something real (a real loss or exclusion) to find a signifier? For the real is generally considered to be unsignifiable. If the real finds a signifier, that signifier must be operating in a way that is highly unusual. For the signifier generally replaces, crosses out, and annihilates the real; it signifies a subject to another signifier, but it does not signify the real as such.

My sense here is that S(A̸) in figure 8.8, which Lacan associates in Seminar XX with specifically feminine jouissance, designates a kind of Freudian sublimation of the drives in which the drives are fully satisfied (this *other* kind of satisfaction is what is behind Lacan's expression "Other jouissance"), and a kind of Lacanian sublimation whereby an ordinary object is elevated to the status of the Thing (see Seminar VII).[37] The Freudian Thing finds a signifier, simple examples of which may include "God," "Jesus," "Mary," "the Virgin," "art," "music," and so on, and the *finding* of the signifier must be understood as an encounter ($\tau\upsilon\chi\acute{\eta}$), that is, as fortuitous in some sense.

Apart from the imaginary satisfaction we may associate with religious ecstasy or rapture, or with the artist's or musician's work, there is nevertheless a *real* satisfaction obtained, and that strikes me as Lacan's "beyond of neurosis" for those with feminine structure. In chapters 5 and 6, I characterized Lacan's first conceptualization of a beyond of neurosis as the subjectifying of the cause, becoming one's own cause, as paradoxical as that may at first sound. By Seminar XX it seems that Lacan views that as *one* path beyond neurosis, the path of those characterized by masculine structure. *The other path—that of sublimation—is particular to those characterized by feminine structure.*[38]

The masculine path might then be qualified as that of desire (becoming one's own cause of desire), while the feminine path would be that of love. And as we shall see, masculine subjectification might then be considered to involve the making one's own of otherness qua efficient cause (the signifier),[39] while feminine subjectification would involve the making one's own of otherness qua material cause (the letter).[40] They would both, then, require subjectification of the cause or otherness, but of different facets thereof. I shall return to this subject momentarily.

### Woman Does Not Exist

The *La̸* in the table under the formulas of sexuation is Lacan's shorthand for the notion that "Woman does not exist": there is no signifier for, or essence of, Woman as such. Woman can thus only be written under erasure: W̶o̶m̶a̶n̶. If, as Lacan suggests, there is no such signifier—the underlying idea presumably being that the phallus is somehow the signifier of Man or Man's essence, since the phallic function is what defines him—the fact that S(Å) is one of Woman's partners suggests that a signifier may be encountered and adopted, in some sense coming to take the place of that missing definition or essence. S(Å) stands in for a signifier that is neither ready-made nor *prêt à porter*, and represents the forging of *a new master signifier ($S_1$), though not one to which a woman is subjected*. While a man is always subjected to a master signifier, a woman's relation thereto seems radically different. A master signifier serves as a limit to a man; not so for S(Å) in relation to a woman.

Socially speaking, Lacan's assertion that there is no signifier of/for Woman is, no doubt, related to the fact that a woman's position in our culture is either automatically defined by the man she adopts as partner or is defined only with great difficulty. In other words, the search for another way of defining herself is long and fraught with obstacles.[41] The Western societal Other never views such attempts very favorably, and thus the satisfaction which could be derived therefrom is often spoiled. Music, art, opera, theater, dance, and other "fine arts" are fairly well accepted by that Other, though less so when a relationship with a man is not proven primary. And whereas in the past, it was fairly well accepted for women to devote themselves to the religious life in convents, eschewing the defining relation to a man, today even that recourse is frowned upon, that is to say, the Other is making certain religious signifiers harder and harder to adopt. For while the relation to S(Å) may be established by encounter, that encounter can be facilitated or thwarted by the culture and subculture(s) in which a woman finds herself.

This by no means implies that there will never be an "automatic" or ready-made signifier for women. If we accept Lacan's diagnosis here, this state of affairs is contingent, not necessary.

Nor does Lacan in any way imply that women have no sexual identity of their own; he does not, as it is sometimes said in the literature, define women simply as men that have something missing.[42] Sexual identity, in Lacanian terms, is constituted on at least two different levels: (1) the successive identifications that constitute the ego (usually identifications with one or both parents), accounting for an *imaginary* level of sexual identity, a rigid level which often comes into very real conflict with (2) masculine or feminine structure as defined above, as related to the different sides of Lacan's formulas of sexuation, any given *subject* being able to situate herself on either side. These two levels, which often come into conflict,[43] thus correspond to the ego and the subject. At the level of ego identifications, a woman may well identify with her father (or a figure who is socially considered to be "masculine"), whereas at the level of desire and of her subjective capacity for jouissance, she may be characterized by feminine structure.

A woman's sexual identity can, in fact, involve many different possible combinations, for unlike masculine and feminine structure, which in Lacan's view constitute an either/or, there being no middle ground between them, ego identifications can include elements from many different persons, both male and female. In other words, the imaginary level of sexual identity can, in and of itself, be extremely self-contradictory.

The very existence of sexual identity (sexuation, to use Lacan's term) at a level *other* than that of the ego, at the level of subjectivity, should dispel the mistaken notion so prevalent in the English-speaking world that a woman is not considered to be a subject at all in Lacanian theory. *Feminine structure means feminine subjectivity.* Insofar as a woman forms a relationship with a man, she is likely to be reduced to an object—object (a)—in his fantasy; and insofar as she is viewed from the perspective of masculine culture, she is likely to be reduced to nothing more than a collection of male fantasy objects dressed up in culturally stereotypical clothes: i(a), that is, an image that contains and yet disguises object (a). That may very well imply a loss of subjectivity in the common, everyday sense of the word—"being in control of one's life," "being an agent to be reckoned with," and so on[44]—but it in no way implies a loss of subjectivity in the Lacanian sense of the term. *The very adoption of a position or stance with respect to* (an experience of) *jouissance involves and implies subjectivity.* Once adopted, a feminine subject will have come into being. The extent to which that particular subject subjectivizes her or his world is another question.

Some of the work being done by certain feminists today might be understood as involving the attempt to present, represent, symbolize, and thereby subjectify a certain real in their experience which has never before been represented, symbolized, or subjectified. Perhaps that previously unspoken, unwritten real is related to what Lacan calls the Other jouissance and the Other sex (Woman constituting the Other sex even for a woman; this point is discussed further below). The latter are Other (foreign or alien to someone) only insofar as they have not been spoken, written, represented, or subjectified. While many feminists view their work in other terms—as having to do with a specifically feminine imaginary or pre-thetic/semiotic level of experience—it might, in more strictly Lacanian terms, and at the risk of being reductionistic, be understood as an attempt to subjectify the real (the real Other or the Other as jouissance).[45]

### Masculine/Feminine—Signifier/Signifierness

Let me pursue my interpretation a step further here. While Lacan never comes right out and says that Man is *defined* by the signifier of desire ($\Phi$), let us suppose, for a moment, that he is so defined. Does this necessarily imply that Woman can never be defined as long as Man is defined? And does that in turn imply that were Woman to be identified with the signifier of desire, Man could not be defined? Is there some structural reason why the signifier of desire may be identified with only one sex at a time, even if either one theoretically? If so, is the opposite sex then necessarily associated with the object as cause of desire? Is there some theoretical reason why one sex should be defined by a signifier and the other as an object?

Perhaps there is. Insofar as separation leads to the division of the Other into barred Other and object (a), the Other (e.g., the parental Other: in the nuclear family, mother and father) breaks down into two "parts," one of which (A) can certainly be associated with the signifier and the other with an object (figure 8.9). In terms of the Lacanian dialectic of desire, as it operates in societies organized like our own, perhaps there *is* a theoretical reason why the roles of signifier and object are embodied in the different sexes.

Figure 8.9

The implication of Lacan's work on sexuation seems to be that subjectification takes place at different levels in differently sexuated beings: those with masculine structure must subjectify or find a new relation to the object, while those with feminine structure must subjectify or find a new relation to the signifier. Both sexes subjectify that which is Other at the outset, yet their approach to this Other, the facet of the Other they deal with, differs. It is as if the Other were instated lock, stock, and barrel in men, their "problem" being with the object; whereas in women the Other is never completely instated as such. Woman's "problem" thus would not be to make the Other exist or to complete it—which is, after all, the pervert's project—but rather to subjectify it, to constitute it within herself. Subjectification for those characterized by feminine structure would thus be quite different from that outlined in chapters 5 and 6 above, and would require an encounter with a signifier.[46]

Men and women are alienated in and by language in radically different ways, as witnessed by their disparate relations to the Other, and to $S_1$ and $S_2$. As subjects, they are split differently, and *this difference in splitting accounts for sexual difference*. Sexual difference thus stems from men and women's divergent relations to the signifier.

Each sex seems to be called upon to play a part related to the very foundation of language: men play the part of the signifier, while women play the part of "*l'être de la signifiance*," as Lacan puts it (Seminar XX, p. 71). To date no other English speaker has, to the best of my knowledge, attempted to translate *signifiance*,[47] yet it is fairly clear from Lacan's usage what he is trying to get at with this term taken over from linguistics. (It is "taken over" in the sense that in linguistics it merely refers to "the fact of having meaning," whereas Lacan turns it on its head.) I have proposed translating it as "signifier*ness*," that is, the fact of being a signifier, the fact that signifiers ex-sist, the subsistence of signifiers, the signifying nature of signifiers.[48] When Lacan uses the term, it is to emphasize the nonsensical nature of the signifier, the very existence of signifiers apart from and separated from any possible meaning or signification they might have; it is to emphasize the fact that the signifier's very existence exceeds its significatory role, that its substance exceeds its symbolic function. The signifier's being goes beyond its "designated role," its role in logos, which is to signify. Thus rather than referring to "the fact of having meaning," Lacan uses it to refer to "the fact of having effects Other than meaning effects."

We should hear *defiance* in Lacan's "signi*fiance*"! The signifier defies the role allotted to it, refusing to be altogether relegated to the task of signification. It has an ex-sistence beyond and outside of meaning-making, sense-making.

Being, in Lacan's work, is associated with the letter—the letter, in the 1970s, being the material, nonsignifying face of the signifier, the part that has effects without signifying: jouissance effects. The letter is related to the *materiality of language*, the "*substance jouissante*," as Lacan puts it in Seminar XX (p. 26):[49] the jouissance or "jouissing" substance, the substance that gets off or enjoys. To associate the masculine with the signifier and the feminine with the letter may seem tantamount to a return to the old form and matter metaphor dating back to at least Plato, but in Lacan's work there is always a twist to the return: substance gets the better of form and teaches it a trick or two.

## Other to Herself, Other Jouissance

In what sense can a woman be considered to be an Other to herself, as Lacan suggests? Insofar as she defines herself in terms of a man (in terms of the phallus, via that man), that other aspect—the potential relation to S(A)—remains opaque, foreign, Other. Consider what Lacan says in 1958/1962: "Man serves here [in relation to castration] as a relay so that woman becomes an Other for herself, just as she is for him" (*Écrits* 1966, p. 732). Seeing herself only in terms of the phallus, that is, in terms of her position as defined in relation to a man, other women who do not seem to be thus defined are cast as Other. Insofar, however, as that Other potential is realized, that is, a relation to S(A) is established, woman is no longer an Other to herself. Insofar as it is not realized, she remains an *hommosexuelle*, as Lacan writes it, conflating man (*homme*) and homosexual: she loves men, she loves like a man, and her desire is structured in fantasy like his.

To those characterized by masculine structure, a woman is cast as Other—as radically Other, as the Other of/as jouissance—insofar as she embodies or is seen as a representative of the Other jouissance Lacan calls indecent. Why "indecent"? Because it requires no relation to the phallus, and shows up the paucity of phallic jouissance, which is the mere pittance of pleasure left after the drives have been thoroughly subjected (in the case of masculine structure) to the symbolic. This subjection of the drives corresponds to a certain Freudian form of sublimation, the one wherein the real is drained off into the symbolic,[50] jouissance being transferred to the Other.

The Other jouissance involves a form of sublimation through love that provides full satisfaction of the drives. The Other jouissance is a jouissance of love,[51] and Lacan relates it to religious ecstasy and to a kind of bodily, corporal jouissance that is not localized in the genitals the way phallic jouissance is (the former is not, he clearly states, so-called vaginal orgasm as opposed to clitoral). According to Lacan, the Other jouissance is *a*sexual (whereas phallic jouissance is sexual), and yet it is *of* and *in* the body[52] (phallic jouissance involving but the organ as instrument of the signifier).

The little Lacan directly says about S(Ⱥ) suggests that the Other jouissance it denotes has to do with the absolute radicality or *otherness* of the Other: there is no Other (i.e., no outside) of the Other. The Other is not just an outside *relative to* a particular, determinate inside; it is always and inescapably Other, "outside" any and all systems.[53]

I will leave a detailed explanation of the Other jouissance for another occasion,[54] suggesting here simply that it is related to Freud's notion that the full satisfaction of the drives provided by one form of sublimation is "desexualized."[55] "Desexualized libido" seems closely related to Lacan's *a*sexual, Other jouissance. Sublimation is, incidentally, situated by Lacan (in a somewhat different context) in the bottom left-hand corner of the logical square I presented in chapters 4 and 6 above (see figure 8.10).

Figure 8.10

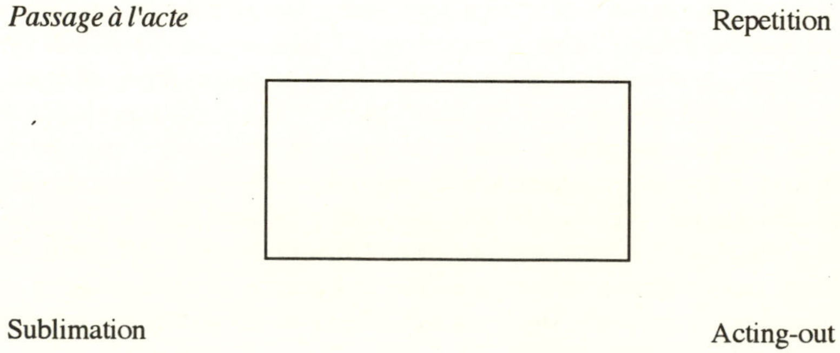

*Passage à l'acte*                                                  Repetition

Sublimation                                                        Acting-out

My comments here amount to no more than the beginning of an interpretation, but this strikes me as a general sense in which figure 8.8 could be understood.

As I indicated earlier, Lacan sets out to show (1) that the sexes are defined separately and differently, and (2) that their partners are neither symmetrical nor overlapping. Man's partner, as seen in figure 8.8, is object (a), not a woman as such. A man may thus get off on something he gets from a woman: a certain way she talks, a certain way she looks at him, and so forth, but it is only insofar as he has invested her with that precious object that arouses his desire. He may thus need a (biologically defined) woman as the substratum, prop, or medium of object (a), but she will never be his partner.

Nor will he ever be hers as such. She may require a (biologically defined) man to embody, incarnate, or serve as prop for the phallus for her, but it is the phallus and not the man that will be her partner. The break or dissymmetry is even more radical when it comes to her Other partner, S(Ⱥ), as that partner is not situated under "Men" at all, and thus a woman need have no recourse to a man to "relate" or "accede" to it.

Had men and women's sexual partners turned out to be identical—had, say, object (a) functioned as the sole partner for both of them—at least their desire as sexuated beings would be structured in some sort of parallel (*hommosexuelle*) way, and we could try to envision a sexual relationship between them on that basis. But the dissymmetry of their partners is utter and complete, and no conceivable relationship between the sexes can thus be postulated, articulated, or written in any form whatsoever.

### The Truth of Psychoanalysis

That is what Lacan generally qualifies as *the* truth of psychoanalysis. Granted, he at times suggests that all truth is mathematizable: "[T]here is no such thing as a truth which is not 'mathematicized,' that is, written, that is, which is not based, qua Truth, solely upon axioms. Which is to say that there is truth but of that which has no meaning, that is, of that concerning which there are no other consequences to be drawn but within [the register] of mathematical deduction" (Seminar XXI, December 11, 1973).

But this comment applies merely to the true (*le vrai*) we see, for example, in "truth tables" and symbolic logic (see chapter 10). The only *truth* of psychoanalysis, according to Lacan, is that there is no such thing as a sexual relationship, the problem being to bring the subject to the point of encountering that truth.

## Existence and Ex-sistence

*N'existe que ce qui peut se dire. N'ex-siste que ce qui
peut s'écrire.*

Given Lacan's many seemingly paradoxical statements involving existence—
"Woman does not exist," "The Other jouissance does not exist"—and involving *il y a* and *il n'y a pas*—"There's no such thing as a sexual relationship," "*Il
y a de l'Un*, "*Il n'y a pas d'Autre de l'Autre*"—I'd like to add a word here
about Lacan's notion of ex-sistence.

To the best of my knowledge, the word "ex-sistence" was first introduced
into French in translations of Heidegger (e.g., of *Being and Time*), as a translation for the Greek *ekstasis* and the German *Ekstase*. The root meaning of the
term in Greek is "standing outside of" or "standing apart from" something. In
Greek, it was generally used for the removal or displacement of something, but
it also came to be applied to states of mind that we would now call "ecstatic."
Thus a derivative meaning of the word is "ecstasy," hence its relation to the
Other jouissance. Heidegger often played on the root meaning of the word,
"standing outside" or "stepping outside" oneself, but also on its close connection in Greek with the root of the word for "existence." Lacan uses it to talk
about "an existence which stands apart from," which insists as it were from the
outside; something not included on the inside, something which, rather than
being intimate, is "extimate."

The Other jouissance is beyond the symbolic, standing apart from symbolic
castration. It ex-sists. We can discern a place for it within our symbolic order,
and even name it, but it nevertheless remains ineffable, unspeakable. We can
consider it to ex-sist because it can be written: $\overline{\forall} x \Phi x$.

Sexual relationships, however, are distinct in this respect: they cannot
be written, and thus neither exist nor ex-sist. There's simply *no such
thing*.

The very notion of ex-sistence, and of the Other jouissance as ex-sisting,
makes Lacan's "economy of jouissance" or "libidinal economy" an open, untotalizable economy. There is no conservation of jouissance, no proportionate
relationship between jouissance sacrificed and jouissance gained, no sense in
which the Other jouissance makes up for or makes good the inadequacy or
paucity of phallic jouissance—in a word, no *complementarity* or commensura-
tion. The Other jouissance is fundamentally incommensurate, unquantifiable,
disproportionate, and indecent to "polite society." It can never be recuperated
into a "phallic economy" or simple structuralism. Like object (a) as ex-sistence, the Other jouissance has an irremediable effect on the "smooth workings
of structure."

## A New Metaphor for Sexual Difference

The signifier . . . is to be structured in topological
terms.
   —Lacan, Seminar XX, p. 22

What are we to make of Lacan's view of sexual difference as I have tried to lay
it out here? Is it to be taken seriously? How is it helpful to us?

Clearly Lacan provides a new metaphor of sexual difference, one that goes
beyond the dialectic of active and passive (with which Freud himself was
unsatisfied), having and being (far more interesting, at least from a grammati-
cal/linguistic standpoint), and so on.[56] One thing most contemporary critics
and psychoanalysts would agree upon is that biological differentiations are
inadequate, too many people seeming to cross over, at the psychical level,
the "hard and fast" lines of biologically determined sexual difference. We
thus begin with the hypothesis that there are males with feminine structure
(defined in some way) and females with masculine structure (defined in some
other way).

What is of interest in Lacan's way of defining masculine and feminine structure? For one thing, it involves a new topology: it breaks with the age-old
Western conception of the world as a series of concentric circles or spheres,
and instead takes as its model such paradoxical topological surfaces as the
Möbius band, the Klein bottle, and the cross-cap. The latter, in particular, is
a fertile surface for revolutionizing the way we think. If there is a "strict equivalence between topology and structure" (Seminar XX, p. 14), then new topological models may be helpful in thinking about systems.

In essence, the cross-cap is a sphere with a twist: *the Lacanian twist*, so to
speak. That little twist changes all of the topological properties of the sphere,
nothing returning upon itself as in the old, familiar conception of things. It is
perhaps the same Lacanian twist which, in the late 1950s and 1960s, shifts
so many of Lacan's terms from the symbolic to the real. (This process finally comes to an end, in a sense, when Lacan encounters the Borromean
knot which takes the three registers—the imaginary, symbolic, and real—as
equally important.) The Lacanian twist is, perhaps, the ability to see something
beyond the symbolic where philosophy and structuralism see nothing but
the same old thing.

Unlike the Möbius band, the cross-cap is an *impossible* surface. The former
can be constructed; thus it is imaginable (or "imaginarizable")—it can be pic-
tured in the mind. The cross-cap, on the other hand, is a surface that can be
described in the same way as are a number of other surfaces in topology, with
little rectangles with arrows along their edges indicating how the opposite

sides go together, yet is impossible to construct. Consider the surfaces represented in figure 8.11, with their symbolic representations:

Figure 8.11

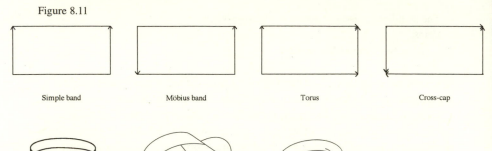

| Simple band | Möbius band | Torus | Cross-cap |

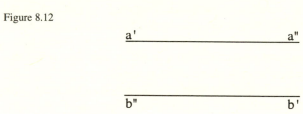

All of these surfaces, except for the cross-cap, lend themselves to accurate visual representation. While the cross-cap can be symbolically expressed in topological terms (see the rectangle above the word), it can neither be accurately visualized nor constructed. To try to imagine it, you can picture to yourself a sphere that is slashed at a certain spot, each point on either side of the cut being reconnected, not to the point directly across from it, as in suturing a wound, but to the *symmetrical* point on the opposite side, as in figure 8.12, where a' would be connected to b' and a" to b".

Figure 8.12

a'                                                             a"
_____

_____
b"                                                             b'

The cross-cap is, in this sense, impossible. Yet it can be written; it is susceptible to symbolic inscription. The symbolic can be used here to describe something real, something extra-symbolic.

If the old notion of concentric circles or spheres ever applied to anything, Lacan seems to suggest that it applies to masculine structure, bounded as it is by the paternal function (figure 8.13). Freud suggests that women have a different relation to the law, which he correlates with a less highly developed

Figure 8.13

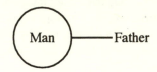

ego-ideal or superego, but which perhaps can be better understood as implying that the relations to boundaries of subjects characterized by feminine structure are fundamentally different: the opposition between inside and outside is inapplicable. Just so, the surface of the cross-cap does not constitute a hermetic boundary, and there is but a locally valid notion of inside and outside, not a definitive one. That little anomalous rent in its "surface" changes all of its properties. Another way to formulate Lacan's new metaphor is with the terms "open" and "closed," as derived from set theory and topology. Like the set constituted by Man, a "closed set" includes its own boundary or limit; like Woman, an "open set" does not include its own boundary or limit. It could be argued that it is at least in part thanks to Lacan's work in set theory, logic, and topology—rather unusual fields of study for most psychoanalysts—that he is able to formulate sexual difference in a new way.[57]

Lacan's new metaphor for sexual difference constitutes a new symptom: a new symptomatic way of viewing sexual difference that is neither any more nor any less symptomatic than earlier ways. A symptom always allows one to see certain things and stops one from seeing other things.

Were I to qualify this symptomatic way of seeing, I might be tempted to call it "Gödelian structuralism," insofar as it maintains the importance of structure, while continually pointing to the necessary incompleteness thereof and the fundamental undecidability of certain statements made within it. Lacan clearly adopts the Gödelian notions that every significant formal system contains some undecidable statements and that it is impossible to define the truth of a language in that same language. In Lacan's work it is not simply the exception that proves the rule but, more radically, the exception that forces us to redefine the rules. His work embodies the very structure of hysteria: the closer he comes to formulating a system, the more vigorously he reexamines it and calls it into question. If it is "a system to end all systems," it is Lacan who teaches us to hear that very expression in a new way.

# Part Four

THE STATUS OF PSYCHOANALYTIC DISCOURSE

# 9

## The Four Discourses

There is no whole. Nothing is whole.
—Lacan, *Scilicet* 2/3 (1970): 93

There's no such thing as a universe of discourse.
—Lacan, Seminar XIV, November 16, 1966

There's no such thing as a metalanguage.
—Lacan, Seminar XIV, November 23, 1966

LACANIAN psychoanalysis constitutes a very powerful theory and a socially significant practice. Yet it is not a *Weltanschauung*, a totalized or totalizing world view,[1] though many would like to make it such. It is a discourse and, as such, has effects in the world. It is but one discourse among many, not *the* final, ultimate discourse.

The dominant discourse in the world today is no doubt the discourse of power: power as a means to achieve x, y, and z, but ultimately power for power's sake. Lacanian psychoanalysis is not, in and of itself, a discourse of power. It deploys a certain kind of power in the analytic situation, a power that is unjustifiable according to many American schools of psychology wherein the "client's" autonomy (read: ego) is sacrosanct and must remain untrammeled and unchallenged. Psychoanalysis deploys the power of the cause of desire in order to bring about a reconfiguration of the analysand's desire. As such, analytic discourse is structured differently from the discourse of power. Lacan's "four discourses" seek to account for the structural differences among discourses, and I will turn to this accounting in a moment.

First let me raise the question of relativism. If psychoanalysis is not somehow the ultimate discourse, being but one discourse among others, what claim can it make to our attention? Why should we bother to concern ourselves with analytic discourse at all, if it is just one of several or one of many? I will provide but one simple answer here: because *it allows us to understand the functioning of different discourses in a unique way.*[2]

Before taking up the particulars of Lacan's four discourses, let me point out that, while Lacan terms one of his discourses the "hysteric's discourse," he does not mean thereby that a given hysteric always and inescapably adopts or functions within the hysteric's discourse. As an analyst, the hysteric may function within the analyst's discourse; as an academic, the hysteric may function within the discourse of the university. The hysteric's psychical structure does not change as he or she changes discourses, but his or her efficacy changes. Situating him or herself within the analyst's discourse, his or her effect on others corresponds to the effect allowed by that discourse and suffers from the obstacles and shortcomings endemic to that discourse. A particular discourse facilitates certain things and hinders others, allows one to see certain things while blinding one to others.

Discourses, on the other hand, are not like hats that can be donned and doffed at will. The changing of discourses generally requires that certain conditions be met. An analyst does not always function within analytic discourse; insofar, for example, as he or she teaches, the analyst could very well adopt the university discourse or the master's discourse, or for that matter the hysteric's discourse (and Lacan's own teaching often seems to come under this latter head).

One thing that is immediately striking is that, while Lacan forges a discourse of the hysteric, there is no such discourse of the obsessive neurotic, phobic, pervert, or psychotic. Their discourses can no doubt be formalized to some extent, and Lacan went a long way towards formalizing the structure of fantasy in phobia, perversion, and so on.[3] Yet they are not primary focuses of the four major discourses he outlines. I will not go into the four discourses in *all* their complexity, especially as concerns their development over time from Seminar XVII, where they are introduced, to Seminar XX and beyond, where they are somewhat reworked. Instead I shall present the basic features of each of the four discourses and then, in the next chapter, discuss a *second* way of talking about different kinds of discourses that Lacan presents in Seminar XXI.

## The Master's Discourse

Lacan's discourses begin in a sense with the discourse of the master, both for historical reasons and because it embodies the alienating functioning of the signifier to which we are all subject. As such, it holds a privileged place in the four discourses; it constitutes a sort of primary discourse (both phylogenetically and ontogenetically). It is the fundamental matrix of the coming to be of the subject through alienation (as we saw in chapters 4–6), but Lacan ascribes to it a somewhat different function in the context of his four discourses:

$$\frac{S_1}{\$} \rightarrow \frac{S_2}{a}$$

In the master's discourse, the dominant or commanding position (in the upper left-hand corner) is filled by $S_1$, the nonsensical signifier, the signifier with no rhyme or reason, in a word, the master signifier. The master must be obeyed— not because we'll all be better off that way or for some other such rationale— but because he or she says so.[4] No justification is given for his or her power: it just is.

The master (represented here by $S_1$) addresses (that addressing is represented by the arrow) the slave ($S_2$), who is situated in the position of the worker (in the upper right-hand corner, also referred to by Lacan as the position of the other). The slave, in slaving away for the master, learns something: he or she comes to embody knowledge (knowledge as productive), represented here by $S_2$. The master is unconcerned with knowledge: as long as everything works, as long as his or her power is maintained or grows, all is well. He or she has no interest in knowing how or why things work. Taking the capitalist as master here and the worker as slave, object (a), appearing in the lower right-hand corner, represents the surplus produced: surplus value. That surplus, deriving from the activity of the worker, is appropriated by the capitalist, and we might suppose that it directly or indirectly procures the latter enjoyment of some kind: surplus jouissance.

The master must show no weakness, and therefore carefully hides the fact that he or she, like everyone else, is a being of language and has succumbed to symbolic castration: the split between conscious and unconscious ($\$$) brought on by the signifier is veiled in the master's discourse and shows up in the position of truth: dissimulated truth.

The various positions in each of the four discourses can now be designated as follows:

$$\frac{\text{agent}}{\text{truth}} \rightarrow \frac{\text{other}}{\text{product/loss}}$$

Whichever matheme Lacan places in one of these four positions, it takes on the role ascribed to that position.

The other three discourses are generated from the first by rotating each element counterclockwise one quarter of a turn or "revolution."[5] One might suppose that these further or "derivative" discourses either came into being, or at least were grasped, later in time; this seems true of at least the last two of the four, for the analyst's discourse only came into being at the end of the nineteenth century, and it was the analyst's discourse that eventually allowed the hysteric's discourse to be grasped. (The master's discourse had long since been recognized by Hegel.)

## The University Discourse

> For centuries, knowledge has been pursued as a de-
> fense against truth.
>     —Lacan, Seminar XIII, January 19, 1966

In the discourse of the university,

$$\frac{S_2}{S_1} \rightarrow \frac{a}{\$}$$

"knowledge" replaces the nonsensical master signifier in the dominant, commanding position. Systematic knowledge is the ultimate authority, reigning in
the stead of blind will, and everything has its reason. Lacan almost goes so far
as suggest a sort of historical movement from the master's discourse to the
university discourse, the university discourse providing a sort of legitimation
or rationalization of the master's will. In that sense he seems to agree with the
argument put forward in the 1960s and 1970s that the university is an arm of
capitalist production (or of the "military-industrial complex," as it was called
at the time), suggesting that the truth hidden behind the university discourse is,
after all, the master signifier.

Knowledge here interrogates surplus value (the product of capitalist econo-
mies, which takes the form of a loss or subtraction of value from the worker)
and rationalizes or justifies it. The product or loss here is the divided, alienated
subject. Since the agent in the university discourse is the knowing subject, the
unknowing subject or subject of the unconscious is produced, but at the same
time excluded. Philosophy, Lacan says, has always *served* the master, has always placed itself in the service of rationalizing and propping up the master's
discourse, as has the worst kind of science.

Note that whereas Lacan at first associates the university discourse with
scientific formalization, with the increasing mathematization of science, he
later dissociates true scientific work from the university discourse, associating
it instead with the hysteric's discourse. Surprising as that may seem at first,
Lacan's view of genuine scientific activity (explained in "Science and Truth,"
for example)[6] does correspond to the structure of the hysteric's discourse, as I
shall try to explain it below.

That shift is reflected in *Television* by an association of the scientific
and hysteric's discourses, and a total equation of them in "*Propos sur
l'hystérie*," a talk given in Belgium in 1975. It implies that the kind of
knowledge involved in the university discourse amounts to mere rationalization, in the most pejorative Freudian sense of the term. We can imagine it,
not as the kind of thought that tries to come to grips with the real, to maintain the difficulties posed by apparent logical and/or physical contradictions,

but rather as a kind of encyclopedic endeavor to exhaust a field (consider Charles Fourier's 810 personality types[7] and Auguste Comte's goal of a total sociology).

Working in the service of the master signifier, more or less any kind of argument will do, as long as it takes on the guise of reason and rationality.


## The Hysteric's Discourse

In the hysteric's discourse (which is actually the fourth generated by the succession of quarter turns, not the third, as I am presenting it here),

$$\frac{\$}{a} \rightarrow \frac{S_1}{S_2}$$

the split subject occupies the dominant position and addresses $S_1$, calling it into question. Whereas the university discourse takes its cue from the master signifier, glossing over it with some sort of trumped-up system, the hysteric goes at the master and demands that he or she show his or her stuff, prove his or her mettle by producing something serious by way of knowledge.[8] The hysteric's discourse is the exact opposite of the university discourse, all the positions being reversed. The hysteric maintains the primacy of subjective division, the contradiction between conscious and unconscious, and thus the conflictual, or self-contradictory, nature of desire itself.

In the lower right-hand corner, we find knowledge ($S_2$). This position is also the one where Lacan situates jouissance, the pleasure produced by a discourse, and he thus suggests here that an hysteric gets off on knowledge. Knowledge is perhaps eroticized to a greater extent in the hysteric's discourse than elsewhere. In the master's discourse, knowledge is prized only insofar as it can produce something else, only so long as it can be put to work for the master; yet knowledge itself remains inaccessible to the master. In the university discourse, knowledge is not so much an end in itself as that which justifies the academic's very existence and activity.[9] Hysteria thus provides a unique configuration with respect to knowledge, and I believe this is why Lacan finally identifies the discourse of science with that of hysteria.

In 1970, in Seminar XVII, Lacan views science as having the same structure as the master's discourse.[10] He seems to see it as serving the master, as did classical philosophy. By 1973, in *Television*, Lacan claims that the discourse of science and the discourse of the hysteric are *almost* identical (p. 19), and in 1975 he identifies them quite unreservedly.[11] What leads him to do so?

Consider Heisenberg's uncertainty principle. In simple terms, it states that we cannot precisely know both a particle's position and its momentum at the same time. If we have been able to ascertain one parameter, the other must necessarily remain unknown. In and of itself, that is a startling proposition for a scientist to put forward. Naively, we often think of scientists as people who relentlessly refine their instruments until they can measure everything, regardless of its infinitesimal proportions or blinding speed. Heisenberg, however, posited a limit to our ability to measure, and thus a true limit to scientific knowledge.

If, for a moment, we view scientific knowledge as a whole or a set, albeit expanding (we could imagine it as an ideal set of all scientific knowledge, present and future), then Heisenberg can be understood as saying that the set is incomplete, the whole is not whole, for there's an "unfillable" hole in the set (figure 9.1).[12]

Figure 9.1

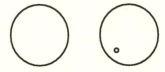

Now that is similar to what Lacan says of the hysteric: the hysteric pushes the master—incarnated in a partner, teacher, or whomever—to the point where he or she can find the master's knowledge lacking. Either the master does not have an explanation for everything, or his or her reasoning does not hold water. In addressing the master, the hysteric demands that he or she produce knowledge and then goes on to disprove his or her theories. Historically speaking, hysterics have been a true motor force behind the medical, psychiatric, and psychoanalytic elaboration of theories concerning hysteria. Hysterics led Freud to develop psychoanalytic theory and practice, all the while proving to him in his consulting room the inadequacy of his knowledge and know-how.

Hysterics, like good scientists, do not set out to desperately explain everything with the knowledge they already have—that is the job of the systematizer or even the encyclopedist—nor do they take for granted that all the solutions will be someday forthcoming. Heisenberg shocked the physics community when he asserted that there was something that structurally speaking could not be known: something that it is impossible for us to know, a kind of conceptual anomaly.

Similar problems and paradoxes have arisen in logic and mathematics, as we saw in chapters 3 and 7 above. In Lacan's terminology, these impossibilities are related to the real that goes by the name of object (a).

Now in the hysteric's discourse, object (a) appears in the position of truth. That means that the truth of the hysteric's discourse, its hidden motor force, is the real. Physics too, when carried out in a truly scientific spirit, is ordained and commanded by the real, that is, by that which does not work, by that which does not fit. It does not set out to carefully cover over paradoxes and contradictions, in an attempt to prove that the theory is nowhere lacking—that it works in every instance—but rather to take such paradoxes and contradictions as far as they can go.

## The Analyst's Discourse

Let us turn now to analytic discourse:

$$\frac{a}{S_2} \rightarrow \frac{\math{\$}}{S_1}$$

Object (a), as cause of desire, is the agent here, occupying the dominant or commanding position. The analyst plays the part of pure desirousness (pure desiring subject), and interrogates the subject in his or her division, precisely at those points where the split between conscious and unconscious shows through: slips of the tongue, bungled and unintended acts, slurred speech, dreams, etc. In this way, the analyst sets the patient to work, to associate, and the product of that laborious association is a new master signifier. The patient in a sense "coughs up" a master signifier that has not yet been brought into relation with any other signifier.

In discussing the discourse of the master, I referred to $S_1$ as the signifier with no rhyme or reason. As it appears concretely in the analytic situation, a master signifier presents itself as a dead end, a stopping point, a term, word, or phrase that puts an end to association, that grinds the patient's discourse to a halt. As we saw in chapter 6, it could be a proper name (the patient's or the analyst's), a reference to the death of a loved one, the name of a disease (AIDS, cancer, psoriasis, blindness), or a variety of other things. The task of analysis is to bring such master signifiers into relation with other signifiers, that is, to dialectize the master signifiers it produces.

That involves reliance upon the master's discourse, or as we might see it here, recourse to the fundamental structure of signification: a link must be established between each master signifier and a binary signifier such that subjectification takes place. The symptom itself may present itself as a master signifier; in fact, as analysis proceeds and as more and more aspects of a person's life are taken as symptoms, each symptomatic activity or pain may present itself in the analytic work as a word or phrase that simply is, that seems to signify nothing to the subject. In Seminar XX, Lacan refers to $S_1$ in the analyst's discourse as *la bêtise* (stupidity or "funny business"), a reference back to the case of Little Hans, who refers to his whole horse phobia as *la bêtise*, as Lacan translates it (p. 17). It is a piece of nonsense produced by the analytic process itself.[13]

$S_2$ appears in analytic discourse in the place of truth (lower left-hand position). $S_2$ represents knowledge here, but obviously not the kind of knowledge that occupies the dominant position in the university discourse. The knowledge in question here is unconscious knowledge, that knowledge that is caught up in the signifying chain and has yet to be subjectified. Where that knowledge was, the subject must come to be.

Now, according to Lacan, while the analyst adopts the analytic discourse, the analysand is inevitably, in the course of analysis, hystericized. The analysand, regardless of his or her clinical structure—whether phobic, perverse, or obsessive-compulsive—is backed into the hysteric's discourse.

$$\frac{\$}{a} \rightarrow \frac{S_1}{S_2}$$

Why is that? Because the analyst puts the subject as divided, as self-contradictory, on the firing line, so to speak. The analyst does not question the obsessive neurotic's theories about Dostoevsky's poetics, for example, attempting to show the neurotic where his or her intellectual views are inconsistent. Such an obsessive may attempt to speak during his or her analytic sessions from the position of $S_2$ in the university (academic) discourse, but to engage the analysand at that level allows the analysand to maintain that particular stance. Instead, the analyst, ignoring, we can imagine, the whole of a half-hour-long critique of Bakhtin's views on Dostoevsky's dialogic style, may focus on the slightest slip of the tongue or ambiguity in the analysand's speech—the analysand's use, for example, of the graphic metaphor "near misses" to describe her bad timing in the publishing of her article on Bakhtin, when the analyst knows that this analysand had fled her country of origin shortly after rejecting an unexpected and unwanted marriage proposal ("near Mrs.").

Thus the analyst, by pointing to the fact that the analysand is not the master of his or her own discourse, instates the analysand as divided between conscious speaking subject and some other (subject) speaking at the same time through the same mouthpiece, as agent of a discourse wherein the $S_1$s produced in the course of analysis are interrogated and made to yield their links with $S_2$ (as in the hysteric's discourse). Clearly the motor force of the process is object (a)—the analyst operating as pure desirousness.[14]

## The Social Situation of Psychoanalysis

I mentioned earlier that psychoanalysis is not, in and of itself, a discourse of power: it does not collapse into the master's discourse. Yet an American's view of the Lacanian psychoanalytic scene—both in France and elsewhere—often encompasses little more than the power struggles engaged in by individual analysts and schools against other analysts and schools.[15] Insofar as psychoanalysis is a social practice, it obviously operates in social and political environments that contain competing and oftentimes antagonistic discourses: medical discourse promoting the physiological basis and treatment of mental "disorders," "scientific" and philosophical discourses aiming at undermining the theoretical and clinical foundations of psychoanalysis, political and economic discourses seeking to reduce the length and cost of psychoanalytic therapy, psychological discourse hoping to attract patients to its own adherents, and so on. In such circumstances, psychoanalysis becomes one political lobbyist among many and can do no more than attempt to defend its right to exist in ever-changing political contexts.

In Paris and other cities where Lacanian psychoanalysis has become a major movement, individuals and schools compete for theoretical and/or clinical dominance, vying for political influence, university support, hospital positions, patients, and simple popularity. Is that a necessary outgrowth of psychoanalytic discourse as we see it operating in the analytic setting? I think not. It may certainly have a negative impact upon an individual analyst's ability to completely adhere to analytic discourse in the analytic setting, but it does not seem to be inherent to analytic discourse as such. This claim will no doubt be disputed by many, given psychoanalysis' long history of schisms and infighting, but I would sustain that the latter results from the adoption of other discourses by analysts as soon as institutionalization begins (the formation of schools, the consolidation of doctrine, the training of new analysts, the stipulation of licensing requirements, etc.), not from analytic discourse itself. There are limits to the extent to which analytic discourse can and should be adhered to in contexts other than the analytic setting!

## There's No Such Thing as a Metalanguage

There is no such thing as a metalanguage or metadiscourse that would somehow escape the limitations of the discourses thus far discussed, for one is always operating within a particular discourse, even as one talks about discourse in general terms. Psychoanalysis' claim to fame does not reside in providing an archimedean point *outside of discourse*, but simply in elucidating the structure of discourse itself. Every discourse requires a loss of jouissance[16] (see chapter 8) and has its own mainspring or truth (often carefully dissimulated). Each discourse defines that loss differently, starting from a different mainspring. Marx elucidated certain features of capitalist discourse, and Lacan elucidates features of other discourses as well. It is not until we have identified the features peculiar to a discourse that we can know how it operates.

When Lacan first presents the four discourses, he seems to suggest there are no others. Does that mean that every conceivable form of discourse activity comes under one of those four? I shall leave that question open until the next chapter, in which I take up the question of science.

# 10

## Psychoanalysis and Science

THE STATUS of psychoanalysis with respect to science is generally discussed in America in the most naive of terms. Science (with a capital S) is assumed to refer to a self-evident set of "bodies of knowledge" (as opposed to a diverse group of hotly disputed social practices) and a fixed set of verification and refutation procedures, model-building methods, concept formulation processes, and so on—that is, when those who discuss science know anything whatsoever of scientific endeavor.

Science is not, however, the monolithic edifice positivists and everyday American common sense make it out to be. Work in the history and philosophy of science in the latter part of the twentieth century, as well as in the individual sciences themselves,[1] has decisively dispelled the notion that every science is based on a set of axiomatic mathematizable propositions, measurable empirical entities, and pure concepts. There is virtually *no* agreement among scientists, philosophers, and historians regarding what constitutes a science and what does not. This has not, however, in any way dampened the esteem for science in the United States, where every affirmation must seek its stamp of approval from the recognized Scientific Authorities, and where the solution to every problem is expected to be provided by "hard science."

### Science as Discourse

The fact remains that *science is a discourse*. As banal as that statement may seem, it implies a dethroning of Science and a reassessment of science as *one* discourse among many. Freud may be interpreted as translating "rationality" into "rationalization," and Lacan's discourse theory suggests that there are as many different claims to rationality as there are different discourses. Each discourse, seeking its own ends and having its own mainspring, attempts to make its own form of rationality prevail.

There are, no doubt, several presently existing forms of scientific discourse, some of which (the worst) can be subsumed under the university discourse discussed in the last chapter (science as a justification for, and means to further expand, the master's power), some under the hysteric's discourse, and so on.

One useful way of understanding the relationship between psychoanalytic discourse and scientific discourse is, it seems to me, in terms of Lacan's contribution to discourse theory in the 1970s, starting in Seminar XXI. Before turning to it, however, let me briefly sketch out his approach to the relationship between psychoanalysis and science in the mid-1960s.

## Suturing the Subject

Lacan, quite interested at the time in establishing psychoanalysis as a science, poses the question as follows: Do all presently existing scientific discourses have something in common? I have already discussed his answer to that question elsewhere, in a commentary on "Science and Truth,"[2] and will summarize it very briefly here: science "sutures" the subject, that is, neglects the subject, excluding the latter from its field. At least it attempts to do so to the fullest extent possible, never fully succeeding.[3] This is as true of Lévi-Strauss' brand of structuralism as of Newtonian physics; the speaking subject is considered irrelevant to the field. While Lacan was at first excited by the prospect of founding psychoanalysis as a science on bases similar to those of linguistics and structural anthropology, he later distinguished psychoanalysis from the latter two disciplines in that they do not take *truth* into account: the *cause*, and thus the subject that will have resulted from that cause.

If science can be said to deal with truth, it is only insofar as it reduces truth to a kind of value. In truth tables, the letters T (true) and F (false) are assigned to various possible combinations of propositions, as in table 10.1. If

Table 10.1

| A | B | A and B | |
|---|---|---------|---|
| T | T | T | line 1 |
| T | F | F | line 2 |
| F | T | F | line 3 |
| F | F | F | line 4 |

I assert that Lacan was French (proposition A) and that he never set foot outside of France (proposition B), in order for my statement as a whole to be true, both A and B must be true individually. The four lines in the truth table represent all four possible combinations taken into account by this kind of propositional logic. A can be either true or false, and B can be either true or false; thus any combination of their *truth values* is theoretically possible. If only one of them is true, my statement as a whole is false. It is only when both of them are true that my statement as a whole is true (top line).

Science relies on the designations "true" and "false," but they take on meaning only within a propositional or symbolic logic: they are values understandable within the field defined by that science and make no claims to independent validity.[4]

"True" and "false" are thus simple values in scientific discourse, like plus and minus, 0 and 1: they are binary opposites that play a role in a specific context. Truth with a capital T, on the other hand, is swept aside, relegated to other disciplines, whether poetry and literature or religion and philosophy.

Psychoanalysis, by contrast, gives precedence to that which throws into question the self-confirming nature of its own axioms: the real, the impossible, that which does not work. That is the Truth taken responsibility for in psychoanalysis. The major form it takes is the impossibility of sexual relationships.

If science can be said to deal with the subject, it is only the conscious Cartesian subject, master of its own thoughts, whose thought is correlative to its being. Existing sciences certainly do not take into account the split subject for whom "I *am* where I am not thinking" and "I think where I am not."

Science, America's foremost de facto metalanguage, sutures the Lacanian subject, suturing its cause (as Truth) in the same gesture.[5] As it excludes the psychoanalytic subject and object, Lacan's view in the 1960s is that science will have to undergo some serious changes before psychoanalysis can be included within its scope. In other words, the formalization of psychoanalysis into mathemes and rigorously defined clinical structures—so characteristic of Lacan's work at that stage—does not suffice to make psychoanalysis into a science, for science itself is not yet capable of encompassing psychoanalysis. Science must first come to grips with the specificity of the psychoanalytic object.[6] At that time, then, Lacan's view is that *science is not yet equal to the task of accommodating psychoanalysis.*

In Seminar X, Lacan associates the supposed progress of science with our increasing inability to think the category "cause." Continually filling in the "gap" between cause and effect, science progressively eliminates the content of the concept "cause," events being understood as leading smoothly, in accordance with well-known "laws," to other events. Lacan understands cause in a more radical sense, as that which disrupts the smooth functioning of lawlike interactions. Causality in science is absorbed into what we might call structure—cause leading to effect within an ever more exhaustive set of laws. A cause as something that seems not to obey laws, remaining inexplicable from the standpoint of scientific knowledge, has become unthinkable, our general tendency being to assume that it will just be a matter of time before science can explain it.

What distinguishes psychoanalysis from the sciences is that it takes into account the cause, and the subject in his or her libidinal relation to the cause, whereas linguistics, for example, takes the subject into account only as determined by the symbolic order, that is, by the signifier. Psychoanalysis thus grapples with the two faces of the subject: (1) the "pure subject" of the combinatory or matrix—the subject without a cause, as it were, and (2) the "saturated subject," as Lacan calls it[7]—that is, the subject in relation to an object of jouissance (a libidinal object), the subject as a stance adopted with respect to jouissance.

The project of Lacanian psychoanalysis is, in the 1960s, to maintain and further explore these two primordial concepts—cause and subject—however paradoxical they may seem. At this stage in Lacan's work, the differences between science and psychoanalysis seem altogether insurmountable.

## Science, the Hysteric's Discourse, and Psychoanalytic Theory

This situation changes to some extent when Lacan identifies true scientific discourse with the hysteric's discourse, as I mentioned in the last chapter. For genuine scientific work does not exclude the cause, as that which interrupts the smooth functioning of lawlike activity, but rather attempts to take it into account in some way, as in the case of Heisenberg's uncertainty principle. Here the real up against which science runs is not neatly skirted, but rather brought within the theory it upsets. Truth, as the encounter with the real, is not elided, but met head on. The physicist here might be said to allow him or herself to be duped, to work as something other than the knowing subject.[8] In that sense, scientific discourse and the hysteric's discourse coincide.

But where does that leave psychoanalysis? Psychoanalytic discourse, *as operative in the analytic setting*, is clearly distinct from the hysteric's discourse and is not involved in theory building, but rather in a praxis defined by specifically psychoanalytic ends; based on the analyst's enigmatic desire, psychoanalysis aims at subjectification, separation, traversing of fantasy, and so on. It is not a practice based on *understanding*, either for the analyst or the analysand, but rather on a certain efficiency (in Aristotle's sense of the word).

Psychoanalytic discourse, *as operative in theory building*, on the other hand, insofar as it takes Truth seriously—attempting to formulate the encounter with the real cause—functions much like the hysteric's discourse and thus like scientific discourse. It seems to me that, just as it is important—even though it involves oversimplification—to distinguish "basic science" from "applied science" (that is, goal-oriented science), it is important to distinguish the strictly theoretical from the clinical aspects of psychoanalysis.

Psychoanalysis as a whole is a praxis. Nevertheless, its different facets can be examined separately in terms of discourse theory. *Psychoanalytic practice*, in other words, in the analytic setting, adopts analytic discourse—in the best of cases, that is, for many analysts clearly adopt something more along the lines of the university discourse. *Psychoanalytic theory and teaching* adopt the hysteric's discourse—once again, in the best of cases, for often they become nothing more than doctrinal enterprises designed to gloss over all unanswered questions.[9] *Psychoanalytic associations*, as social-political institutions, may adopt a variety of discourses (hysteric's, master's, or university), and while Lacan clearly believed that they should function in a particular way, I shall leave for another occasion a discussion of the discourse they should ideally adopt, according to Lacan, and the discourse(s) they do in fact adopt.

This multiplicity of discourses adopted by analysts should not surprise us, for the same is true in other praxes:

- In clinical practice, the medical doctor may well employ suggestion, threats, placebos, inflated fees, white lies, and whatever else it takes to get his or her patients back on the road to health. In his or her more theoretical enterprises, the medical doctor may adopt the scientific discourse accepted at a particular historical moment. And in his or her search for power, prestige, or sheer survival, the medical doctor may turn into a political lobbyist, adopting the discourse of expediency (the master's discourse).

- The politician adopts the discourse of power (the master's discourse) in the "war room," the discourse of democracy and justice (the university discourse) before the public eye, and perhaps even the hysteric's discourse in his or her probing discussions with advisors.

- Even the theoretical physicist, whose field is not constituted as a praxis in my sense of the term (a praxis aims at changing the real, not simply studying it),[10] adopts different discourses depending on whether he or she is in the laboratory, in the classroom, at a department meeting, in discussion with a funding source like the National Science Foundation, or in an interview with Pentagon officials.

In any praxis, and in virtually any field, different discourses are appropriate at different moments and in different historical, social, political, economic, and religious contexts.

## The Three Registers and Differently "Polarized" Discourses

The real is what does not depend on my idea of it.
—Lacan, Seminar XXI, April 23, 1974

You can't do whatever you want with it.
—Lacan, Seminar XIII, January 5, 1966

As I mentioned earlier, another useful way to understand the relationship between psychoanalytic discourse and scientific discourse is in terms of Lacan's contribution in the 1970s to discourse theory. In Seminar XXI, Lacan provides a way of thinking about discourses that is slightly different from that provided in "the four discourses" and subsists alongside the latter, albeit perhaps only at the very beginning of that one seminar.

This new way of thinking about different discourses defines each discourse according to the *order* in which the three registers—imaginary, symbolic, and real—are taken up in it (figure 10.1). The discourses that go around the circle in a clockwise direction (RSI, SIR, and IRS) are to be distinguished from those that go around in a counterclockwise direction (RIS, ISR, and SRI). Lacan adopts the term "right polarization" (*dextrogyre*) for clockwise directions and "left polarization" for counterclockwise directions (*lévogyre*), terms used to describe the "orientation" of knots like his Borromean knot (see Seminar XXI, November 13, 1973).

Figure 10.1

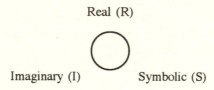

Real (R)

Imaginary (I)          Symbolic (S)

To the best of my knowledge, Lacan never provides a detailed account of *all* the discourses covered by this particular combinatory. He mentions only two: religious discourse, which realizes the symbolic of the imaginary (RSI), and psychoanalytic discourse, which imagines the real of the symbolic (IRS). According to Lacan, these two discourses have something in common, as they are both "right polarized." But rather than discuss their possible similarities, what I would like to do here is elucidate what Lacan means by "imagining the real of the symbolic," and suggest how science might be situated in terms of this new combinatory.

Mathematics, according to Lacan, was the first discourse to imagine—that is, glimpse, perceive, conceive—that the symbolic order itself contains elements of the real. There are kinks in the symbolic order that constitute logical aporias or paradoxes, and they are ineradicable: a better, "purer" symbolic system does not eliminate them. There are impossibilities in the symbolic order—such as those laid bare by Gödel (briefly discussed in chapters 3 and 7 above)—and mathematicians were among the first to imagine them and attempt to conceptualize them.

Psychoanalysis follows in the footsteps of mathematics—the former thus constituting an IRS discourse as well—by "extending the mathematical process" (Seminar XXI, November 13, 1973). By recognizing object (a), psychoanalysis imagines, or takes cognizance of, the real of/in the symbolic.

This is another way of saying that psychoanalytic *theory building* ideally comes under the hysteric's discourse, as I said earlier. But it also allows us to talk about the psychoanalytic *process* in the same breath: the analyst, in the analytic setting, listens for the real (impossibilities) in the analysand's symbolic and attempts to hit that real with interpretation.[11] The IRS classification thus allows us to talk about psychoanalytic theory *and* practice in the same terms: it characterizes psychoanalysis as a *praxis*.

Lacan never says how he would classify science in terms of this new combinatory, but I would venture to suggest that the best science, like mathematical logic à la Gödel, could be considered an IRS discourse.[12] Heisenberg's uncertainty principle certainly recognizes and grapples with the real of the symbolic order constituted by modern physics, as does other work in the sciences.

Physics will never constitute a praxis in the sense that psychoanalysis does. While psychoanalysis aims, not at the analysand's good (as understood by most current social and political discourse), but at his or her greater Eros,[13] physics does not seek to change the real it studies: it has no aims in mind for space, time, and matter. Nevertheless, both constitute IRS discourses and thus have a certain *orientation* in common.

### Formalization and the Transmissibility of Psychoanalysis

In the late 1950s and 1960s, Lacan makes a considerable effort to formulate and abbreviate psychoanalytic concepts in the guise of symbols or "mathemes," as he calls them. The term "matheme" is modeled on phoneme, semanteme, and mytheme, the smallest units of speech, meaning, and myth, respectively, and the symbols Lacan invents are quasi-mathematical in nature, providing formula-like expressions.

In the 1960s, Lacan takes formalization/mathematization to be one of the main characteristics of science, that being a key to 100 percent transmissibility, the ability to integrally transmit *something* from one person to another. Each matheme condenses and embodies, in a sense, a considerable quantity of conceptualization, yet each is also highly polyvalent, as the reader will have noticed in the course of this book. While mathemes or formulas cannot, in and of themselves, guarantee the integral transmission of an idea or concept from one person to another—a sort of ideal communication ("I see what you mean") that Lacan himself decisively critiques, the essence of all "communication" being miscommunication—*what is transmitted is the matheme itself.* As a bit of writing, as a written trace, mathemes can be handed down from generation to generation, or even buried in the sand, dug up again millennia later, and interpreted as signifying a subject to another signifier.

Early on, Lacan's concern with the transmissibility of psychoanalysis is clearly based on English and American misinterpretation of Freud's work in particular, his hope being that such misinterpretation can be avoided by formulations and formalization akin to those of the "hard sciences." At the same time, however, he sought to avoid saying things in a simplistic manner and to discourage his students from all too quickly thinking they understood Freud's texts, their analysands' speech, or Lacan's own words.

While Lacan at one point boasts that he has reduced psychoanalysis to set theory, that is, an integrally transmissible discourse, Lacanian psychoanalysis remains anything but a finite system of definitions and axioms. Nevertheless, it does move in the direction of increasing "literalization"[14]—formulations involving letters and symbols, in other words, mathemes—a process of symbolization that inscribes qualitative relations, not quantitative ones. Like the figures discussed at the end of chapter 8, whose dimensions can be varied indefinitely without ever changing their fundamental topological properties, the relations written or ciphered using Lacan's algebra are qualitative, structural relations.

Lacan's search for a nonquantitative kind of formalization can be seen in what he terms the "pass." The pass is a process wherein someone who has gone through analysis talks about his or her analysis in detail with two other people (*passeurs*) who in turn report on what they have heard to a committee (*Cartel de la passe*). The process was devised in part to gather information on the analytic process independent of what the analyst him or herself provides, and to thus confirm or refine notions about what actually occurs in analysis. The pass could be understood as a way of establishing psychoanalysis as a practice involving a number of "generic procedures," as Alain Badiou calls them,[15] procedures that are repeated again and again with different analysands. Thus understood, the pass could be considered part of a larger attempt to establish a kind of scientificity particular to psychoanalysis.

## The Status of Psychoanalysis

[P]sychoanalysis is to be taken seriously, even though
it is not a science.
—Lacan, Seminar XXV, November 15, 1977

Lacan's discussion of right and left polarized discourses suggests that "the four discourses" are not the only discourses imaginable. The latter do, nevertheless, cover a great deal of ground and are extremely useful in examining the mainsprings and aims of various discourses. Most notably for our purposes here, they allow us to situate "true" scientific endeavor as part and parcel of the hysteric's discourse.

While science and psychoanalytic theory building have that much in common, and while both are IRS discourses, psychoanalysis is not a science, but a discourse that allows us to understand the structure and operation of scientific discourse at a certain fundamental level. Thus, while psychoanalysis, in its

Lacanian version, seeks its own proper forms of scientificity—formalization ("mathemization"), generic procedures, rigorous clinical differentiations, and so on—it is nevertheless an independent discourse requiring no validation from science. After all, Science with a capital S does not exist: "it is but a fantasy."[16] Science is but one discourse among others.

## The Ethics of Lacanian Psychoanalysis

> [T]he ethical limits of psychoanalysis coincide with
> the limits of its practice.
> —Lacan, Seminar VII, pp. 21–22.

Lacan provides a sustained attempt to examine ever further the aims of analysis on the basis of advances in theory, and to develop ever further theorization on the basis of revised views of the aims of analysis. Analysis is not pragmatic in its aims, if pragmatism means compliance with social, economic, and political norms and realities. It is a praxis of jouissance, and jouissance is anything but practical. It ignores the needs of capital, health insurance companies, socialized health care, public order, and "mature adult relationships." The techniques that psychoanalysts must use to deal with jouissance wreak havoc on the principle that time is money and on accepted notions of "professional conduct." While therapists in our society are expected to interact with their patients in ways that are considered by dominant contemporary social, political, and psychological discourses to be for their own *good*,[17] analysts act instead so as to further their analysands' *Eros*. That aim is constitutive of the praxis that is psychoanalysis.

# Afterword

MARX SAYS of the capitalist system that one can begin one's examination of it at any point, without missing any of its features. The order in which one's study proceeds is thus of no importance; one can pick up the thread of the fabric of capitalism anywhere. The same is no doubt true of Lacanian psychoanalysis, and the logic of my presentation of it here is certainly contingent, based only on the order in which certain of Lacan's notions sorted themselves out in my own mind.

This book was never conceived as a *whole*, representing instead a compilation of papers or talks on specific themes prepared for widely varying audiences, worked together after the fact to establish a semblance of unity. That unity remains somewhat ad hoc, but it had to be provided to satisfy the requirements of the Other (in this case, the American publishing industry).[1] The book's best moments are, it seems to me, tucked away in certain subsections and notes where I associate at some length without regard to the appropriateness of such ruminations at the particular points in the whole at which they appear.

The ununified nature of the whole may, however, be troublesome to some readers in certain respects. In my early work on Lacan, I was quite concerned about grasping the "true distinctions" between the Name-of-the-Father, $S(\bar{A})$, $\Phi$, $S_1$, and so on, being troubled by their multiple meanings and uses, the constant introduction of homonyms (*le non du père*, the Father's "No," as a homonym for *le nom du père*, the Name-of-the-Father), and ubiquitous grammatical ambiguities (*le désir de la mère*, the mother's desire or the desire for the mother). Here, on the other hand, I have played fast and loose with many of these terms, interpreting them as seemed fit for each different context. This allows for a certain fluidity in the use of concepts, but I shall, on the other hand, perhaps be taxed for a lack of rigor. If mathematicians use symbols that mean nothing, psychoanalysts use symbols that can mean so many different things, and positivists unsuccessfully attempt to assign one single, unambiguous meaning to each term, what is to be done?

A closer look at the work of mathematicians nevertheless suggests that, like the proverbial three rabbis with four different opinions, there are virtually as many different theories of the foundations of mathematics as there are of the Big Bang, the origin of life on earth, and so on. Perhaps the symbols used by mathematicians, meaning nothing, are open to any and all interpretations.

That is certainly not the case with Lacan's symbols. Their meanings may be multiple, but there is a definite logic to their transformations or shifts in meaning. Object *a* begins as imaginary and moves into the real in the late 1950s and early 1960s; S($\mathbb{A}$) begins in the symbolic and moves towards the real. The shift is always towards the real. Each symbol thus has its own historical/conceptual contexts and undergoes discernible transformations.

No one can ultimately be satisfied with this book, as everyone will think that I have not adequately dealt with the theoretical issues most important to them in their respective fields. The literary critic will feel that I have scanted Lacan's style and rhetoric and his notion of metaphor; the philosopher, that I have blithely glossed over tremendous debates in logic and set theory, presenting old formulations as if they were the latest advances; the psychoanalyst, that the attention I pay to speculative, logical systems is greater than that granted clinical issues, and that subjects such as death and jouissance receive short shrift; the feminist, that I have not sufficiently developed Lacan's views of sexual difference and thus have not exposed the shortcomings therein; the student, that I have provided needless commentary on the oftentimes abstract origins of Lacan's notions instead of presenting a clearer, more straightforward version of them; the academic, that I have devoted hopelessly little space to situating my views with respect to those put forward by others writing on Lacan today.

   To these critiques, all of which are no doubt justified in part, I can only reply that Lacan is of interest to scholars and practitioners in far more fields than I could ever hope to familiarize myself with. As an analyst, I only come to understand what Lacan is getting at through experience, being ineluctably led to certain notions by my analysands. Quite often it is my clinical practice that allows me to come up with a glimmer of an interpretation of a particularly striking but obscure passage in Lacan's work. I hope to rectify in future writings some of the obvious inadequacies and imbalances of this one; nevertheless, I suspect that certain readers will still feel that I am skirting the issues most important to them. But it is for those most knowledgeable in a field to draw out the implications for that field of Lacan's (or anyone else's) work.

The very idea of a *book* was quite foreign to Lacan's mind. The writings he brought out were often published grudgingly, at the entreaty of others. Was he simply being coquettish? In part, perhaps; but more profoundly he seems to have wished his "system" to remain an open system, almost an antisystem. Publication means fixity, the formation of doctrine, and ultimately an approach to psychoanalysis that begins with nothing but preconceived ideas, set notions about what one should find in an analysis and what should occur in the process—in a word, standardization. Just as Freud, in his papers on "Technique," cautioned practitioners not to fill their minds with ideas about and goals for their analysands, but rather to be open to everything they say and do—by paying free-floating or evenly-hovering attention to the analysand—Lacan reminds his students over and over to stop trying to understand everything, because understanding is ultimately a form of defense, of bringing everything back to what is already known. The more you try to understand, the less you hear—the less you can hear something new and different.

It is absolutely clear from their work that Freud and Lacan experimented with both psychoanalytic practice and theory all their lives. Lacan is, indeed, one of the few analysts who followed the spirit of Freud's work, even as he paid incredible attention to the letter of it as well. That spirit requires a certain openness—not incompatible with trenchant critique of the work of others who return to *pre-analytic* notions—an openness we might associate with Lacan's own teaching style: attacking orthodoxy, exploding his own emerging orthodoxy, challenging the master signifiers of his own field, some of which were of his own making.[2] Lacan's discourse as a teacher seems to come under the discourse of the hysteric, a discourse that never accepts authority for authority's sake. Lacan takes Freud very seriously, but nevertheless contradicts him at times after careful consideration. The point is not merely to avoid criticizing without prior reflection on the basis of preconceived notions, but also not to be obsessed with formulating a system that explains everything (as is required by the university discourse). The best teaching discourse is the hysteric's discourse, which Lacan associates with the best scientific activity. It is not always an easy discourse to sustain for those who do not adopt it spontaneously, nor for those in the publish or perish world of American academia.

> [R]eading in no way obliges you to understand. You
> have to read first.
>     —Lacan, Seminar XX, p. 61

My reading of Lacan's work here apparently calls for some explanation in the context of contemporary American intellectual trends. While this book was still in manuscript, virtually everyone selected by publishers to read it remarked that I was not critical enough of Lacan, implying that it was not sufficient to provide a close reading of his work, or a detailed explanation thereof, without immediately launching into critique. In the end I began to view the situation as quite comical, maddening as it was: it was becoming quite evident that, in the world of American academic publishing, the time had passed when one could seriously study a thinker (at least a contemporary thinker) without simultaneously "correcting" his or her views. Nevertheless this particular privilege is above all refused to scholars writing on Lacan, not so much to those writing on Derrida, Kristeva, Foucault, and other contemporary figures. Why is that?

Reading Lacan is an infuriating experience! He almost never comes right out and says what he means, and the explanations that have been proffered for this run the gamut: "The man couldn't write, much less think straight," "He never wanted to be pinned down or held to a specific theoretical position," "He did it all on purpose, deliberately making it difficult, if not downright impossible, to figure out what he was getting at," "His writing operates on so many levels at once, and requires knowledge of so many areas in philosophy, literature, religion, mathematics, etc., that you can only grasp what he is saying after having read all of the background material," and so on.

All of those statements are both true and false. Having translated five of his *Écrits* now, I find him an unbearable writer to translate, but a pleasure to read in French. Which does not mean that he no longer drives me to distraction at times with his ambiguities and vague formulations, but his work is so evocative and provocative that there are few texts I enjoy more. It may well be true that he was *unable* to express his thought very clearly at times, but is that not true of everyone, and is it not belied by the brilliant clarity of certain of his formulations? His multitudinous allusions and references may trouble certain readers, but the key to understanding him is not to read all of the background material first; that only leads to more confusion.

No, the problem is that *a peculiar temporal logic is involved in reading Lacan*: you cannot read his *writings* (in particular the *Écrits*) unless you already know more or less what he means (this is less true of his seminars). In other words, in order to get anything out of his writing, you already have to understand a good deal of what he is talking about. And even then!

Therefore, you either have to learn about Lacan from someone else—with all the biases that entails—and then try to verify or refute what you have learned by examining his texts. Or you have to read and reread and reread his work until you can begin to formulate hypotheses of your own, and then reread yet again with those hypotheses in mind, and so on. Not only is that a problem in terms of the publish-or-perish economic reality of most academics—leading to serious temporal tension around understanding and "production"—but it also runs counter to a certain American pragmatism and independence. If I cannot put someone's work to use for me in a relatively short space of time, what is the point? Above all I need to prove that I am an independent thinker, and thus I must criticize it as soon as I think I have begun to understand it. Therefore I must read it with a view to critiquing it, short-circuiting the "time for comprehending" and proceeding directly to the "moment of concluding."

In the 1960s, Lacan ridicules those who talked about understanding Freud *before* translating his work (which is merely common sense, after all)—as if one could understand anything about Freud before engaging in the complicated task of translation. The same is obviously true of Lacan: translation has to come first, in some sense, in understanding him, but you cannot even begin to translate without certain keys and reference points. You think you begin to understand as you translate, and as your understanding grows, your translations evolve—though, inevitably, not always in the right direction. You must jump to conclusions about his work and formulate hypotheses if anything is to take on meaning for you in his texts, and yet at the same time "what [you] understand is a bit precipitated" (Seminar XX, p. 65). All understanding involves jumping the gun, jumping to conclusions, but that does not make all conclusions correct!

The reaction in the United States to an author like Lacan is:

1. If I can't figure him out myself, then he's not worth thinking about.
2. If he can't express himself clearly, then it must be muddled thinking.
3. I never thought much of French "theory" anyway.

Which is reminiscent of the threefold denial concocted by the man accused by his neighbor of having returned a kettle in damaged condition:

1. I returned it undamaged.
2. The kettle had a hole in it when I borrowed it.
3. I never borrowed the kettle in the first place.[3]

If an author is worth reading seriously, you have to take for granted at the outset that, as crazy as certain ideas may at first seem, considered in greater detail they may become more convincing, or at least lead you to understand the aporias that gave rise to them. That is more credit than most people are willing to give an author, and a love-hate ambivalence gets played out around reading. To assume that it is not as crazy as it sounds is to love the author ("I love the person I assume to have knowledge," Seminar XX, p. 64), whereas to read it critically comes off as hate (Are you with him or against him?). Perhaps hate is the condition for a serious reading: "Perhaps I would read [Aristotle] better if I assumed he had less knowledge" (ibid.). If that indeed is the condition, it had better be preceded by a prolonged period in which the reader loves the author and presumes him or her to have knowledge!

That love is hard to sustain in the United States. The work by Lacan that has thus far appeared in English has, for the most part, been poorly translated. There is no psychoanalytic context in which clinicians can observe Lacanian practitioners at work and see the immediate benefits at the clinical level of Lacan's distinctions and formulations. And learning from someone else about Lacan in the United States generally means learning from someone who started reading these hermetic texts only a couple of years before you did.

The French man or woman in the street understands nothing of Lacan and cannot explain a single one of his formulations. Lacan may be typically French, and closer in spirit to the "French mind" than to the American, but virtually no one in France comes to understand Lacan by reading the *Écrits*! As Lacan says, "[T]hey were not meant to be read" (Seminar XX, p. 29). The

French learn about Lacan in academic and/or clinical contexts, where they are taught by one or more of the thousands of Lacanians who worked with him and his associates, attended lectures, went to case presentations at the hospitals, spent years on the couch, and so on. They learned about Lacan's work first hand—as a praxis.

In the United States, Lacanian psychoanalysis is little more than a set of texts, a dead discourse unearthed like ancient texts in archeological finds, the context of which has been washed or eroded away. No quantity of publications can change that. For Lacan's discourse to come alive here, his *clinical approach* will have to be introduced alongside his texts, through analysis, supervision, and clinical work, that is, through subjective experience.

## The Language of the Unconscious

IN THIS appendix, I examine the elaborate four-symbol "language" presented in Lacan's as yet untranslated postface to the "Seminar on 'The Purloined Letter'" (*Écrits* 1966, pp. 41–61). A far simpler model of such a language was provided in chapter 2 above, which allowed me to bring out a number of the essential features of such languages. The elaborate discussion of Lacan's more complex model here is a prerequisite to the exploration of the *caput mortuum* found in appendix 2, the *caput mortuum* being an avatar (one of the most difficult to unearth, I dare say) of object (a).

The work included in both appendices here should be viewed as an attempt to take Lacan *literally*, in other words, to pay as great, if not even greater, attention to the *letter* of his postface than has previously been paid by others to the "Seminar on 'The Purloined Letter.'"[1] Indeed, virtually no one ever reads Lacan's postface to that seminar.[2] Yet, by presenting a relatively simple model of language that includes *overdetermined* symbols, Lacan is able to show how and where the real manifests itself within the symbolic, and thus point to the limits of "literalization."

### "Recreational Mathematics"

Lacan's exposition here (*Écrits* 1966, pp. 41–61) is confusingly laconic, but his moves can nevertheless be laid out rather simply:

*Step One*: coin tosses are grouped by threes, each grouping falling into one of the categories represented in table A1.1.

Table A1.1

| 1 | 2 | 3 |
|---|---|---|
| (identical) | (odd) | (alternating) |
| + + + | + + −    − − + | + − + |
| − − − | + − −    − + + | − + − |

Lacan refers to the triplets falling under categories 1 and 3 as "symmetrical," and to those falling under category 2 as "asymmetrical" (thus the appellation "odd" for the latter). These designations will be important further on.

Taking a string of toss results, we thus group and label them as indicated in figure A1.1.

Figure A1.1

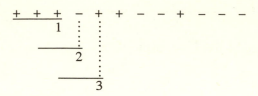

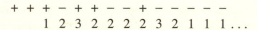

The first three toss results (+ + +) fall into category 1; the next *overlapping* group of three (+ + −) falls into group 2; the third (+ − +) is of type 3; and so on. I will abbreviate this as follows:

$$+ \ + \ + \ - \ + \ + \ - \ - \ + \ - \ - \ - \ - \ -$$
$$1 \ \ 2 \ \ 3 \ \ 2 \ \ 2 \ \ 2 \ \ 2 \ \ 3 \ \ 2 \ \ 1 \ \ 1 \ \ 1 \dots$$

The reader will easily observe that one cannot move directly from a 1 to a 3 (or from a 3 to a 1) without a 2 intervening to begin (or remove) alternation of signs. All other direct succession combinations are possible. Lacan provides the graph in figure A1.2 (called the "1–3 Network," *Écrits* 1966, p. 48) to visualize all the allowable moves:

Figure A1.2: 1–3 Network

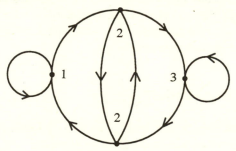

(Note that this same graph applies in all respects to the simplified two-sign toss-grouping matrix described in chapter 2.)

*Step Two*: We now lay a symbolic matrix upon this numeric one (table A1.2).

Table A1.2: Greek Letter Matrix I

| α | β | γ | δ |
|---|---|---|---|
| 1_1, 1_3 | 1_2 | 2_2 | 2_1 |
| 3_3, 3_1 | 3_2 | | 2_3 |

Here the blank space between the pairs of numbers must be filled by a third number. Each Greek letter thus regroups the first-level groupings by *threes*. For example, α covers the cases where we find two 1s (under the plus/minus line) *separated by another number*:

$$+\ +\ +\ +\ +\ -\ -\ -\ +\ -\ -\ -\ -\ -$$
$$\underline{1\ \ 1\ \ 1\ \ 2\ \ 2\ \ 1\ \ 2\ \ 3\ \ 2\ \ 1\ \ 1\ \ 1}\dots$$
$$\alpha$$

In this case, the middle number must be a 1, for, as we saw above, it cannot be a 3, it being impossible to go directly from a 1 to a 3 configuration (there must be a 2 in between); nor can it be a 2, as we need two 2s in a row to be able to return to a 1 (a single 2 is not sufficient). If we fill in the blanks correctly, we can now provide a more detailed table (table A1.3). For the moment, however, the most important things for us to keep track of are the first and third numbers in each triplet.

Table A1.3: Greek Letter Matrix II

| α | β | γ | δ |
|---|---|---|---|
| 111, 123 | 112, 122 | 212, 232 | 221, 211 |
| 333, 321 | 332, 322 | 222 | 223, 233 |

Lacan does not say this in so many words (or not explicitly enough, at any rate, to be easily understood),[3] but any other way of regrouping these first-order symbols reduces the rest of what follows to sheer nonsense. The strings of numbers must be regrouped as follows. Considering once again our toss-result line (i.e., the +/− line) and the number coding line (second line), first we group the first and third numbers, then the second and fourth, then the third and fifth, and so on, adding a symbol below each linked pair to represent it, as in table A1.4.

Table A1.4

Slot Numbers:

| | | | | | 1 | 2 | 3 | 4 | 5 ... |
|---|---|---|---|---|---|---|---|---|---|
| + | + | + | − | + | + | − | − | +... | |
| *1* | 2 | *3* | 2 | 2 | 2 | 2... | | | |
| | | α | | | | | | | |
| | 2 | 3 | 2 | | | | | | |
| | | γ | | | | | | | |
| | | 3 | 2 | 2 | | | | | |
| | | | β | | | | | | |
| | | | 2 | 2 | 2 | | | | |
| | | | | γ | | | | | |

I will abbreviate this schema as follows:

$$+\ +\ +\ -\ +\ +\ -\ -\ +\ -\ -\ -\ -\ -$$
$$1\ 2\ 3\ 2\ 2\ 2\ 2\ 3\ 2\ 1\ 1\ 1$$
$$\alpha\ \ \gamma\ \ \beta\ \ \gamma\ \ \gamma\ \ \delta\ \ \gamma\ \ \alpha\ \ \delta\ \ \alpha$$

Note that in defining his Greek Letter Matrix, Lacan says that an α goes from a symmetrical three-toss grouping (i.e., category 1 or 3) to another symmetrical one; a β goes from a symmetrical to an asymmetrical (i.e., category 2); a γ from an asymmetrical to another asymmetrical; and a δ from an asymmetrical to a symmetrical. I shall come back to this point further on.

What must be pointed out next is that while any one letter may follow *directly* upon any other (this can be checked by inspection of table A1.3, Greek Letter Matrix II), any one letter may not follow *indirectly* upon any other. The case we will look at here, to begin with, is the determination of, or limitation imposed upon, the *third* position.

Suppose we begin with the letter α; the next letter can be α, β, γ, or δ, but we always get an α or a β in the third slot. Why so? The four possible α combinations (viz. 111, 123, 333, 321) all end in either 1 or 3. As the last number of these triplets will become the first number of the third-slot triplets, and as α and β are the only letters to comprise combinations beginning with 1 and 3, only α and β can fill the third slot.

This whole reasoning process can be repeated if, instead of α, we begin with the letter δ, for all δ combinations also end in 1 or 3.

On the other hand, all β and γ combinations *end* in 2, and as only δ and γ combinations *begin* with 2, only they can fill slot three if there is a β or a γ in slot one.

This accounts for the emblematically laconic formula that appears in *Écrits* (1966, p. 49) and that I have reproduced in table A1.5. We see on the top line that, in the case of α and δ, regardless of what letter we put at time 2, we still get α or β at time 3; and the lower line shows that, in the case of γ and β, every letter we try at time 2 gives us γ or δ at time 3.

Table A1.5: AΔ Distribution

$$\frac{\alpha,\delta}{\gamma,\beta} \quad \longrightarrow \quad \alpha,\beta,\gamma,\delta \quad \longrightarrow \quad \frac{\alpha,\beta}{\gamma,\delta}$$

| Times: | 1 | 2 | 3 |

Which is to say that the third slot is already to some extent determined by the first—the first "bearing within itself" the "kernel" of the third. Before developing this notion further, let us examine Lacan's *four-time* schema on page 50 of *Écrits* 1966.

Let us look first at Table O, where the slots are numbered in the top line and a sample number line (coding the coin toss results) is provided in the second line down (table A1.6). Lacan *does not* claim that the only way to get from δ in slot one to β in slot four is by inserting two α's between them. There are in

Table A1.6: Lacan's Table O

Slot Numbers:

| 1 | 2 | 3 | 4 | | | | Greek letter lines: |
|---|---|---|---|---|---|---|---|
| sample number line: | | | | | | | |
| 2   1 | 1 | 1 | 1   2 | | | | |
| δ | α | α | β | γ | γ | δ | 1 |
| | γ | | | | α | | 2 |
| β | δ | | δ | β | | | 3 |

fact a number of different ways to get from δ to β; Lacan's point here is that *none of them* include the letter γ (Greek letter line 2), a fact one can check by trying all the various possible combinations (a fastidious task at best), or by simply noticing that, as all δ's end in 1 or 3, a γ is not possible in the third slot (we saw above, in table A1.5, the AΔ Distribution, that only α and β can follow δ in the third slot), and that a γ in the second slot automatically means that the slot-4 triplet will begin with a 2, whereas no β begins with a 2.

Greek letter line 3 of the table shows that if you try to put a β in slot 2, you never get a β in slot 4 (for a β puts a 2 at the beginning of the slot-4 triplet, and no β begins with a 2); and that if you should be so foolhardy as to try to put a δ in slot 3, you come up against what we already saw in the three-time example: a δ can never be found in slot 3 if there is a δ in slot 1.

The rest of Greek letter line 1 to the right of δααβ shows us the excluded terms for the series βγγδ, which works exactly like the left-hand side.[4]

On the pages that follow Table O, Lacan mentions other syntactic features of the Greek letter overlay. For example, if one comes across two β's following one another without a δ in between, they must either be immediate successors (i.e, ββ) or be separated by one or more αγ pairs (e.g., βαγβ, βαγαγβ, βαγα . . . γβ). What is more immediately pertinent for us here is to note that, whereas it is theoretically possible for a random series of coin tosses to indefinitely reproduce α's or γ's, as in the following two samples—

```
+ + + + + + + + + + + +
1 1 1 1 1 1 1 1 1 1 1 1
 α α α α α α α α α α
- - + + - - + + - - + + -
2 2 2 2 2 2 2 2 2 2 2
 γ γ γ γ γ γ γ γ γ
```

—no random series whatsoever could possible endlessly produce δ's or β's in this way, for δ's always go from even numbers at the beginning of triplets to odd numbers at the end (e.g., 223) and must thus exhaust themselves after but two repetitions, and β's do just the opposite (going from odd to even) and thus similarly exhaust themselves. In other words, they can only replenish themselves through the interpolation of other letters, and in fact every β couple requires at least *two* other successive letters before it can come up again. The same is true for δ couples.

## Probability and Possibility

One of the conclusions that can be drawn from Lacan's second-order matrix is that, try as one might, regardless of how loaded the coin used may be or how much one cheats, certain of the letters defined, namely β and δ, can *never* turn up more than 50 percent of the time. By contrast, with a great deal of luck or a little coin loading, α, like γ, *could* turn up more than half the time. While this two-tier symbolic matrix was designed in such a way as to give each Greek letter *exactly* the same probability of showing up as the others,[5] a restriction in terms of possibility and impossibility has arisen, as it were, ex nihilo.

*Probability and possibility are not one and the same thing.* Hence Lacan's assertion that prodigiously propitious combinations of coin tosses *could* lead α or γ to utterly overrun the series, while even the most preposterously propitious combinations *could never* lead β or δ to do so, is a significant result of the combinatory, surpassing all considerations of probability.

But the most important outcome, to my mind, is the *syntax* produced, which allows certain combinations and prohibits others. We see here that the laws generated by our numeric overlay (barring direct moves from 1 to 3 and from 3 to 1) blossom into an intricate apparatus with the introduction of the alphabetic matrix. In chapter 2, note 6, I explored some of the similarities between this kind of apparatus and language. The grammar generated here can be represented on a graph similar to Lacan's 1–3 Network, as shown in the next subsection.

## Network Mappings

In the remainder of this appendix and in appendix 2, I examine the "Parenthesis of Parentheses" added by Lacan in 1966, which splits this introduction/afterword to the "Seminar on 'The Purloined Letter'" in two. I will begin my discussion of this section with the footnote which ends it, wherein we see the 1–3 Network transformed, and the α, β, γ, δ Network laid out for the first and only time. The new network is depicted in figure A1.3.

In this retranscription of the 1–3 Network, all the arrows have changed directions, and instead of finding the numbers 1, 2, and 3, we find the following four combinations: 00, 01, 10, and 11. The diagram has thus been reversed, and the coding system once again tinkered with—to the point of being unrec-

Figure A1.3: 1–3 Network (slightly modified)

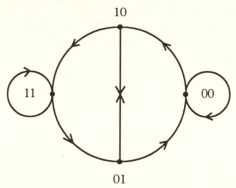

ognizable! One is obliged to return to the table showing which toss result combinations are grouped under each number (table A1.7) to discover the logic behind the new code.

Table A1.7

| 1 | 2 | 3 |
|---|---|---|
| (identical) | (odd) | (alternating) |
| + + + | + + −   − − + | + − + |
| − − − | + − −   − + + | − + − |

Lacan has *not* simplified this diagram to a two-sign matrix (i.e., + +, + −, − +, and − −) as it might appear at first glance (though, as I mentioned above, the 1–3 Network is a perfectly adequate schematization of this simplified two-sign matrix). The combination 11 evidently refers to the former category one, covering + + + and − − −. How is this possible? Let us suppose that 1 here denotes "same," in other words, that the first two toss results are both either plus or minus; 11 thus implies that the second overlapping pair of toss results are also the same; in this way we can account for both combinations which previously fell under category one. The symbol 0 will then obviously denote "different," and 00 will thus account for both + − + and − + −, the two pairs of toss results included therein both involving different signs. And while 10 will cover + + − and − − + (same and then different), 01 will cover + − − and − + + (different and then same).[6]

If this new coding works in the way I have just suggested, there is a typographical error on the graph provided on page 56 of the *Écrits*. For assuming the chain of toss results goes from left to right (and this is the way it goes in Lacan's own example in the footnote on page 47), each new term will be added on the right, and thus + + + and − − − will become + + − and − − +, respectively, as they move towards the top of the circle, both of which must be coded as 10. The 01 and 10 combinations are thus erroneously inverted on page 56, and I have therefore made the necessary modifications to figure A1.3.[7]

Lacan now proceeds to establish a higher-order graph which he blithely claims all mathematicians know how to derive—as though his text, now appearing in the collection of his "psychoanalytic" writings known as *Écrits*, were to be primarily perused by accomplished mathematicians! Let us try to "unpack" this graph one step at a time.

Breaking in half the fours arcs composing the quadrants of the main circle in the 1–3 Network and placing a point (or vertex) at each of the breaks, we obtain a square defined by these four new points (figure A1.4).

Figure A1.4

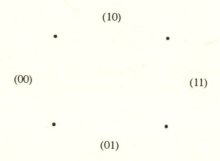

(10)

(00)                                                                (11)

(01)

We then define two more points by breaking the right and left loops around 00 and 11 in half, and two further points by breaking the central straight line between 10 and 01 (which, as we recall by looking at the old 1–3 Network, actually consisted of two arrows). We then reconnect these points to one another with new arrows, oriented as in the 1–3 Network (figure A1.5). Thus we have accounted for the graph's *form* by *breaking down each step of the 1–3 Network into two separate steps.*

Figure A1.5

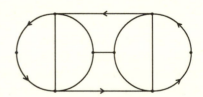

The numbers Lacan goes on to assign to each of the new points, though seemingly similar to those found in the 1–3 Network, derive from yet another, though related, code! Had Lacan maintained the same code, his new $\alpha$, $\beta$, $\gamma$, $\delta$ Network would correspond to sequences of four signs (i.e., plus and minus signs) and not to sequences of five, as is in fact the case.

The higher-order graph, understood as breaking down each step of the 1–3 Network into two separate steps, accounts for twice as many combinations of signs. In the case of a three-slot binary combinatory—one which takes three consecutive plus or minus signs as its basic building block or unit—there are $2^3$ (viz. 8) possible combinations, but if we add an additional slot, we get $2^4$ (viz. 16) possible combinations. Now as we saw above, using the 1/0 (same/different) overlay, each point on the 1–3 Network corresponds to two different combinations: for example, 10 corresponds to + + − and − − +, the first two signs being the same, the second two different. Thus in the case of a three-slot combinatory (such as the 1–3 Network), there are 8 possible combinations corresponding to 4 points or vertices (numbered 11, 10, 01, and 00). In the case of a four-slot combinatory, we have 16 possible combinations associated with 8 vertices; and in a five-slot combinatory we have 32 possible combinations and 16 vertices (the best graph for which involves three dimensions).

Now *Lacan's* α, β, γ, δ *Network has 8 vertices and would thus normally correspond to four-slot sequences of signs.* And the fact that he numbers these vertices with 1/0 sequences with three slots each (i.e., 000, 001, 010, 011, 100, 101, 110, and 111) would seem to confirm the idea that the Network maps four-sign plus/minus sequences. But then how do we account for the fact that α, β, γ, and δ all refer to five-sign sequences?

This can be done in three ways:

> **1**. Whereas in the 1–3 Network, 1 and 0 referred to *same and different*, respectively, here they refer to *odd and even*.[8] In other words, instead of coding strings of four toss results (e.g., 111 denoting + + + + and − − − −, 000 denoting + − + − and − + − +, and so on), they recode our old numeric matrix: 1 stands for our numeric-matrix categories one and three (the *odd-numbered* categories in table A1.7) and 0 for numeric-matrix category two (the *even-numbered* category).
>
> **2**. Alternatively, we could say that 1 refers to all *symmetrical* configurations (grouped under numeric-matrix categories one and three in table A1.7) and 0 to all *asymmetrical* configurations (grouped under category two in table A1.7). That is, 0 would refer to all the categories Lacan refers to as "odd" (here in the sense of "bizarre"). Thus while recoding the numeric matrix, it also simplifies the coding of strings of three toss results.[9]

I mentioned above that, in defining his Greek Letter Matrix, Lacan stipulated that an α goes from a symmetrical three-toss grouping (i.e., category one or three) to another symmetrical one; a β goes from a symmetrical to an asymmetrical (i.e., category two); a γ from an asymmetrical to another asymmetrical; and a δ from an asymmetrical to a symmetrical. The α, β, γ, δ Network can be rewritten by filling in the different triplets designated by each of the new triplets employing only 0s and 1s (figure A1.6).

From each point on the graph one can follow the chain in the two different directions pointed out by the addition of an odd or an even number (and thus a 0 or a 1) at the end of the triplet, or ultimately (if one has the enthusiasm to work out all the combinations), a plus or a minus at the end of a five-sign sequence. The graph has the advantage of pointing out all the permitted paths (and thus,

Figure A1.6

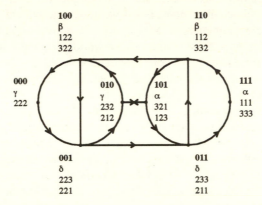

by implication, all the prohibited ones), and the 1/0 code it uses reduces all the various plus/minus combinations and triplets to a three-slot 1/0 combinatory.

Note here that the annotations for α, β, γ, and δ provided by Lacan with this table (p. 57) are once again cryptically laconic. The periods function as blanks to be filled by either symbol, 1 or 0: 1.1 is thus to be read as 111 or 101, 1.0 as 110 or 100, and so on. Here we see most clearly that each Greek letter is defined in terms of its symmetrical-asymmetrical configuration. Note also that though it might now seem that the old 1–3 Network, including 11, 10, 01 and 00 as its vertices, could adequately represent the α, β, γ, δ system, it is able to represent neither the prohibited moves nor the memory circuits.

Lacan seems to have been led to the final *form* of this complex network by first putting the eight possible 1/0 triplets on the corners of a cube (or parallel-epiped). As a cube has exactly eight corners, it no doubt came to Lacan's mind as a likely representational device (see Seminar IV, March 20, 1957). If we put 000 at one extreme and 111 at the other, successively adding 0s in going around one way and 1s in going around the other (figure A1.7), we have but to fill in the arrows, flatten out the cube into two dimensions, and round out the square ends to find Lacan's final graph (figure A1.6).[10]

Note for future reference that the numeric triplets situated on the top and bottom levels of the α, β, γ, δ Network are *mirror images*: 322/223, 122/221, 233/332, 211/112. The same goes for the new 1–0 binary triplets: 100/001, 110/011. These mirror images all include the necessary *right to left reversal* implied by Lacan's mirror stage. β *and* δ *are thus mirror reflections of each other*. (They are, after all, defined as going from symmetrical to asymmetrical and from asymmetrical to symmetrical, respectively.) This will be of importance in analyzing Lacan's "L Chain" in appendix 2.

**3.** There is yet another way to explain how the α, β, γ, δ Network covers five-sign sequences of pluses and minuses: first we code these sequences using the 1–3 Network code, and then we *recode* the coding using the same code! Let me explain:

*The same/different 1/0 code can be applied twice*: first to a five-sign sequence

Figure A1.7

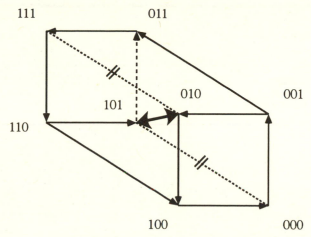

(e.g., + + − + +) and then to the 1/0 code corresponding to it (e.g., 1001). For, taking overlapping pairs in the number sequence, we can recode them according to whether we find two identical *numbers*, which will be coded as 1, or two different numbers, which will be coded as 0. In the example above (+ + − + +, to which 1001 corresponds), we recode 1001 as different-same-different, in other words, as 010. This allows us to reduce five-sign plus/minus sequences to three-sign 1/0 sequences, and, strangely enough, every sequence thus coded fits precisely into the $\alpha$, $\beta$, $\gamma$, $\delta$ schema: every single +/- sequence which is grouped (by the twice-applied same/different code) under 111 and 101, for example, is in fact an $\alpha$ sequence (going from 1 to 1, 1 to 3, 3 to 3 or 3 to 1).[11]

This is easily explained by observing that a 1 in the second application of the code accounts for *all four symmetrical* plus/minus three-sign *combinations* (i.e., covers 00 and 11 in the first application, which in turn covered + − + and − + −, and + + + and − − − respectively). A 0 in the second application designates *all asymmetrical* three-sign *combinations* (designated by 10 and 01 in the first application, they in turn designating + + − and − − +, and + − − and − + +, respectively).

Thus, a double application of the same/different code has exactly the same effect as the symmetrical/asymmetrical coding, assigning as it does a 1 or a 0 to each successive set of symmetrical or asymmetrical triplets.

The same kind of diagram can be constructed with the help of a flow-chart. One begins with + + + and charts the different directions in which one is led by adding a + or a − at the end of the series. This splits the flow-chart into two branches with every addition, as we see in table A1.8. Here we notice that line 2 of the flow-chart provides the right-hand circle of figure A1.6, the connection between lines 14 and 15 (211 → 112) providing the oriented diameter of this same circle; line 10 provides the left-hand circle, line 8 providing its diameter; line 6 presents the pulsation linking the two circles together; lines 1 and 8 give us the $\alpha\alpha\alpha$ and $\gamma\gamma\gamma$ loops; and so on.

**TABLE A1.8**

Line numbers

| Line | | | | | | | |
|---|---|---|---|---|---|---|---|
| 1 | ++++ | → +++++<br>111 | | | | | α loop |
| 2 | | → ++++−<br>112 | → +++−+<br>123 | → ++−+−<br>233 | → +−+−+<br>333 | → −+−+−<br>333 | right-hand circle |
| 3 | | | | | | → −+−++<br>332 | |
| 4 | | | | | → +−+−−<br>332 | → −+−−+<br>332 | top line |
| 5 | | | | | | → −+−−−<br>321 | |
| 6 | | | | → ++−++<br>232 | → +−+++<br>321 | → −+++−<br>212 | connects the two circles |
| 7 | | | | | | → −++++<br>211 | |
| 8 | | | | | → +−++−<br>322 | → −++−+<br>223 | left-diameter |
| 9 | | | | | | → −++−−<br>222 | |
| 10 | | | → +++−−<br>122 | → ++−−+<br>222 | → +−−+−<br>223 | → −−+−−<br>232 | left-hand circle |
| 11 | | | | | | → −−+−+<br>233 | |
| 12 | | | | | → +−−++<br>222 | → −−++−<br>222 | γ loop |
| 13 | | | | | | → −−+++<br>221 | |
| 14 | | | | → ++−−−<br>221 | → +−−−−<br>211 | → −−−−−<br>111 | bottom line |
| 15 | | | | | | → −−−−+<br>112 | |
| 16 | | | | | → +−−−+<br>212 | → −−−+−<br>123 | conncects the two circles |
| 17 | | | | | | → −−−++<br>122 | |

To actually construct such a graph, one would take all of the above moves, recode the numeric triplets into odds (1s) and evens (0s), and then link all of the identical entries (new triplets) together, drawing in all the possible moves. Given that in a three-slot combinatory with but two choices for each slot, we know that there are eight points to be linked up (000, 001, 010, 011, 100, 101, 110, and 111), and while there are a whole variety of ways of drawing this sort of "Network," Lacan's is one of the most elegant. As J.-A. Miller points out, this Network is closely related to Lacan's "graph of desire" (*Écrits*, p. 315).

# *Appendix 2* _____

## Stalking the Cause

LACAN begins one part of the afterword to his "Seminar on 'The Purloined Letter,'" the "Parenthesis of Parentheses" (added in 1966), with the rather disingenuous remark that he is "perplexed" by the fact that none of the people who tried to decipher his "clearly enunciated" numeric and alphabetic matrixes ever "dreamt" of translating them in terms of parentheses—as if that were the very first thing that should come to mind.

His intent seems to be to give a retranscription of his well-known Schema L,[1] while at the same time updating it in such a way as to bring out the role of object *a*, a concept he spent a good deal of time elaborating between 1956 and 1966. Let us follow his retranslation step by step here; only then shall we be in a position to see how object *a* as cause is introduced therein.

I mentioned in appendix 1 that to go from a β to a β, one can either proceed directly or, barring the appearance of a δ, through the interpolation of αγ pairs. The example Lacan provides on page 51 of *Écrits* 1966, (βαγα . . . γβ), is totally recoded in the course of this retranscription. We take the following parenthetical structure, never theoretically motivated by Lacan's text, but rather simply posited, ( ( ) ( ) ), where β and δ have been transformed into parentheses (β being an opening parenthesis, δ a closing parenthesis, as I shall demonstrate below), and proceed to fill in the various blanks. Numbering the blanks as follows,

$$( 1 ( 3 ) 2 ( 3 ) 1a )$$

we see that Lacan places an indefinite number of αγ pairs in blank 1, and of γα pairs in blank 1a. Lacan refers to these first sequences as the *lining*, as of a coat, but the French *doublure* suggests a sort of doubling as well; it seems clear that it is this *twofold* structure—in other words, the double opening and closing parentheses, (( ))—which is crucial here, as the stuffing (the αγ and γα pairs) can, according to Lacan, be reduced to nothing. Lacan also refers to these double parentheses as quotes or quotation marks, a suggestive nomenclature to say the least.

In position 2 we place an indefinite number of γα pairs, with an additional γ at the end so as to make the total number of signs odd (there may also be no signs whatsoever here). In the two 3-positions we put zero or more γ's; in other words, as many as we like. Thus far we have:

$$(αγαγ . . . (γγ . . . γ) γαγα . . . γ (γγ . . . γ) . . . γαγα)$$

which, if we choose no signs wherever possible, can be reduced to (( ) ( )).

In the next step, outside of the first and last parentheses we place a series of α's, once again as many as we like, engulfing zero or more parentheses filled either with nothing or with αγ strings ending in α to make for an odd number of signs. These strings can be situated on one or both sides of the main string shown above. For example:

(αγαγ . . . (γγ . . . γ) γαγα . . . γ (γγ . . . γ) . . . γαγα) ααααα (αγαγ . . . α)ααα . . .

Now we replace the α's and γ's with 1s and 0s respectively:

(1010 . . . (00 . . . 0) 010101 (00 . . . 0) . . . 0101) 11111 (1010 . . . 1) 111

In the L Chain (corresponding to "Schema L") Lacan provides, he writes this just slightly differently:

Chain L: (10 . . . (00 . . . 0) 0101 . . . 0 (00 . . . 0) . . . 01) 11111 . . . (1010 . . . 1) 111 . . .

One more condition is, according to Lacan, necessary to make Chain L correspond to Schema L: the 000 strings in parentheses shall be taken as moments of silence, while the 0s found in alternating strings shall be taken as scansions or cuts; for 0 does not play the same role in these two positions.

Perplexing *indeed* that we never even for an instant dreamt of rewriting Lacan's α, β, γ, δ chain in this way! Before going on to attribute a part of Lacan's Schema L to each part of Chain L, let us try to dissect, ever so little, the Chain as it stands.

Outside of the main double set of parentheses (or quotes: « ») we find a sequence we can simplify as follows: 111(101)111. Knowing (for Lacan stipulates at least this much) that 1 = α and 0 = γ, we can unilaterally determine that the sign for the opening of the parentheses is β and that that for the closing is δ. For the first part of the sequence, ααα, is only possible on the basis of an all plus, all minus, or uniformly alternating sequence (corresponding to all 1s or all 3s in our first numeric matrix). As the next part, (αγα), shows a γ in the second position after the opening of the parentheses, and as a γ designates 2-to-2 moves, the parenthesis necessarily begins an alternation (+ to −, or vice versa), taking us from a 1 to a 2, or interrupts uniform alternation (putting two pluses or two minuses in a row), taking us from a 3 to a 2, both of which are β configurations. For example:[2]

$$
\begin{array}{ccccccccccc}
+ & + & + & + & + & + & + & - & + & + \\
1 & 1 & 1 & 1 & 1 & 2 & 3 & 2 & & \\
& & & \alpha & \alpha & \alpha & \beta & \alpha & \gamma & \\
& & & \mathbf{1} & \mathbf{1} & \mathbf{1} & \mathbf{(} & \mathbf{1} & \mathbf{0} &
\end{array}
$$

The closing of the parenthesis can be determined in the same way, for we know that a γ always ends with a 2 and that if two positions further on we are to have another sign which is not a γ, it must be a δ, as two slots down from a γ there can only be a γ or a δ (cf. the AΔ Distribution in appendix 1). This can be seen by continuing the above chain:

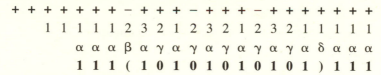

$$+ + + + + + - + + + + + +$$
$$1\ 1\ 1\ 1\ 1\ 2\ 3\ 2\ 1\ 1\ 1\ 1\ 1$$
$$\alpha\ \alpha\ \alpha\ \beta\ \alpha\ \gamma\ \alpha\ \delta\ \alpha\ \alpha\ \alpha$$
$$\mathbf{1\ 1\ 1\ (\ 1\ 0\ 1\ )\ 1\ 1\ 1}$$

The equation of β and δ with opening "(" and closing ")" parentheses is further confirmed by the fact, discovered in the discussion of the α, β, γ, δ Network in appendix 1, that β and δ are mirror images of each other.

Let us note here that odd-numbered αγ strings always result in 12321 cyclical patterns. Consider for example the string below:

$$+ + + + + + - + + + - + + + - + + + + + +$$
$$1\ 1\ 1\ 1\ 1\ 2\ 3\ 2\ 1\ 2\ 3\ 2\ 1\ 2\ 3\ 2\ 1\ 1\ 1\ 1\ 1$$
$$\alpha\ \alpha\ \alpha\ \beta\ \alpha\ \gamma\ \alpha\ \gamma\ \alpha\ \gamma\ \alpha\ \gamma\ \alpha\ \gamma\ \alpha\ \delta\ \alpha\ \alpha\ \alpha$$
$$\mathbf{1\ 1\ 1\ (\ 1\ 0\ 1\ 0\ 1\ 0\ 1\ 0\ 1\ 0\ 1\ )\ 1\ 1\ 1}$$

Here, in the plus/minus line, we see an alternation of three signs with one opposing sign.[3]

Now these (10 . . . 1) groupings—about which Lacan says we can have zero or more of them, of whatever length, inserted into the 1111 chain, placed (in Lacan's example) after the main quotes—are taken, along with this 1111 chain, as corresponding to the Other on Schema L. The Other here is thus represented as a homogeneous sequence of pluses or minuses (or a uniformly alternating sequence of pluses and minuses), interrupted, if we like, by sequences of three of one sign and one of the other, which take the form of sinusoidal curves in the numeric matrix: 11123212321232111. In the α = 1, γ = 0 overlay, these (10 . . . 0) groupings only momentarily break up the endless repetition of 1s, this repetition of the "unary trait," as Lacan terms Freud's *einziger Zug* (in the chapter on "Identification" in *Group Psychology and the Analysis of the Ego*). The 1 here thus seems to be the one of pure difference, of an as yet undifferentiated mark, and the parentheses engulfed within them, if there are any, are simply momentary suspensions, seemingly without importance, which, starting from 1, return the chain to the same point, 1, after a longer or shorter series of cycles.

If we look for a moment back at the α, β, γ, δ Network in appendix 1, we notice that at the extreme right we have 111, whereas to the extreme left we have 000. The 0–1 binary code used in this Network (where 1 = symmetrical, and 0 = asymmetrical) should not be conflated with the 0–1 binary code which generates the L Chain (where 1 = α, and 0 = γ). The Network does, however, provide an interesting visual prop, for if we allow ourselves to momentarily confound the two binary matrices, substituting the unbarred subject for 000, the Other for 111, and parentheses for β's and δ's, we get either the configuration in figure A2.1 or that in figure A2.2.

Figure A2.1

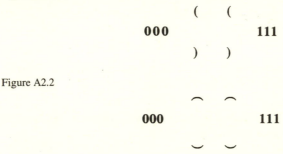

Figure A2.2

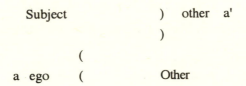

Rotating the Network forty-five degrees we get figure A2.3,

Figure A2.3

| Subject | | ) other a' |
|---------|---|------------|
|         | ( | )          |
| a ego   | ( | Other      |

where the mirror-reflected parentheses could easily represent the ego (small *a*) and the other (*a'*). This schematization is, obviously, strikingly similar to Lacan's Schema L.

The γ–α alternation in the middle of the network—not shown here—could perhaps be equated with the *drive* as it turns itself inside out (going from 123 in step one to 232 in step two, and on to 321 in step three; or simply back and forth from 101 to 010). Lacan mentions, for example, that drives are such that an incorporative drive, in other words, a drive to devour, can flip-flop into a fear of being devoured (he likens this to the turning inside out of a glove and to the two never ultimately distinct "sides" of a Möbius strip).[4]

This interpretation of the pistonlike γ–α pulsation as representative of the drive gains added weight from Lacan's statement that what is between the "quotes" (the double parentheses)—for example, 000)010(000—amounts to the S(Es) in Schema L, that is, the subject completed by the addition of the Freudian *Es* or id, the id being the seat of the drives (the French for drive being *pulsion*). He does, however, equate the 01 alternation between the 00 . . . 0 strings with the *a-a'* imaginary axis of Schema L.

Let us now examine more closely what we find within the "quotes" of Lacan's L Chain:

$$(10 \ldots (00 \ldots 0) \, 0101 \ldots 0 \, (00 \ldots 0) \ldots 01)$$

The 0s in parentheses correspond to an indefinitely long sequence of γ's, in other words, 2s, and thus to repeating series of two pluses and two minuses. Whereas the γ's or 2s that we examined earlier (in the 1010 . . . 1 chains) were part of sinusoidal wave patterns, even numbers surrounded on all sides by odd numbers (in the numeric matrix) or 0s always kept apart by 1s (in the 1/0 binary matrix), here the chain is monotonous, the barriers constituted by the parentheses at either end presenting the only *relief* (in both senses of the term) or heterogeneity. Simplifying the above quote to (10 (000) 010 (000) 01), we see that we can assign it a sample numeric line below it:

$$\begin{array}{cccccccccccccccccccc}
\beta & \alpha & \gamma & \beta & \gamma & \gamma & \gamma & \gamma & \delta & \gamma & \alpha & \gamma & \beta & \gamma & \gamma & \gamma & \delta & \gamma & \alpha & \delta \\
( & 1 & 0 & ( & 0 & 0 & 0 & 0 & ) & 0 & 1 & 0 & ( & 0 & 0 & 0 & ) & 0 & 1 & ) \\
\end{array}$$

(...1 1) 2 3 2 2 2 2 2 2 3 2 1 2 2 2 2 2 1 2 3 3

The alternating 0s and 1s in the center represent Schema L's *a–a′* imaginary grid; everything outside of the two main sets of parentheses represents the field of the Other (capital A), clearly dominated here by repetition of the unary trait; and the 10 and 01 pairs in the right- and left-hand "lining" concern the privileged status—which Lacan claims to have more adequately explained in his later topological investigations—of *a* and *a′* themselves.

$$\begin{array}{ccccc}
 & & a\text{-}a' & & \\
(10\ldots & (000)\ 01010\ (000) & & \ldots 01) & 1111\ (10101)\ 111\ldots \\
\hline
a & & & a' & \\
 & \text{S(Es)} & & & A
\end{array}$$

The right- and left-hand parts of the lining taken together, (10 . . . . . 01), isolated from the rest of the chain, represent the psychological ego of the cogito, in other words, what Lacan calls the false cogito. The ego is here equated with a kind of *lining* or *screen*—from which the subject is momentarily being subtracted (for theoretical purposes)—that *isolates* the subject from the Other.

Having posited these relationships between his L Chain and Schema L, Lacan then goes on to say:

> The only **remainder** which imposes itself in this attempt [to reformulate Schema L as Chain L] is the formalism of a certain remembering [*mémoration*] linked to the symbolic chain, whose law can be easily formulated using Chain L.
>
> ([This law is] essentially defined by the relay (or shift) constituted in the alternation of 0s and 1s by the surpassing or hurdling [*franchissement*] of one or several parenthetical signs [opening or closing parentheses, taken singly or in combination, and so on].)
>
> What must be kept in mind here is the rapidity with which one achieves a formalization that is suggestive both of primordial remembering in the subject and of a structuration in which it is remarkable that stable disparities can be distinguished (in

effect, the same dissymmetrical structure persists if, for example, we reverse all the quotes).

This is but an exercise, but it fulfills my intent to inscribe therein the sort of **contour** in which what I called the *caput mortuum* of the signifier takes on its **causal** aspect.

An effect which is as manifest here as in the fiction of the purloined letter. (*Écrits* 1966, p. 56; highlighting mine)

There is thus a remainder to be accounted for here, and Lacan often speaks of his object *a*, cause of desire, as a remainder, scrap, leftover, or residue. Let us look once again at Table O (here table A2.1).

Table A2.1

|   | Slot Numbers | | | | | | | |   |
|---|---|---|---|---|---|---|---|---|---|
|   | 1 | 2 | 3 | 4 | | | | | |
| sample number line: | | | | | | | | | Greek |
| 2 | 1 | 1 | 1 | 1 | 2 | | | | letter lines: |
|   | δ | α | α | β | γ | γ | δ | | 1 |
|   |   | γ |   |   |   | α |   | | 2 |
|   | β |   | δ |   | δ | β |   | | 3 |

We observed in appendix 1 that in going from δ to β in four steps, γ had to be thoroughly barred from the circuit, β from the second step, and δ from the third. These barred letters constitute a residue, in a sense, as they cannot be used in the circuit here. They must be pushed aside, and we can thus say that the chain works around them, in other words, that the chain forms by circumventing them, thus tracing their contour. They are what Lacan calls the *caput mortuum* of the process (see chapter 2).

## Parenthetical Structures

Looking back at the quotation translated above, we see that the law in question in the second paragraph is that incarnated by the combinations of signs needed to "hurdle" the L Chain parentheses each time they come up. For example, after a series of 0s and a closed parenthesis, we need pairs of 01 signs if we are to hurdle the next closed parenthesis and attain an indefinitely long series of 1s. It is precisely the sets of 01 and 10 *pairs* found between the sets of parentheses—for example, (10 . . . (—which do all the work of ordering and hurdling here, for the unbroken series of 0s in parentheses—for example, (00000)—can be of any length whatsoever; whereas the number of 0-1 alternations is always crucial: there must be an odd number of signs between the two sets of 0s—for example, (000) 01010 (00)—and an even number of them between the sets of "quotes."

What happens if, as Lacan suggests in the above-quoted text, we reverse all the "quotes"? We get:

) 1 0 ..) 0 0 0 ( 0 1 0 1 0 ) 0 0 0 (.. 0 1 ( 1 1 1 ) 1 0 1 0 1 ( 1 1 1
δ α γ δ γ γ γ β γ α γ α γ δ γ γ γ β γ α β α α α δ α γ α γ α β α α α

That sequence is *forbidden* by the very definitions of the Greek letters. What is then the "dissymmetry" Lacan has in mind in the fourth paragraph down? If we not only reverse the parentheses, but also switch 0s for 1s—

) 01 . . . ) 111 (10101) 111 ( . . . 10 (000) 01010 (000 . . .

—we obtain a series which *is* possible and where we see (trivially) the same lack of symmetry as in the L Chain: what is on the left cannot be made to "balance" what is on the right.

| | | |
|---|---|---|
| left: | ) 01 . . . ) 111 (10101) 111 ( . . . 10 ( | Subject |
| right: | 010 (000) 01010 (000) 010 . . . | Other |
| or | 000) 010 (00000) 010 (000 . . . | |

In a certain sense, we can equate the left-hand side with the subject and the right-hand side with the Other—the upshot being that there is no simple symmetry and thus, we might hazard the term, no *harmony*, between them. If so, one must ask oneself "Why?" The answer here seems to be "Because of the cause"—the cause here being identified with the *caput mortuum*, the letters scrapped in any movement from one predefined letter to another (from a δ, for example, to another δ).

Let us consider again for a moment the right and left sides of the nonreversed chain:

| | | |
|---|---|---|
| left: | (10 . . . (000) 01010 (000) . . . 01) | Subject |
| right: | . . 111 (101) 11111 (101) 111 . . . | Other |

On the left-hand side we find an extra, and structurally necessary, set of parentheses, ( ), viz. those at the extremes. Now does not Lacan very often write object *a* as "object (a)"? This may seem a bit farfetched, but Lacan does say that the left-hand side corresponds to the subject (completed by the Freudian id) in addition to *a* and *a'*. The status of *a* and *a'* was not yet fully accounted for at the Schema L stage in his development, but he claims that his later topology does account for them. That topology situates object (a) through use of the cross cap (cf., for example, Seminar IX). From the 10/01 mirror images related to the very status of *a* and *a'*, Lacan seems to shift his attention to the parentheses alone.

Why does Lacan involve parentheses in such conceptualizations at all? Something is clearly being *bracketed* here: the subject is doubly bracketed in the L Chain, and object (a) is bracketed in a multitude of mathemes and graphs. Something is being *mis entre parenthèses*, that is, suspended or put into abeyance.

Let us consider for a moment the function of an opening parenthesis, (, in a variant of the L Chain:

$$\underbrace{1\,1\,1\,1\,1\,1\,1\,1\,1\,1}_{A} \quad \underbrace{(101010\ldots\ldots)}_{a} \quad \underbrace{1\,1\,1\,1\,1\,1\,1\,1\,1}_{A}$$

The 1s to the left correspond to the repetition of the unary trait, which Lacan associates with the Other. Without the parenthesis—in other words, $\beta$ in Lacan's alphabetic matrix—a 0 could never intervene in the chain: no variation at all would be possible. A chain of $\alpha$'s can be broken only by a $\beta$ (if we think back to our numeric matrix, a chain of 1s or 3s can only be broken by a 2, as direct 1-3 and 3-1 shifts are prohibited).

Thus only a parenthesis can introduce heterogeneity into the otherwise unbroken monotony of the repetition of the unary trait. Only with the intervention of a parenthesis does something split off from or separate out from the Other; only with its appearance is the Other momentarily held at bay (just waiting to resume, reasserting its rights, at the far side of the double parenthesis), just long enough for something to hollow out a sort of hole in the Other (the endless 1 Chain).

This kind of image fits very nicely with Lacan's notions of alienation and separation, whereby the subject comes to dwell within the Other, hollowing out a place for itself in the Other's lack (cf. Seminar XI). It is, of course, an approximate image, with which we could easily find fault if we so desired, but it does seem to account for some of Lacan's claims here.[5]

The letter can then be seen to force upon the subject a parenthetical structure: the autonomous workings of the letter—the letter seeming to derive from, and to be necessarily and wholly situated within, the realm of the Other—allow him or her no other choice.

# Glossary of Lacanian Symbols _____

$\text{\$}$ — (Read "barred S.") The subject has, as I argue, two faces: (1) the subject as alienated in/by language, as castrated (= alienated), as precipitate of "dead" meaning; the subject here is devoid of being, as it is eclipsed by the Other, that is, by the symbolic order; (2) the subject as spark that flies between two signifiers in the process of subjectivization, whereby that which is other is made "one's own."

$a$ — Written object $a$, object (a), *petit a*, *objet a*, or *objet petit a*. In the early 1950s, the imaginary other like oneself. In the 1960s and thereafter, it has at least two faces: (1) the Other's desire, which serves as the subject's cause of desire and is intimately related to experiences of jouissance and loss thereof (examples include the breast, gaze, voice, feces, phoneme, letter, nothing, etc.); (2) the residue of the symbolization process that is situated in the register of the real; logical anomalies and paradoxes; the letter or signifierness of language.

$S_1$ — The master signifier or unary signifier; the signifier that commands or as commandment. When isolated, it subjugates the subject; when it is linked up with some other signifier, subjectivization occurs, and a subject of/as meaning results.

$S_2$ — Any other signifier, or all other signifiers. In the four discourses, it represents knowledge as a whole.

A — The Other, which can take on many forms: the treasure-house or repository of all signifiers; the mOther tongue; the Other as demand, desire, or jouissance; the unconscious; God.

$\text{\AA}$ — (Read "barred A.") The Other as lacking, as structurally incomplete, or as experienced as incomplete by the subject who comes to be in that lack.

S($\text{\AA}$) — Signifier of the lack in the Other. As the Other is structurally incomplete, lack is an inherent characteristic of the Other, but that lack is not always apparent to the subject, and even when apparent, cannot always be named. Here we have a signifier that names that lack; it is the anchoring point of the entire symbolic order, related to every other signifier ($S_2$), but foreclosed (as the Name-of-the-Father) in psychosis. In Lacan's discussion of feminine structure, it seems to have more to do with the materiality or substance of language (and thus is related to object $a$ as signifierness).

$\Phi$ — The phallus as signifier of desire or jouissance; not negativizable.

$\Phi x$ — The phallic function, associated with symbolic castration: the alienation to which speaking beings are subjected due to their being in language.

$\exists x$ — Logical quantifier meaning "There exists at least one x." It is usually followed in Lacan's work by a function, for example, $\Phi x$, where it can be read, "There is at least one x such that the phallic function is operative."

$\overline{\exists x}$ — In classical logic, the sign of negation (~) precedes the quantifier. Lacan, however, creates a different kind of negation by placing a bar over the quantifier (a negation related to discordance); it generally indicates "There does not exist even one x" (such that . . .). To say that no such x exists, however, does not in any way imply that no such x ex-sists.

$\forall x$ — Logical quantifier meaning "for every x" (whether it be an apple, a person, an element, or whatever) or "for (any and) all x's." Lacan allows for a new gloss on this old quantifier: "for the whole of x."

$\overline{\forall x}$ — According to Lacan's revamping of negation, when the bar of negation is placed over this quantifier, it means "not the whole of x" (a woman, for example) or "not all of x," as well as "not all x's." This matheme is often used independently to refer to the Other jouissance that may potentially be experienced by those with feminine structure.

$\lozenge$ — This diamond or lozenge (*poinçon*) designates the following relations: "envelopment-development-conjunction-disjunction" (*Écrits*, p. 280), alienation ($\vee$) and separation ($\wedge$), greater than ($>$), less than ($<$), and so on. It is most simply read, "in relation to," or "desire for," as in $\$ \lozenge a$, the subject in relation to the object, or the subject's desire for the object.

$\$ \lozenge a$ — Matheme or formula for fantasy, usually the "fundamental fantasy." It can be read as "the barred subject in relation to object $a$," that relation being defined by all the meanings the lozenge takes on. With object $a$ understood as the traumatic experience of jouissance that brings the subject into being in the encounter with the Other's desire, the formula for fantasy suggests that the subject tries to maintain just the right distance from that dangerous desire, delicately balancing the attraction and the repulsion.

$\$ \lozenge D$ — Matheme for drives (often referred to as "instincts" in translations of Freud's work) that involves the subject in relation to demand (not need or desire). The formula of fantasy—implying desire—is often reduced to that of the drive in neurosis, as the neurotic takes (or mistakes) the Other's demand for his/her desire.

# Acknowledgments ─────────────────────────────

Jim Ovitt introduced me to Lacan's work in the early 1980s, and Richard Klein, a professor of Romance studies at Cornell University, gave me my first taste of the pleasures and horrors of the Lacanian text.

Jacques-Alain Miller taught me the lion's share of what I know about Lacanian psychoanalysis, and I am greatly indebted to *Orientation lacanienne*, his weekly seminar given under the auspices of the University of Paris VIII, Saint-Denis, which I attended from 1983 to 1989. He provided many of the keys that allowed me to begin to read Lacan's *Écrits*, and a great many of the formulations found in my book represent *my interpretation* of things Miller said about Lacan in his *Orientation lacanienne*. Other teachers influential in my grasp of Lacan's work include Colette Soler, one of the most experienced Lacanian psychoanalysts affiliated with the École de la Cause freudienne, and Alain Badiou, professor of philosophy at the University of Paris VIII, Saint-Denis. This book is in no sense a summary of their views: indeed, they would no doubt all take issue with various interpretations proffered here.

Marc Silver bears the dubious honor of having gotten me involved in translating Lacan's work and having encouraged me to spend countless hours deciphering one Lacanian model after another.

Kenneth Reinhard (professor of English at UCLA), Julia Lupton (professor of comparative literature and English at UC Irvine), and John Smith (professor of German at UC Irvine) were enthusiastic supporters of my work on Lacan throughout the writing of this book and worthy interlocutors. Their help in providing me a forum in which to develop interpretations of certain of Lacan's texts, and to learn something about teaching, will always be greatly appreciated.

Howard Kushner, professor of history at San Diego State University, coached me through a crucial part of the publication process and invited me to give an introductory paper that led to the writing of the first chapter of this book.

Richard Knowles, chairman of the Department of Psychology at Duquesne University, graciously eased my teaching load to enable me to finally finish writing this book.

# Notes

## Preface

1. For example, his letters to Fliess and the "Project for a Scientific Psychology," first published in 1950, *The Standard Edition of the Works of Sigmund Freud* (hereafter SE), edited by James Strachey (New York: Norton, 1953–74), vol. I. Some of the more crucial letters only became available in 1954, in particular, letters 29 and 30; see *The Origins of Psychoanalysis* (New York: Basic Books, 1954).

2. Two faces of the subject, two references to Freud: the Freud of 1895–96 (parts of the correspondence with Fliess [SE I]), and the Freud of 1933 (the *New Introductory Lectures on Psychoanalysis* [SE XXII, p. 80]).

3. *The San Diego Union*, July 12, 1990.

4. "Psychoanalysis . . . may even enlighten us as to what we should understand by 'science'" (Seminar XI, p. 7).

5. See my forthcoming *A Clinical Introduction to Lacanian Psychoanalysis* (Cambridge: Harvard University Press, 1996).

6. See, for example, Colette Soler's discussion of them in the collection of lectures from the first Lacan Seminar in English, *Reading Seminars I & II: Lacan's Return to Freud*, edited by Bruce Fink, Richard Feldstein, and Maire Jaanus (Albany: SUNY Press, 1995).

7. The present book was written before the new English translation of the complete *Écrits* was published. The reader is referred to *Écrits*, translated by Bruce Fink in collaboration with Héloïse Fink, with the assistance of Russell Grigg and Henry Sullivan (New York: Norton, forthcoming).

## Chapter 1
## Language and Otherness

1. The French term *discours* has uses in ordinary French conversation that the term "discourse" in English does not. "*Ça c'est ton discours*," someone might tell you in French: that's your side of the story, that's your account of what happened. "*Son discours à lui, c'est qu'elle ne l'aime pas assez*": his story is that she doesn't love him enough. Here we might even go so far as to say that it's his "schtick"; in the sixties we might have translated it as his "rap" or his "line," it being understood that the same point of view has been expressed by that person *time and again*. It's the same old "schtick" or "spiel," the same old complaint about a blocked situation where the speaker is not getting what he wants. It's almost a "hang-up," a frustration he keeps harping on. The French term *discours* of course also has the more academic and philosophical meanings of "discourse" in English. See chapter 9 for a detailed discussion of various forms of discourse.

2. The relationship between ego talk and the Other will be spelled out further on.

3. This phrase is repeated endlessly in Lacan's work; see, for example, *Écrits*, p. 312.

4. Or "unconscious thinking"; see, for example, SE V, pp. 468, 493, and 613.

5. See, for example, *The Purloined Poe*, edited by John Muller and William Richardson (Baltimore: Johns Hopkins University Press, 1988).

6. The fundamental incompleteness of the Other—that is, its ultimate nature as lacking—and the overall logic behind some of Lacan's crucial concepts will be discussed at length in chapters 3 and 8.

7. See Lacan's various formulations in Seminar II: "*Je est un autre*," "I is an other" (p. 9); "*le moi est un objet*," "the ego is an object" (p. 44); and so on. "*Je est un autre*" is also found in *Écrits* 1966 on page 118 (*Écrits*, p. 23). The multiple implications of these phrases will be spelled out further on.

8. This is implied by all of Lacan's work on Freud's *Vorstellungsrepräsentanz*; see, for example, *Écrits* 1966, p. 714, and Seminar XI, pp. 216–22.

9. Detailed discussions of this term are found in chapters 2, 4, and 5.

10. See, for example, Seminar VII, p. 61.

11. Freud's term is *unterdrückt*, literally, repressed, suppressed, put down, restrained, held back, and so on. See Seminar XI, p. 219, and Seminar III, p. 57, where Lacan translates it as *chû en dessous*.

12. See, for example, Seminar XI, pp. 149 and 203.

13. Cf. the words uttered by Freud's father: "The boy will come to nothing," in *The Interpretation of Dreams*, SE IV, p. 216.

14. See Seminar II, pp. 175–205, and *Écrits* 1966, pp. 41–61.

15. What Lacan refers to as a "purloined letter" is essentially a snatch of conversation you were not supposed to hear but did, or a sight, not intended for your eyes, that is indelibly etched in your memory. Unable to "read" such letters, the analysand brings them to analysis. See *The Purloined Poe*, p. 49.

16. See *The Purloined Poe*, p. 38.

17. The expression "subject position" (*position de sujet*) can be found in "Science and Truth," translated by Bruce Fink, *Newsletter of the Freudian Field* 3 (1989): 5; *Écrits* 1966, p. 856.

18. The reader interested in an in-depth discussion of Lacanian diagnostic categories and criteria is referred to my forthcoming book, *A Clinical Introduction to Lacanian Psychoanalysis* (Cambridge: Harvard University Press, 1996), and to Jacques-Alain Miller's "An Introduction to Lacan's Clinical Perspectives" in *Reading Seminars I & II: Lacan's Return to Freud*, edited by Bruce Fink, Richard Feldstein, and Maire Jaanus (Albany: SUNY Press, 1995). In the present study, I do not *systematically* lay out the different clinical structures, though I do briefly indicate how Lacan differentiates neurosis and psychosis (chapter 5) and obsession and hysteria (chapter 7).

## Chapter 2
## The Nature of Unconscious Thought

1. Just as Freud eschews the notion that each element in a dream has a one-to-one relation with one of the dream thoughts.

2. A great many nonconscious thought processes are carried out at what Freud calls the "preconscious" level, but I am not concerned with them here.

3. See Seminar V, *Formations de l'inconscient* [Unconscious Formations], unpublished, 1957–58.

4. This ciphering might be fruitfully compared with distortion, as Freud describes it in *The Interpretation of Dreams*.

5. Still we should not lose sight of what Lacan claims in Seminar IV: "there is a minimum of terms necessary to the functioning of a symbolic system . . . [and] it is certainly not only three" (March 27, 1957), a similar point being stated rather differently in *Écrits*: "A quadripartite structure can always be required—from the standpoint of the unconscious—in the construction of a subjective ordering" (*Écrits* 1966, p. 774). Which suggests that our three-sign system (1,2,3) is *not* ultimately adequate. In appendix 1, I provide a detailed explanation of the workings of the *numeric* matrix found in the postface to the "Seminar on 'The Purloined Letter,'" as well as of Lacan's laconically laid out second *alphabetic* overlay, bringing out the pertinent features of this four-sign system (along with a couple of typographical errors in the French text). See the end of chapter 6 for a discussion of the importance of quadripartite (four-term) structures in metaphor, and chapter 9 for an explanation of some of Lacan's more sophisticated four-part structures.

6. To hone in as closely as possible on what exactly it is that gives rise to Lacan's syntax, let us look in some detail at what we *put into* this model as we constructed it:

We assumed the "real" event in question—the tossing of a coin—to be *random*, that is, we presupposed that the coin was not loaded. But what does it mean for a coin *not* to be loaded? Generally speaking, it means that it is exactly as likely to turn up heads as tails. How is this determined? By throwing it over and over, and counting up the number of times each possibility turns up; an acceptable coin is one which, out of one thousand tosses, gives us five hundred heads and five hundred tails. This is tantamount to saying that it is our already existing symbolic system which determines whether the event in question is considered random or not. The qualification "random" is thus attributed through use of a symbolic matrix involving a rudimentary form of probability theory. Thus nothing is to be taken to be random without having first satisfactorily undergone the test of a symbolic system. (In fact one's results virtually never show exactly 50 percent heads and 50 percent tails: randomness is more of a limit, something a coin or an event approaches as the number of trials approaches infinity.)

Which is to say that the "raw event" with which we began was already symbolically determined, and that symbolic matrices are never "innocent," that is, never lacking in incidence on our supposedly "pregiven reality." The event is thus retroactively constituted as random by the signifier (that is, by the words we use to talk about it).

There is no ideal coin which weighs exactly the same amount on both sides of an imagined plane through its middle, and which thus provides "absolutely random" results. Perhaps a computer can provide perfect 50/50 results (though only after even numbers of "throws": i.e., heads or tails generations). In any case, the point is simply to recognize the symbolic inputs we supplied at the outset.

For our purposes, virtually any coin will do, as will virtually any other method for choosing pluses and minuses. We can begin from almost any series of pluses and minuses, and by grouping them in certain ways—*chaining them together symbolically*—rules are generated concerning the order of the symbols used to group them. The syntax seems to already be there *in statu nascendi* in the grouping strategies adopted—for indeed, *if the groupings do not overlap, syntax disappears.* Consider the following nonoverlapping grouping strategy:

$$\frac{+\ +\ -\ -\ +\ -\ +\ -\ -\ +\ +\ +}{1\quad 3\quad 2\quad 2\quad 2\quad 1}$$

Here no rules arise as to which symbol can or cannot follow another symbol, and the symbols are totally independent of one another in terms of what signs they cipher. For example, the 3 in the above chain no longer ciphers half of what the preceding 1 had ciphered, and can thus easily follow that 1 immediately without an intervening 2. In the overlapping system, a chain is formed (figure 2.2), while in the nonoverlapping system, no links are established between the units to be grouped: they remain utterly independent (figure 2.3).

Figure 2.2

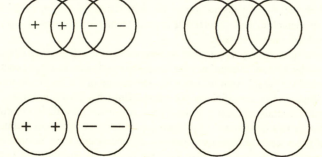

Figure 2.3

Overlapping means that there is no one-to-one or even two-to-one correspondence between elements of the event to be ciphered or symbolized (the series of pluses and minuses) and the symbols employed. Instead of a situation whereby each set of two signs would be designated by one and the same symbol (that set would be its sole and unique "referent," loosely speaking),

$$\frac{+\ +\ -\ -\ +\ -}{1\quad 3\quad 2}\quad \text{Situation } A$$

more than one symbol is used to designate each set of plus or minus signs. In the example in figure 2.4, three symbols represent the two plus and two minus signs, *overrepresenting* them, so it might seem, in that two symbols sufficed for the same job in "Situation A" above.

Figure 2.4

Situation B

If, however, we consider that the symbol 2 designates *two different combinations*, + − and − +, we see that the overlapping is necessary to *completely represent* the plus/minus series, that is, to distinguish a + − combination from a − + (figure 2.5). The overlapping symbolization system is able to distinguish between series 1 and 2, while the nonoverlapping system is not.

Figure 2.5

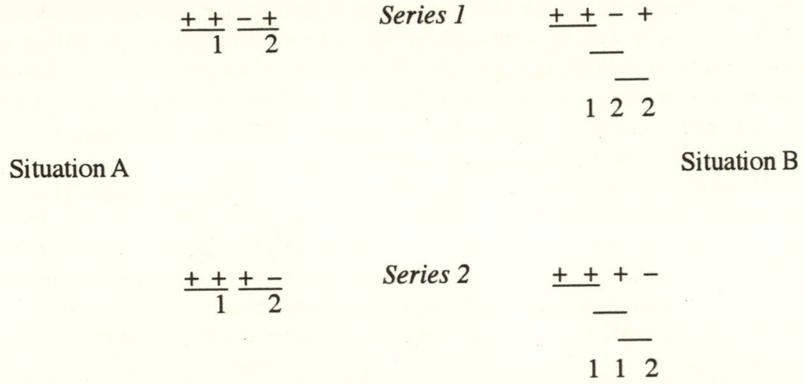

$$\frac{+\ +\ -\ +}{1\quad\ 2}\qquad\textit{Series 1}\qquad\frac{+\ +\ -\ +}{\dfrac{-}{1\ 2\ 2}}$$

Situation A                                                      Situation B

$$\frac{+\ +\ +\ -}{1\quad\ 2}\qquad\textit{Series 2}\qquad\frac{+\ +\ +\ -}{\dfrac{-}{1\ 1\ 2}}$$

Had we, however, assigned different numbers to the two different combinations + − and − +, no such problem would have arisen in the first place, and it seems that it is the *double meaning* (or two different referents) of the symbol 2 that gives rise to two situations: Situation A, under- or ambiguous representation, and situation B, complete representation.

Thus, if we no longer assign two different combinations to the same symbol, we *can* exhaustively represent the plus/minus series with a nonoverlapping string of letters that generates no discernible laws, syntax, or memory. Syntax and memory thus seem to arise only from a specific way of applying the symbols to the series, and the grammar of Lacan's "language" stems, then, not so much from the symbolic material or stuff itself as from this specific mode of application.

But to what extent is the plus/minus series an appropriate model of "reality"? For, after all, Lacan's model takes on value in that it seeks to establish a sort of analogy between the "random events" of a child's early experience, say, and the random chain formed by the string of pluses and minuses. Were a child a computer, such an analogy might suffice, but as a child's experience is not symbolized at all at the outset, that which is to be symbolized apparently bears no resemblance to the clean-cut alternation of pluses and minuses.

But consider Freud's grandson's "*Fort-Da*" (absent-present) game (described in *Beyond the Pleasure Principle*), where the first two words the child speaks seem, in Freud's interpretation, to symbolize the comings and goings of his mother, a considerable event in the child's life. Two terms ("gone" and "here")—which are interdependent in that the mother can only be designated as "here" by the very possibility of her being "gone," and vice versa—code or cipher her appearances and disappearances, constituting "the simplest symbolic sequence, a linear series of signs connoting the alternative, absence or presence" (*Écrits*, p. 141).

Lacan's model, on the other hand, *presupposes* such a first-level coding. It can perhaps be seen as making up in its symbol application strategy what it lacks by way of a "complex reality" to begin from.

We can, as we have seen, cipher the "reality" of coin tossing in a way that *seems to add nothing* to the initial event, but in any case adds another level of meaning to the integers (1, 2, and 3) we used to cipher it.

In the afterword to his "Seminar on 'The Purloined Letter,'" Lacan provides a method of ciphering that assigns double meanings/referents (and sometimes quadruple ones) to all symbols, thus requiring overlapping for complete representation—a form of overdetermination, perhaps. In this respect, his symbolic matrix seems to quite closely mimic natural languages, which regularly assign more than one meaning to the same word and generally require a surplus of words to precisely represent anything. I discuss this more complex language in detail in appendix 1.

7. Freud leads us to wonder whether the expressions "unconscious thought" and "unconscious idea" are not simply oxymorons: "The process of dream-work is something quite new and strange, the likes of which have never before been known. It has given us our first glimpse into those processes which go on in our unconscious mental system . . . we hardly dare call them 'thought processes'" (SE XXII, pp. 17–18).

8. Jacques-Alain Miller, *1, 2, 3, 4,* unpublished seminar, class of February 27, 1985.

9. See *Écrits*, p. 150.

10. Meaning is supplied retroactively, as indicated in later chapters.

## Chapter 3
## The Creative Function of the Word

1. "The letter kills, but we learn this from the letter itself" (*Écrits* 1966, p. 848); in English see my translation of "Position of the Unconscious" in *Reading Seminar XI: Lacan's Four Fundamental Concepts of Psychoanalysis* (Albany: SUNY Press, 1995). The notion that the letter kills is first found in *Écrits* 1966 on p. 24, and in English in *The Purloined Poe*, edited by John Muller and William Richardson (Baltimore: Johns Hopkins University Press, 1988, p. 38).

2. "*Le réel est sans fissure*," "The real is without fissures": it has no cracks, gaps, or holes; it is unrent. For a similar point, see Seminar II, p. 313: "There is no absence in the real." See also Seminar IV, p. 218: "By definition, the real is full."

3. Lacan's notion of reality does not necessarily coincide in all respects with Freud's.

4. See Peter Berger and Thomas Luckmann, *The Social Construction of Reality* (Garden City: Doubleday, 1966).

5. Lacan even goes so far as to say that there would be no being at all were it not for the verb "to be": "'[S]peaking being' . . . is a pleonasm, because there is only being due to speaking; were it not for the verb 'to be,' there would be no being at all" (Seminar XXI, January 15, 1974).

6. Concerning this term of Heidegger's, see chapter 8 of the present book.

7. The latter always and inescapably comports a degree of fantasy, and if it is not the patient's fantasy, then it will simply be the analyst's. The point is not to replace the patient's fantasy-based reality with the analyst's fantasy-based reality, but rather to bring the patient to symbolize his or her real.

8. On metaphorization and substitution in relation to subjectivity, see the end of chapter 6.

9. Dialectization is discussed at length at the end of chapter 5.

10. See appendices 1 and 2 of the present book.

11. I owe this theorization to Jacques-Alain Miller's class, *Orientation lacanienne*.

12. Formulations of this kind are extremely common in Lacan's work: a *class* is

distinguished not in terms of what it contains (as Bertrand Russell would have it; see chapter 2 of his *Introduction to Mathematical Philosophy*) but rather in terms of what it excludes (see Seminar IX); the primal repression of a signifier is what holds in place the whole system of signifiers; the subject has a relation of internal exclusion to its object—the object being that which is excluded, but on the inside, in a sense (it is what is most intimate, but at the same time ejected out of oneself, hence extimate; it is thus exterior while remaining terribly intimate, and interior though remaining utterly foreign). We shall examine this logic in some detail further on.

13. This is related to Lacan's notion of *lalangue*, introduced in his later work.

14. One of his discussions of this paradox may be found in Seminar IX, January 24, 1962.

15. Bertrand Russell and Alfred North Whitehead, *Principia Mathematica*, vol. 1 (Cambridge: Cambridge University Press, 1910).

16. This could be understood in terms of recursive/alternating logics introducing a temporal component. See, for example, Raymond Kurzweil, *The Age of Intelligent Machines* (Cambridge: MIT Press, 1990).

17. There is always an excess or surplus in the autonomous working of the signifier, related, Lacan suggests, to its stuff, its "material" nature: something inherent in the signifier, something "within" the signifier itself (whether sound or letter), leads to its going beyond, exceeding, or surpassing itself.

**Chapter 4**
**The Lacanian Subject**

1. See Lacan's paper, "The Mirror Stage as Formative of the Function of the I as Revealed in Psychoanalytic Experience," *Écrits*, pp. 1–7.

2. See chapters 23–24 of Seminar VIII. The visual images correspond to Lacan's understanding of the "ideal ego," as elaborated by Freud, the figurative (i.e., linguistically structured) images to the "ego ideal."

3. "Shifters, Verbal Categories, and the Russian Verb" (1957) in Roman Jakobson, *Selected Writings*, vol. 2 (The Hague: Mouton, 1971), pp. 130–147.

4. This is a fairly complicated point upon which I will not dwell here. Suffice it to say that a great deal of study has been devoted to the role of proper names, and that Lacan's views are closest to those of Kripke and Jakobson, who hold that a name signifies nothing more than the person who is known by that name. My discussion here closely follows J.-A. Miller's in his unpublished seminars.

5. Otto Jespersen, *Language: Its Nature, Development, and Origin* (New York: 1923).

6. Jacques Damourette and Edouard Pichon, *Des mots à la pensée : Essai de grammaire de la langue française*, 7 vol. (Paris: Bibliothèque du français moderne, 1932–51).

7. This latter is particularly close in connotation to the French use of *ne* with *craindre*.

8. See Seminar IX and "Subversion of the Subject and Dialectic of Desire" in *Écrits*.

9. The reference here is to Heidegger's *Being and Time*, though Heidegger talks about *hupokeimenon* in many other of his works as well. Lacan was somewhat influenced by Heidegger and even translated his article "Logos" into French. It seems clear

that Heidegger's critique of the reified subject was influential in Lacan's thinking, especially in the 1950s (the era of his translation).

10. Better defined as a *breach (not in discourse or other activities, but rather) between one signifier and another, that is, the forging of a link between two signifiers.* The specificity of his subject derives from his work on the signifier, to which I will turn below.

11. See the most recent English translation of Descartes' *Philosophical Writings* by J. Cottingham (Cambridge: Cambridge University Press, 1986): "I am thinking, therefore I am."

12. I explain the use of such Venn diagrams at length in my paper "Alienation and Separation: Logical Moments of Lacan's Dialectic of Desire," in *Newsletter of the Freudian Field* 4 (1990). Here it should simply be noted that the shaded parts are considered valid or true, while the parts left blank are excluded.

13. In a manner of speaking, the Other might be said to have broken down into *imaginary* other—the ego as a crystallization of internalized images—and (decompleted) *symbolic* Other. In chapter 5, however, we will consider the barring of the Other in terms of a split between desiring Other and object *a*, cause of desire.

14. Note that a significant notational change takes place in Lacan's *Écrits* from his "Mirror Stage" article to the "Subversion of the Subject" that is related to the French personal pronoun *je*. In English, when we talk about a word qua word, we tend to put it in quotes. "I" is the first-person personal pronoun; "I" here goes in quotes. The French rarely do so; I say rarely, because there is always a variety of typographical styles, and French writers who read many books in English have a tendency to develop quirky punctuation. Lacan, in any case, in his "Mirror Stage" article, begins with the function of the I, but at that point in his work rarely capitalizes the *j* of *je*. When he discusses Jakobson's work on shifters, the *je* remains in italics, suggesting both that it is being cited—in French one puts in italics any words that are being quoted—and that it is considered imaginary (Lacan often italicizes imaginary elements, such as *a* for other, *i(a)* for image of the other, and so on). However, in translating and retranslating Freud's "*Wo Es war, soll Ich werden,*" *je* tends to be capitalized and is not italicized. Whenever you come across "Je," with a capital J, you can be pretty sure Lacan has in mind his subject of the unconscious; that "Je" is, in a sense, the missing signifier: it is the subject's signifier, but remains unpronounceable as such.

15. "Science and Truth," *Newsletter of the Freudian Field* 3 (1989): 7.

**Chapter 5**
**The Subject and the Other's Desire**

1. I am using the term "child" here instead of "subject" since it does not presuppose subjectivity on the child's part, subjectivity being a result of alienation and separation. "Child" has the disadvantage of suggesting a strictly developmental stage here, which I qualify below.

2. In "Formulations on the Two Principles of Mental Functioning" (1911), SE XII, p. 224. The same expression is found in the case of the Rat Man (SE X).

3. The reader interested in Lacan's attempt to formalize alienation and separation is referred to my article in *Newsletter of the Freudian Field* 4 (1990), entitled "Alienation and Separation: Logical Moments of Lacan's Dialectic of Desire."

4. Akin to that assigned {∅} in set theory.

5. The subject is called upon to assume or subjectify that name, make it his or her own; the frequency with which people fail to do so is witnessed by the large number of people who change their names (when this is not done for strictly political or commercial purposes).

6. In Seminar IX, Lacan exemplifies the intrication of demand and desire with two intertwined toruses (figure 5.8), where a circle drawn around the tubelike surface of one torus (the circle of demand) coincides with the smallest circle around the central void in the other (the circle of desire).

Figure 5.8

7. See, for example, Seminar XI, p. 38.

8. The term "paternal function" can be found in Freud's "Female Sexuality," SE XXI.

9. In the case of single parents, a lover (past or present) or even a friend or relative can, at times, fill the father's "shoes," signifying that part of the parent's desire that goes beyond the child. It is certainly *conceivable* that one of the partners in a homosexual couple might fill this role as well, one of the partners adopting the more nurturing role, the other intervening in the parent-child relationship as third term. In "heterosexual" couples one occasionally finds biological males playing the maternal role and biological females representing the law, but it is clear that social norms do not currently foster the effectiveness of such reversals in replacing the Name-of-the-Father or paternal function.

10. Here I am obviously interpreting Freud's notion of reality as implying a socially defined, socially constructed reality.

11. See his *Naming and Necessity* (Cambridge: Harvard University Press, 1972), which Lacan discusses in Seminar XXI.

12. One cannot help but be reminded here of the father's role in the break-up of the mother-child dyad. I have mentioned the introduction of a *third* element, but that element is in fact always already there, structuring the apparent privacy of the initial relationship. The infant experiences an *intrusion* from the outside, an intrusion—effectuated by what one can variously characterize as the father, the Father's Name, or the phallus—ousting it from a total intersection with the mother, impeding a kind of total overlap.

The intrusion may take the form of a prohibition of its monopoly rights to its mother, which forces its interest to seek beyond her the source of the prohibition, the source of its mother's fascination—her boyfriend, lover, husband, family, neighbors, state, law, religion, God: something which may be totally undefinable and yet quintessentially fascinating.

13. Lacan refers to this as a "fallacious [sense of] completeness" in Seminar XII, June 16, 1965.

14. If we think of the Other as a simple strip (of paper, for example) whose two ends are attached directly, we can think of the subject as the Other with a twist (figure 5.9). The surface that would fill the hole or lack created by the first strip is a simple circle; the surface that would fill the hole or lack created by the second is a more complex topological surface: an "inner eight" (see Seminar XI, p. 156).

Figure 5.9

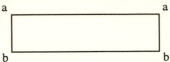
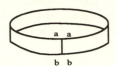

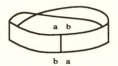

15. Analysis must involve "this repositioning of the ego as subject in the *a* that I was for the Other's desire" (Seminar XII, June 16, 1965).

16. *Sexual über* is generally translated as "surplus of sexuality"; see, for example, SE I, p. 230. See chapter 7 below on Freud's view of the child's reaction to its sexual encounter with the foreign person that sees to its needs.

17. English thus requires a combination of a past tense and an infinitive to achieve the same effect. On the French imperfect, see *Écrits* 1966, p. 840, and in English, "Position of the Unconscious," translated by Bruce Fink, in *Reading Seminar XI: Lacan's Four Fundamental Concepts of Psychoanalysis,* edited by Bruce Fink, Richard Feldstein, and Maire Jaanus (Albany: SUNY Press, 1995).

18. *Écrits* 1966; English translation by Bruce Fink and Marc Silver in *Newsletter of the Freudian Field* 2 (1988). For a detailed analysis of that article, see my paper "Logical Time and the Precipitation of Subjectivity" in *Reading Seminars I & II: Lacan's Return to Freud* (Albany: SUNY Press, 1995).

19. Lacan's discussion of Hamlet can be found in English in *Yale French Studies* 55/56 (1977): 11–52. See also my article "Reading *Hamlet* with Lacan," in *Lacan, Politics, Aesthetics,* edited by Richard Feldstein and Willy Apollon (Albany: SUNY Press, 1995).

20. *Écrits*, p. 289; the phallus or phallic signifier will be discussed at length in chapter 8.

21. We can, of course, situate what I am referring to here as separation and as a "further separation" in terms of Lacan's 1964 articulation of alienation and separation. Rather than saying that the neurotic is in need of a further separation—that is, needs to traverse fantasy—Lacan, in the late 1950s and early 1960s, says that the neurotic confuses "the Other's lack [i.e., desire] with the Other's demand. . . . [T]he Other's demand takes on the function of the object in the neurotic's fantasy" (*Écrits*, p. 321). The idea here is that, in the neurotic's fantasy, ($ ◊ D) instead of ($ ◊ *a*), the subject adopts as his

or her "partner" the Other's demand—that is, something that is static, unchanging, ever revolving around the same thing (love)—instead of the Other's desire, which is fundamentally in motion, ever seeking something else. That essentially means that the subject does not have full access to a third term, to a point outside of the mother-child dual relation. Separation would then be understood as the process whereby the Other's demand (D) is replaced in the neurotic's fantasy by the Other's desire (object *a*). The neurotic subject would have already come into being, in some sense, in his or her truncated fantasy ($\math$ ◊ D), but would achieve a greater degree of subjectivity through separation.

22. I prefer to use the neologistic "scanding" as the verb form of scansion, since "scanning," the accepted verb form, has rather different connotations which could lead to considerable confusion here: looking over rapidly, quickly running through a list, taking ultrathin pictures of the body with a scanner, or "feeding" text and images in digital form into a computer. All of the latter should be clearly distinguished from Lacan's idea of cutting, punctuating, or interrupting something (usually the analysand's discourse or the analytic session).

23. See chapters 17 and 18 of Seminar XI on this point.

24. On analytic interpretation as oracular in nature, see Seminar XVIII, January 13, 1971, and *Écrits*, p. 13.

## Chapter 6
## Metaphor and the Precipitation of Subjectivity

1. Repeated endlessly in Lacan's work; see, for example, p. 207 of Seminar XI.

2. *Newsletter of the Freudian Field* 2 (1988).

3. *Écrits*, p. 157.

4. For example, Max Weber; consider also the very title of critical theorist John O'Neill's *Making Sense Together* (New York: Harper and Row, 1974), a clear contradiction from a Lacanian perspective, given that the essence of communication is miscommunication, misunderstanding. On *verstehen*, see Seminar III, p. 216.

5. *Écrits* 1966, p. 835; in English see "Position of the Unconscious," translated by Bruce Fink, in *Reading Seminar XI: Lacan's Four Fundamental Concepts of Psychoanalysis*, edited by Bruce Fink, Richard Feldstein, and Maire Jaanus (Albany: SUNY Press, 1995).

6. On the substitution of demand for desire in the neurotic's fantasy, see note 21 of chapter 5.

7. They also serve to separate the organ which provides pleasurable stimuli from the symbol used to describe it, in other words, real jouissance from the dead letter.

8. Consider what he says about Alcibiades in *Écrits*, p. 323: "Alcibiades is certainly not a neurotic."

9. Guilt is the one exception Freud makes, speaking as he does of *unconscious* feelings of guilt. It seems, however, more consistent to speak of unconscious thoughts that are associated with guilt feelings. See, in particular, "Repression," SE XIV.

10. SE XIV, p. 148, translation modified; *Trieb* in the Standard Edition is usually treated just like *Instinkt* (instinct), but Lacan translates it into French as *pulsion* and into English as "drive" (as in "death-drive").

11. In this way, Lacan implicitly eliminates an element of Freud's thinking that remains tied, in a sense, to ancient cosmology: the notion of concentric spheres, one

sphere being embedded within another. Freud's term *Vorstellungsrepräsentanz*, which Lacan first translates as *représentant de la représentation*, representative of (the) representation, suggests that there is, first, a level or sphere of thought or representation (which is, no doubt, closest to reality, the phenomenon, or the thing-in-itself) and, secondarily, a level or sphere of ideational representatives thereof. This implies that we can somehow think or represent things to ourselves without the help of any representatives, in some pure, unmediated way—an implication which, from a linguistic standpoint, is patently absurd. Freud's term might be more usefully understood in terms of the distinction between the signifier (representative) and the signified (representation), but it nevertheless suggests some kind of radical distinction between the two, as if the signified were not, somehow, made up of or constituted by the signifier.

When *Vorstellungsrepräsentanz* is translated as psychical representative of the drive, things seem clearer, because we do not think of the drive as consisting of words or signifiers alone, but rather as that which crosses the mind/body gulf or continuum. Yet Lacan stresses that the drive is not unrelated to language: unlike "instinct," drives are, in some sense, embedded in language. But when *Vorstellungsrepräsentanz* is used in other cases, what could it possibly be the psychical representative of? Drives, instincts, and their representatives all remain, it seems to me, to be far better elucidated.

12. For a far more complete discussion of psychosis (e.g., the failure of the paternal metaphor and its consequences), see my *A Clinical Introduction to Lacanian Psychoanalysis* (Cambridge: Harvard University Press, 1996).

13. In the 1960s, Lacan says that it is $S_2$ that is primally repressed, for he reasons that there is no repression, and thus no subjectivity, without two signifiers. It is only upon the appearance of the second that the first becomes operational as a signifier (giving rise to meaning). The precise status of $S_1$ at that stage in his work seems unclear, however; as I mentioned in chapter 5, it seems to be correlated with the mother's desire.

14. SE I, pp. 295–387.

15. See, for example, SE IV, p. 101. In Seminar XI, $S_1$ and $S_2$ are introduced in the discussion of primal repression, $S_1$ designating the mother's desire, and $S_2$ the Name-of-the-Father that is primally repressed through the functioning of the paternal metaphor. By Seminar XVII, virtually any signifier can, at one time or another, play the role of a master signifier ($S_1$), and the Name-of-the-Father might be viewed as one $S_1$ among others, as opposed to an $S_2$, the latter being "just any old signifier."

16. It should be noted that this is my own notation: Lacan never situates the subject along the arrow between $S_1$ and $S_2$.

17. See the last pages of "Analysis Terminable and Interminable," SE XXIII.

18. The "beyond of castration" is further refined in Seminars XVIII, XIX, XX, and XXI, in the course of Lacan's work on sexual difference. In chapter 8, I suggest that there are *different* paths that lead beyond castration for men and for women.

## Chapter 7
## Object (a): Cause of Desire

1. See, for example, his comments in Seminar XXI, April 9, 1974.

2. Significant elaborations of the concept are to be found in Seminars IV, IX, X, XI, XIII, XIV, XV, XVI, XVII, XVIII, the "Suite" to the "Seminar on 'The Purloined Letter' " that appears in *Écrits* 1966, and elsewhere.

3. Other readers are referred to my article "The Nature of Unconscious Thought or

Why No One Ever Reads Lacan's Postface to the 'Seminar on "The Purloined Letter" ' " (in *Reading Seminars I & II: Lacan's Return to Freud*, edited by Bruce Fink, Richard Feldstein, and Maire Jaanus [Albany: SUNY Press, 1995]), which offers a detailed account of object (a) as that which determines the kinks in the symbolic order. See also the appendices to the present book, "The Language of the Unconscious" and "Stalking the Cause."

4. See J.-D. Nasio's *Les Yeux de Laure. Le concept d'object a dans la théorie de J. Lacan* (Paris: Aubier, 1987) for a book-length discussion of object *a* which strikes me as unsatisfactory from numerous points of view.

5. In the case of human beings, that is, speaking beings, it is always difficult to completely separate the imaginary from the symbolic, in the sense that so many of the images that come to us in fantasies, daydreams, and dreams are already symbolically determined or structured. The same is true of "imaginary objects" (or objects as they play a role at the imaginary level), the most important of which is the ego. In the first subsection of chapter 4, I described the formation of the ego, as Lacan understands it, referring to the end of Seminar VIII, in which Lacan rereads the mirror stage from a symbolic perspective. Imaginary objects are thus always symbolically constituted, at least in part, and imaginary relations are thus always already symbolically determined in part as well.

6. While Saussure teaches us that language is essentially structured by difference, we cannot assume that all difference is perceived by virtue of language alone. The animal kingdom—in which the imaginary predominates, the symbolic generally playing little or no part—proves that difference is already operative at the level of the imaginary.

7. The crucial "object" here is the analyst as an avatar of the parental Other, the Other of (or as) demand. Note that Lacan never talks about "symbolic objects": he never situates the *psychoanalytic* object at the symbolic level. The latter shifts in his theory from imaginary other to real cause, never coming to rest, even for but a short moment, in the symbolic register. It is thus not strictly correct to speak of anything other than symbolically constituted objects, or objects qua constituted by the signifier.

Such objects are often objects of the Other's demand. They play a part in the demands addressed by the Other to the subject, for example, by parents to their children, and often involve the achievement of socially valorized positions (beginning with as basic a status as that of being toilet-trained), diplomas, salaries, recognition, fame, and so on. These are objects to be attained, conquered, or obtained, like a piece of paper (diploma, license, Nobel prize), objects prized by the Other, associated with the Other's approval or disapproval. They are objects upon which the child may become fixated, remaining alienated with respect to them and with respect to his or her own efforts to obtain them. If they are to be referred to as objects of desire, they in no sense inspire desire, but more often dread or anxiety. The subject's desire for them is foreign to him or her, not his or her own. Nor can they ultimately be said to be satisfying.

8. In, for example, "Direction of the Treatment," in *Écrits* and Seminar VIII.

9. See, for example, the case of the Rat Man (SE X).

10. Her now well-known dream, taken to illustrate the desire in hysteria for an unsatisfied desire, can be found in SE IV, pp. 146–51.

11. *L'Autre de la demande* is both the Other to whom the subject addresses his or her demands and the Other who demands certain things of the subject; I generally translate the former as the Other *of* demand and the latter as the Other *as* demand.

12. Indeed, all speech, according to Lacan, constitutes a demand for love.

13. Note that Lacan does not always strictly associate love and demand. In Seminar VIII, he begins sketching out object (a) as *agalma*, and what he terms love there is far more closely associated with what he later calls desire. Cf. his discussion of love in Seminar XX.

14. See, in particular, pp. 196–99.

15. "I'm asking you to refuse what I'm offering you, because that's not it!" (repeated throughout the late 1960s and early 1970s in Lacan's seminars).

16. This could also be translated: It is not always what someone asks you for that he or she really wants you to give.

17. Lacan himself might well have said, "Desire is not without an object" (*Le désir n'est pas sans objet*), just as he did in the case of anxiety ("*L'angoisse n'est pas sans objet*" [Seminar X]), but that object would nevertheless have been the object understood as cause.

18. In other words, Lacan clearly implies that "object relations theory" is barking up the wrong tree.

19. The objects in question here are generally symbolically constituted objects, in other words, objects demanded by the Other in speech, or desired by the Other insofar as this desire is made known through speech.

20. See, for example, "Direction of the Treatment" in *Écrits*.

21. This is an overly simplistic view, most ethologists now espousing a more interactive view that still allows us to draw a fairly sharp distinction in this regard between *homo sapiens* and other animal species.

22. I have deliberately left in the above-cited passage of the English translation of Freud's "Negation" something not found in the German, but which is reproduced in the translation provided in the *Collected Papers* (New York: Basic Books, 1959): a future perfect. "[A]n essential precondition . . . is that objects shall have been lost." (Actually it is both a future perfect and a past subjunctive, adding the kind of ambiguity Lacan always relishes.) Put this way, the object is only constituted as lost ex post facto. On refinding, see also *Écrits* 1966, p. 389.

23. Insofar as object (a) plays a visual part in people's fantasies in the form of the breast, it generally appears dressed up or clothed: it takes on a particular visual form or image that Lacan designates as i(a), image of (a). It is not the phantasmatic breast as such that appears, but a dressed-up version thereof. "What is under the clothes—what we call the body—is perhaps but the remainder I call object *a*" (Seminar XX, p. 12).

24. See, in this regard, chapter 10 below on the constitution of the "object of science."

25. See Lacan's expression, "In you more than you" (*En toi plus que toi*) in Seminar XI, p. 263.

26. Freud's term is *Überwältigung*; see SE XIX, p. 57.

27. See, above all, letters 29 and 30 and those from 1896. Further discusssion of these points can be found in my forthcoming book, *A Clinical Introduction to Lacanian Psychoanalysis* (Cambridge: Harvard University Press, 1996).

28. This highlights one of the "shortcomings" of using "over-coming" as a translation for *plus-de-jouir*, as the translators of *Television* (Annette Michelson, Denis Hollier, and Rosalind Krauss [New York: Norton, 1989]) have done (p. 32). Jonathan Scott Lee, in his otherwise fairly cogent discussion of jouissance in *Jacques Lacan*

(Boston: Twayne Publishers, 1990), oddly enough finds this a "wonderful" translation (p. 185). While one could interpret the *plus* here in the sense of *non plus* (no longer; thus, "over"), the expression *plus-de-jouir* is constructed on the model of *plus-value*, the traditional French translation of Marx's *Mehrwert* (surplus value). While Lacan was clearly fond of playing on the literal equivalence of words (*plus* [no longer] and *plus* [extra or bonus] are literally the same, and are often pronounced identically), "over-coming" does not render Lacan's use of the word from 1967 to 1980: a surplus, extra, or supplemental jouissance, not an end to jouissance or too much jouissance. *Plus-de-jouir* does not in any way suggest that jouissance is coming to an end; the *plus* should, rather, be understood as virtually a synonym for *Encore!*—More! Give me more! *Plus-de-jouir* is also one of Lacan's translations for Freud's *Lustgewinn* (see Seminar XXI, November 20, 1973), translated in the Standard Edition as "bonus of pleasure" or "yield of pleasure" (see SE XIX, p. 127). Note that in Seminar XVII (p. 56) Lacan provides his own German translation of *plus-de-jouir*: *Mehrlust* (obviously echoing Marx's *Mehrwert*). The more sensual sense of being "overcome" with or "overwhelmed" by pleasure seems more closely related to the Other jouissance (see chapter 8 below), which has little if anything to do with the *plus-de-jouir*. Indeed, *plus-de-jouir* has none of the connotations of the unhyphenated "overcome": to be overwhelmed (*accablé, dépassé, excédé*), to surmount (*franchir, surmonter*), master, defeat, overthrow, and so on. While "over-coming" has a certain nice polysemy about it, it renders very little of Lacan's French term. I consistently use "surplus jouissance" to translate it; like surplus value, to be considered a plus in one register, it must be considered a minus in another.

29. On this point, see Seminar XIV, April 12, 1967. Note that Lacan says almost exactly the same thing in Seminar XX, *Encore*, translated by Bruce Fink (New York: Norton, forthcoming):

> I will briefly shed light on the relationship between law [*droit*] and jouissance. "Usufruct"—that's a legal notion, right?—brings together in one word what I already mentioned in my seminar on ethics, namely the difference between utility and jouissance. . . . "Usufruct" means that you can enjoy [*jouir de*] your means, but must not waste them. When you have the usufruct of an inheritance, you can enjoy it [*en jouir*] as long as you don't use it up too much. That is clearly the essence of law—to divide up, distribute, and "retribute" everything that counts as jouissance.
>
> What is jouissance? It is reduced here to being nothing but a negative instance. Jouissance is that which serves no purpose.

## Chapter 8
### There's No Such Thing as a Sexual Relationship

1. A reference to the "axiom of specification" in set theory. It should be pointed out that I am overgeneralizing on the question of the part and the whole, but I am doing so to make a point. Lacan *does* in many places talk about the nonexistence of the set of *all* women, the fact that women can only be considered *one by one*, not as a class, etc. Nevertheless, I consider it more important here to emphasize the part/whole dialectic, as what Lacan says about women applies to *each* subject characterized by feminine structure as well.

2. *Écrits* 1966, p. 843; in English, "Position of the Unconscious," translated by Bruce Fink, in *Reading Seminar XI: Lacan's Four Fundamental Concepts of Psychoanalysis*, edited by Bruce Fink, Richard Feldstein, and Maire Jaanus (Albany: SUNY Press, 1995), p. 271.

3. See, for example, Jane Gallop, *Reading Lacan* (Ithaca: Cornell University Press, 1982), and Nancy Chodorow, *Feminism and Psychoanalytic Theory* (New Haven: Yale University Press, 1989).

4. Some of the material contained in this chapter served as the basis for lectures given since 1987 at Cornell, Yale, UCLA, and UC Irvine, and in London and Melbourne; a very early version of it appeared in the *Newsletter of the Centre for Freudian Analysis and Research* (London) 10 (1988); a later version appeared in the *Newsletter of the Freudian Field* 5 (1991). Those versions (above all the first) included certain levels of interpretation of Lacan's formulas of sexuation that are not provided here.

5. "Castration means that jouissance must be refused in order to be attained on the inverse scale of the Law of desire" (*Écrits* 1966, p. 827; *Écrits*, p. 324).

6. Jacques-Alain Miller uses expressions of this kind in his work on the Rat Man: "$H_2O$," in *Hystoria* (New York: Lacan Study Notes, 1988).

7. See, for example, his preface to Roman Jakobson's *Six Lectures on Sound and Meaning* (Cambridge: MIT Press, 1978), p. xviii.

8. Claude Lévi-Strauss, *Structural Anthropology* (New York: Basic Books, 1963), p. 83.

9. See *The Ego and the Id*, SE XIX, p. 54.

10. As Lacan says in Seminar XX, "[T]he apparent necessity of the phallic function turns out to be merely contingent" (p. 87).

11. And, barring significant social upheaval, it looks as though the phallus will continue to serve as at least *a* signifier of desire for some time. Perhaps others will come into being alongside it; perhaps they already have.

12. See his comment on the *impotence* of Dora's father and the role it plays in the exchange of women in Dora's complex familial/extrafamilial configuration (*Écrits* 1966, p. 219; *Feminine Sexuality*, pp. 65–66). Consider also the functioning of certain puzzles made up of little squares with letters, numbers, or images on them, with one square missing, allowing the player to reposition all of the others, one at a time, in the attempt to achieve a predetermined phrase, configuration, or picture (*Écrits* 1966, pp. 722–23).

13. This structure of lack is at the root of Lacan's whole theory of the signifier—the latter originating as the marking of a place where something has disappeared (see Seminar IX, in which the logic of the advent of the signifier is developed at length)—and explains Lacan's considerable interest in Frege's work on the logic of numbers (0 and 1, in particular), for the same basic structure can be seen to be at work there as well.

14. It should already be clear to what extent most contemporary readings of Lacan on sexual difference are misguided, confusing as they do the father and the phallus, the phallus and the penis, and so on. I will cite but one example here, that of Nancy Chodorow in her *Feminism and Psychoanalytic Theory* (New Haven: Yale University Press, 1989). Chodorow has the merit of indicating that her discussion concerns "Lacanian feminists," not Lacan himself (whom she never once quotes). Her sources, mentioned in a footnote (p. 264), are Juliet Mitchell, Jacqueline Rose, Jane Gallop,

Shoshana Felman, Toril Moi, Naomi Shor, and others. On the basis of her reading of their work on Lacan, Chodorow writes that Lacanians sustain the following:

> The father [is] symbolized by his phallus. . . .
> Sexual constitution and subjectivity is different for he who possesses the phallus and she who does not.
> As the phallus comes to stand for itself in the theory of desire, and not even to stand in relation to the mother's desire, the woman becomes not a subject in her own right—even one who can never have the phallus—but simply a symbol or a symptom in the masculine psyche. (p. 188)

The confusion as to Lacan's position is, it seems to me, so utter and complete that I have preferred to lay out his position as I understand it in this chapter, rather than critique other writers' interpretations thereof.

15. Just as everything changes in a narrow view of capitalism as a closed system when stock market phenomena owing to the subjective nature of "value" are taken into account.

16. This sentence, based on the better-known "*l'analyste ne s'autorise que de lui-même*" (an analyst's only authorization comes from himself, an analyst is only authorized by himself, or the only authorization one has to be an analyst comes from oneself), can be rendered as "One's only authorization as a sexuated being (man or woman) comes from oneself."

17. Note that I have been unable to find a way in English to sidestep the problem of using the verb "to be" to translate this phrase. Lacan's *il n'y a pas* here is stronger than saying "Sexual relationships do not exist," for it implies that "Sexual relationships do not ex-sist" either; indeed, "There ain't no such thing." This point is taken up later in the chapter; here let me simply say that Lacan uses two different kinds of formulations for two different notions: when he says "*L'Autre n'existe pas*," we can still suppose that the Other perhaps ex-sists, but when he says "*Il n'y a pas d'Autre de l'Autre*," he does not leave us the option of speculating whether or not this Other of the Other (beyond or outside of the Other) might in fact ex-sist: it neither exists nor ex-sists. Note that Lacan says virtually the same thing at least as early as 1967: "the big secret of psychoanalysis is that there is no such thing as a sexual act" (Seminar XIV, April 12, 1967). What he means by "sexual act" has nothing to do with sexual intercourse: instead of being a genuine action or an action in the "full" sense of the term, the sexual act is always a bungled action, an *acte manqué*.

18. I am leaving aside here a parallel gloss Lacan gives on his formulas of sexuation that seems to me (1) to distract from his most incisive and far-reaching conclusions about sexual difference, and (2) to have been superseded in the course of his own work. His parallel gloss is not without interest (and the reader is referred to my earliest paper, mentioned in note 4 to this chapter, for a detailed discussion of it) but strikes me as somewhat less useful than the one I have focused on in the present study.

19. In Seminar XI, Lacan associates $S_1$ with the mother's desire, which is barred by $S_2$, the Name-of-the-Father, in primal repression. Here I am associating $S_1$ with primal repression and $S_2$ with secondary repression; this is, however, no more than a convention adopted for convenience's sake. As I mentioned in note 15 to chapter 6, $S_1$ shifts in Lacan's theory from designating the mother's desire in the paternal metaphor to designating any signifier that comes to serve as a master signifier.

20. Or, as Lacan puts it in Seminar XXI, "semiotic jouissance" (June 11, 1974): the jouissance of meaning ("jouis-sense") derived from *lalangue*.

21. This view of object (a) is at work in Lacan's "Suite" to "The Seminar on 'The Purloined Letter'" (*Écrits* 1966); I discuss it at some length in appendices 1 and 2 below and at greater length in "The Nature of Unconscious Thought or Why No One Ever Reads Lacan's Postface to the 'Seminar on "The Purloined Letter,"'" a lecture given at the Lacan Seminar in English in Paris in June 1989 and published in *Reading Seminars I & II: Lacan's Return to Freud*, edited by Bruce Fink, Richard Feldstein, and Maire Jaanus (Albany: SUNY Press, 1995).

22. This could perhaps be written: "not all-together" subject to the symbolic order.

23. The difficulty one encounters in attempting to characterize the Other jouissance in any more concrete way stems from the very ineffability and inaccessibility of $S_1$ qua point of origin that cannot be directly grasped in any articulable, discursive way. Rather than viewing $S_1$ here as the father's "No!" we could, in fact, think of it as the mother's desire that is barred by the father's "No!" ($S_2$). Understood in that way, the Other jouissance would, in some sense, "hark back" to a pleasure before the instituting of language ($J_1$), thus "realizing the symbolic."

24. In the remainder of this book, "male" and "female" always refer to biological/genetic determinations, whereas "man" and "woman," "men" and "women," "masculine" and "feminine" always refer to psychoanalytic determinations.

25. An interesting conclusion is that one could go so far as to say that the analyst, qua analyst, is sexless. The same holds true for the master.

26. Readers familiar with the quantifiers ∀ and ∃ should realize right from the start that Lacan's use of them deviates quite significantly from current usage in logic; in particular, he uses ∀x variously to mean all x's and the whole of x at different times. His adoption of a different symbolism for negation should also be understood as implying something other than the simple tilde (~) used in symbolic logic. The different meanings of the bar of negation when placed over the quantifier and over the function are briefly outlined below.

27. *Scilicet* 4 (Paris: Seuil, 1973): 7.

28. And thus it seems that there must be an exception to the universal claim just enunciated! Lacan echoes Charles Sanders Peirce here: "a rule has no meaning without a limit."

29. On discordance and foreclosure in grammar, see Jacques Damourette and Edouard Pichon, *Des mots à la pensée: Essai de grammaire de la langue française*, 7 vols. (Paris: Bibliothèque du français moderne, 1932–51), especially vol. 1; vol. 6 is useful in understanding Lacan's distinction between the subject of the statement and the subject of enunciation.

30. "Comes" should be understood here in both senses.

31. The father of the primal horde should, in this sense, be considered psychotic.

32. Just as $\exists x \overline{\Phi x}$, in the case of masculine structure, does not in the end posit an existence but rather an ex-sistence. It could thus be argued that in Lacan's symbolism, as opposed to classical logic's, $\exists x$ means "there ex-sists an x," while $\overline{\exists x}$ simply denies the possibility of x's existence, without stipulating anything about its ex-sistence.

33. He is certainly not whole in any other sense without his partner, object (a), and the plenitude achieved when he is united with his partner remains phantasmatic at best ($\math$ ◊ $a$).

34. "If something ex-sists with respect to something else, it is precisely inasmuch as it is not coupled, but rather 'tripled' to it, if you will allow me this neologism."

35. At the time I wrote this chapter, I was not aware of the recent issue of the journal *La Cause freudienne* (put out by the École de la Cause freudienne) devoted to *L'Autre sexe* (The Other [or Opposite] Sex, 24 [June 1993]). A number of interesting remarks are made therein about $S(\text{\AA})$ that suggest other possible interpretations than the one I provide below.

36. This might be written $S(a)$. Let it be noted that at least one of the things Lacan says about $S(\text{\AA})$ may not confirm my interpretation: "$S_1$ and $S_2$ are precisely what I designate by the divided A, which I make into a separate signifier, $S(\text{\AA})$" (Seminar XXIV, May 10, 1977). This quote at least makes it clear that $S(\text{\AA})$ is, at that point in Lacan's thinking, the signifier of the divided or barred Other, that is, the Other as incomplete. Insofar, however, as that equates $S(\text{\AA})$ with the signifier of the Other as lacking or desiring, it is related to the *signifier of the Other's desire*, which could, as I am suggesting, be written $S(a)$. Thus stated, however, it could be equated with the phallus ($\Phi$), whereas my sense is that what is in question here is the mOther's desire *as lost*, or the lost mother-child unity.

37. On sublimation, see the recent issue of the journal *La Cause freudienne* devoted to sublimation (*Critique de la sublimation*, 25 [September 1993]), which came out after the present chapter was written.

38. This should not be understood to imply that sublimation of the drives never occurs in those characterized by masculine structure. According to Freud, all desexualization implies sublimation of the drives, though he does not suggest that all ego and superego functions—which require desexualization—provide full satisfaction. Obsession could be offhandedly characterized as the category wherein the drives are utterly and completely desexualized (thought alone, perhaps, remaining sexualized). Nevertheless, there is obviously something different about the sublimation involved in turning id into ego or superego (i.e., turning from "pleasure" to "reality") and that involved in the sublimation that leads to full satisfaction of the drives.

39. See *Écrits* 1966, p. 839; in English, see "Position of the Unconscious," translated by Bruce Fink, in *Reading Seminar XI: Lacan's Four Fundamental Concepts of Psychoanalysis*, edited by Bruce Fink, Richard Feldstein, and Maire Jaanus (Albany: SUNY Press, 1995), p. 268.

40. See *Écrits* 1966, p. 875 (in English, *Newsletter of the Freudian Field* 3 (1989): 22), and "Masculine/Feminine—Signifier/Signifierness" in chapter 8.

41. The most common definition adopted throughout the ages has been "motherhood," yet in many ways it takes on meaning only via the phallic signifier. What are we to make of names that assume a certain social status, like "Madonna" or "Marilyn Monroe"? Do Madonna's and Marilyn's own names (which are adopted names, after all) function as $S(\text{\AA})$ for them? On this point, see my book on *Modern Day Hysteria* (Albany: SUNY Press, forthcoming).

42. Luce Irigaray forcefully expresses the view that women have become defined as non-men in our culture, though she does not attribute it to Lacan: "[I]nstead of remaining a different gender, the feminine has become, in our languages, the non-masculine, that is to say, an abstract nonexistent reality. . . . [T]he feminine grammatical gender itself is made to disappear as subjective expression, and vocabulary associated with women often consists of . . . terms which define her as an object in relation to the male

subject" (*Je, tu, nous: Towards a Culture of Difference*, translated by Alison Martin [New York: Routledge, 1993], p. 20).

43. One could argue that there are indeed three separate levels: love, desire, and jouissance.

44. This conception of subjectivity is extremely common and leads to a great deal of confusion among readers of Lacan who think in terms which are perhaps more political than Lacanian. The most widespread conception of the "subject" in cultural studies, film studies, comparative literature, and philosophy is, it seems to me, that of an *active agent* who takes initiative and runs his or her own life, defines his or her own universe, and (re)presents him or herself in his or her own terms. Such characterizations are all terribly problematic from a psychoanalytic perspective (neglecting alienation, the unconscious, the nature of the ego, desire as the Other's desire, and so on), and the gap between such notions and Lacan's notion of the subject should be quite evident by now. Nevertheless, a bridge between the two views could, perhaps, be constructed through the notion of *subjectivization*: the subject coming into being with the symbolization of a certain real.

45. What I am referring to as subjectification is very nicely expressed by Luce Irigaray when she says that a woman in patriarchal culture "must go through a complex and painful process, a *real conversion* to the female gender" (my emphasis; *Je, tu, nous: Towards a Culture of Difference,* translated by Alison Martin [New York: Routledge, 1993], p. 21). The subjectification of the specifically feminine (or Other sex) is perhaps more difficult and painful in Western than in certain non-Western societies.

46. This statement should no doubt be qualified to some extent: feminine subjectification proceeds in much the same way as masculine subjectification to the extent that a woman does not realize her potential relation to S(Ⱥ), i.e., remains a *hommosexuelle*, not a *hétérosexuelle* (someone with a relation to the Other sex).

47. Jacqueline Rose leaves it in French, as do numerous other translators. Rose's explanation of the term is more confusing than anything else, whereas Jean-Luc Nancy and Philippe Lacoue-Labarthe's discussion in *The Title of the Letter*, translated by David Pettigrew and François Raffoul (Albany: SUNY Press, 1992), is very useful, showing the tension implicit in Lacan's early use of the concept. The latter unfortunately do not consider Lacan's more explicit use of the concept in the 1970s.

48. See *Newsletter of the Centre for Freudian Analysis and Research* 10 (1988).

49. See the whole dialectic of the signifier and the four Aristotelian causes which follows on pp. 26–27.

50. Or the id is drained off into the ego, as Freud says in *The Ego and the Id* (SE XIX, p. 56), where (unlike in the *New Introductory Lectures on Psychoanalysis*, the translation of which Lacan criticizes throughout the *Écrits*) he writes, "*[W]elches dem Ich die fortschreitende Eroberung des Es ermöglichen soll*" (*Studienausgabe*, vol. 3 [Frankfurt: Fischer Taschenbuch Verlag, 1975], p. 322).

51. "[O]nly love allows jouissance to condescend to desire" (Seminar X, March 13, 1963).

52. *Jouissance du corps* (Seminar XX, p. 26) suggests both jouissance of the body (of another person) and jouissance experienced in the body (one's own or an Other's).

53. This description of the Other as radically heterogeneous obviously likens it to object (a) in many respects.

54. See my *Modern Day Hysteria* (Albany: SUNY Press, forthcoming); I take up there the connection Lacan draws between the Other jouissance and love: the love of God, "divine love," and "private religions."

55. If "masculine sublimation" might be characterized as *symbolizing the real object*, "feminine sublimation" might be characterized as *realizing the signifier*. Formulated in Lacan's terms of Seminar XXI, those with masculine structure might be said to symbolize the real (object) of the imaginary (fantasy), which corresponds to SRI, while those with feminine structure realize the symbolic of the imaginary, which corresponds to RSI, associated by Lacan with religion in that seminar. One would then involve a "clockwise" or "right-polarized" discourse, while the other would involve a "counter-clockwise" or "left-polarized" discourse (see chapter 10 below).

56. Many contemporary writers nevertheless continue to tax Lacan with remaining stuck within the old Freudian model. Consider, for example, Elizabeth Grosz's comment in *A Reader in Feminist Knowledge*, edited by Sueja Gunew (New York: Routledge, 1991): "[In Lacan's work,] masculine and feminine remain, as in Freud's work, defined by the relations between active and passive, subject and object, and phallic and castrated" (p. 86). The reader of the present work will by now, I hope, realize that that is akin to saying that Lacan died sometime around 1960.

Consider, for example, the following passage from "Position of the Unconscious," written in 1964: "The vacillation psychoanalytic experience reveals in the subject regarding his masculine or feminine being is not so much related to his biological bisexuality, as to the fact that there is nothing in his dialectic that represents the bipolarity of sex apart from activity and passivity, i.e., a drive versus outside-action polarity, *which is altogether unfit to represent the true basis of that bipolarity*" (*Écrits* 1966, p. 849, my emphasis; in English see "Position of the Unconscious," in *Reading Seminar XI: Lacan's Four Fundamental Concepts of Psychoanalysis*, edited by Bruce Fink, Richard Feldstein, and Maire Jaanus [Albany: SUNY Press, 1995], p. 276).

57. In many ways, Lacan remains a structural thinker, and his way of understanding masculine structure and feminine structure (as bounded/unbounded, closed/open, finite/infinite) makes them strict contradictories, not simple contraries: there is no middle ground or continuum between them (just as there is no "borderline" category between neurosis and psychosis in his version of psychoanalysis). This undoubtedly leaves Lacan open to the feminist and deconstructionist critiques of binary thinking, one of the clearest expressions of which, in my experience, is found in Nancy Jay's fine paper on "Gender and Dichotomy" (in *A Reader in Feminist Knowledge*, edited by Sueja Gunew [New York: Routledge, 1991], p. 95). Interestingly enough, to express her point, Jay relies on Aristotle's logical categories "contradictories" and "contraries" (the same categories Apuleius situated on the "logical square" Lacan often refers to and uses as a model) between which there is no middle ground—that is, *the dichotomy between those two categories is itself a binary opposition or contradictory*. Does not the goal of eliminating all contradictories or binaries entail, for example, viewing psychopathology as a continuum, there being no sharp dividing line between neurosis and psychosis? Clinically speaking, that is a view Lacan would hardly have been inclined to accept. Cf. Roland Barthes' interesting discussion of binaries in *Elements of Semiology* (New York: Hill and Wang, 1967), pp. 80–82.

**Chapter 9**
**The Four Discourses**

1. See Lacan's remarks on this point in Seminar XI, p. 77.
2. Without itself constituting a "metalanguage."
3. See, in particular, Seminar VI.
4. Indeed, Lacan says that the first function of language is the "imperative."
5. Note that other discourses than the four discussed here could be generated by changing the *order* of the four mathemes used here. If, instead of keeping them in the order in which they are found in the master's discourse (figure 9.2), we changed the order to that in figure 9.3, four different discourses could be generated. In effect, a total of twenty-four different discourses are possible using these four mathemes in the four different positions, and the fact that Lacan only mentions four discourses suggests that he finds something particularly important about the *order* of the elements. As is true of many of his quadripartite structures, it is this particular configuration, and not just any old combination of its constitutive elements, that Lacan considers of value and interest to psychoanalysis.

Figure 9.2

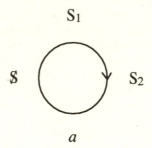

Figure 9.3

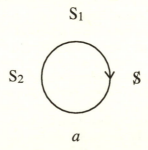

6. *Newsletter of the Freudian Field* 3 (1989).
7. See Charles Fourier, *The Passions of the Human Soul* (New York: Augustus M. Kelley Publishers, 1968), p. 312.
8. See *Scilicet* 2/3 (1970): 89.
9. Indeed, the academic, rather than getting off on knowledge, would seem to get off on alienation.
10. He makes the same point in *Scilicet* 2/3 (1970): 395–96.

11. *Scilicet* 5 (1975): 7, and *"Propos sur l'hystérie," Quarto* (1977).

12. This could be associated with S($\mathbb{A}$), which Lacan, in Seminar XX (p. 118), qualifies as the "one-less" (*l'un-en-moins*).

13. Recall that in the case of Little Hans, Hans suffers from a kind of generalized anxiety state before latching onto the horse phobia; the latter appears *after* he has already begun a kind of analytic treatment with his father, under Freud's tutelage.

14. Object (a) as cause occupies four different positions in the four discourses, and at the end of "Science and Truth" Lacan associates four other discourses with the four Aristotelian causes:

science: formal cause

religion: final cause

magic: efficient cause

psychoanalysis: material cause

It seems to me a fruitful venture to compare the four disciplines, thus analyzed in this text from 1965, and their causes, with the four discourses outlined in 1969 and object (a)'s position in each of them. The four components of the Freudian drive might help situate the different objects at stake at the different levels.

15. Provided by numerous books, including Sherry Turkle's *Psychoanalytic Politics: Freud's French Revolution* (New York: Basic Books, 1978) and Elizabeth Roudinesco's *Jacques Lacan & Co.: A History of Psychoanalysis in France, 1925–1985*, translated by Jeffrey Mehlman (Chicago: University of Chicago Press, 1990).

16. Analytic discourse, for example, requires the analysand to give up the jouissance associated with his or her symptoms or master signifiers.

## Chapter 10
## Psychoanalysis and Science

1. I cannot possibly summarize that voluminous literature here. The reader is referred to works by such authors as Alexandre Koyré, Thomas Kuhn, Paul Feyerabend, and Imre Lakatos.

2. "Science and Psychoanalysis," in *Reading Seminar XI: Lacan's Four Fundamental Concepts of Psychoanalysis* (Albany: SUNY Press, 1995).

3. Indeed, what remains is the "subject of science," that Lacan equates in the mid-1960s with the "subject of psychoanalysis."

4. The distinction between truth and true as a value can already be found in Pascal's *Pensées*, ¶ 233.

5. Certain sciences take into account the positional subject (e.g., game theory à la von Neumann), which in Gottlob Frege's terms might be described as an "unsaturated" function, that is, a function whose gap is not filled by an object. Lacan adopts the term "unsaturated" in "Science and Truth."

6. A useful way of thinking about the difference between "scientific objects" and the "psychoanalytic object" is suggested by a passage in Jonathan Scott Lee's interesting chapter on "Sexuality and Science" in his *Jacques Lacan* (Boston: Twayne Publishers, 1990): "[W]here positivism defines a science in terms of the preexisting objects studied by that science, Lacan offers a definition of a science in terms of the kinds of signifiers, of formal vocabularies, that it adds to the objects it studies and that, in turn, transform

those objects into the objects of science" (p. 188). As such, "scientific objects" are cut out of the real, or hewn therefrom, by "scientific language"; in psychoanalysis, on the other hand, object (a) is the remainder of that process, in other words, what is left over "after" the constitution of science's objects. There is always a limit to formalization: the progressive symbolization of the real always leaves a remainder. As Lacan says in Seminar XXV, "[W]ords make the thing. . . . But our concern [as analysts] is precisely with the lack of correspondence [*inadéquation*] between words and things" (November 15, 1977).

7. "Science and Truth," *Newsletter of the Freudian Field* 3 (1989). Lacan may well have borrowed this term from Frege.

8. Though the specifically psychoanalytic subject no doubt continues to be sutured. According to some, Heisenberg's uncertainty principle heralded the return of the importance placed on the activity of the scientist cum subject in the encounter with, and formulation of, the workings of Nature; nevertheless, the scientist as understood in such accounts seems to be no more than a positional notion.

9. "[G]etting involved in teaching, analytic discourse leads the analyst to the analysand's position," which, as I mentioned in chapter 9, requires the adoption of the hysteric's discourse (*Scilicet* 2/3 [1970]: 399).

10. "What is a praxis? . . . It is the broadest term for designating a concerted action of whatever kind by man, that enables him to change [*traiter*] the real via the symbolic" (Seminar XI, p. 6).

11. "*L'interprétation porte sur la cause du désir*" ("Interpretation bears on the cause of desire"), "*L'Étourdit*," *Scilicet* 4 (1973): 30.

12. A taxing discourse to support, to say the least!

13. See Seminar VIII, translated by Bruce Fink (New York: Norton, forthcoming).

14. I am borrowing this term from Jean-Claude Milner, one of the most astute contemporary writers on linguistics, psychoanalysis, and science. See, in particular, his fine article "Lacan and the Ideal of Science," in *Lacan and the Human Sciences*, edited by Alexandre Leupin (Lincoln: University of Nebraska Press, 1991), p. 36, and his far more in-depth discussion in *Introduction à une science du langage* (Paris: Seuil, 1989) pp. 92ff.

15. See, for example, his *Manifeste pour la philosophie* (Paris: Seuil, 1989). The most complete account I know of, however, was provided in the class he gave under the auspices of the University of Paris VIII, Saint-Denis and the Collège International de Philosophie from 1987 to 1989.

16. Seminar XXV, November 15, 1977.

17. Among the things some of these discourses view as for the patient's own good, one finds: turning the patient into a "productive member of society," removing his or her "antisocial tendencies," making him or her more reflective and insightful, and enabling him or her to find love, desire, and sexual satisfaction with one and the same partner.

## Afterword

1. Indeed, it took me some five years to overcome my own qualms about presenting my work in the guise of a kind of unified, finished "system," as opposed to a series of in-depth *readings* of Lacan's work, and to provide what that Other clearly required in

the case of a previously unknown author like myself. While the main outlines of what I have presented in this book had already been worked out by the time I left France in 1989 after having trained as an analyst at the École de la Cause freudienne, it took me until 1994 to work it into a form a press would agree to publish!

2. "[T]rue teaching, that is, teaching which never stops subjecting itself to what is known as innovation" (*Écrits*, p. 145).

3. See SE IV, p. 120.

## Appendix 1
## The Language of the Unconscious

1. Cf. *The Purloined Poe: Lacan, Derrida & Psychoanalytic Reading*, edited by John Muller and William Richardson (Baltimore: Johns Hopkins University Press, 1988).

2. One notable exception is Jacques-Alain Miller, who provided a fine reading in his unpublished seminar *1,2,3,4*, given under the auspices of the University of Paris VIII, Saint-Denis, in 1984–85.

3. In the first publication of Lacan's "Seminar on 'The Purloined Letter'" (*La Psychanalyse* 2 [1956]), things are spelled out a bit more clearly. There Lacan writes that "Consideration of the 1–3 Network alone suffices to show that, in accordance with the terms whose succession it fixes, the middle [term] will be unequivocally determined—otherwise stated, the said group will be sufficiently defined by its two extremes. Let us thus posit the following extremes (1) and (3) in the [(1)(2)(3)] group" (p. 5).

Yet in more clearly stating how the terms are to be grouped, Lacan lapses into inaccuracy: fixing the extreme terms does *not* in all cases unequivocally determine the middle term (e.g., as we saw in the Greek Letter Matrix II, the blank in the 2__2 configuration can be filled by 1, 2, or 3.

4. Note here, however, that this latter series cannot follow directly upon the former without the interpolation of a second β, for two γ's in a row necessitate two 2s in a row, and they can only be generated here by two β's. Cf. the α, β, γ, δ Network on p. 57 of the *Écrits* 1966, reproduced further on in this appendix.

Important note: there are mistakes in this part of Lacan's *Écrits*, and they can be extremely misleading.

The table one finds directly above this one on page 50 of the *Écrits* (here table A1.9) is misleading in that (1) it clearly contains a typographical error, and (2) while the toss-result and number coding lines run left to right, and thus the Greek letter line normally would as well, Lacan seems to be running the latter right to left here. We saw

Table A1.9: Lacan's Table Ω

| Slot Numbers: | | | | | | | | | |
|---|---|---|---|---|---|---|---|---|---|
| | | 1 | 2 | 3 | 4 | | | | |
| sample number line: | | | | | | | | | Greek |
| 1 | 2 | 3 | 3 | ? | ? | ? | ? | ? | letter lines: |
| | | α | δ | δ | γ | β | β | α | 1 |
| | | | δ | | | | β | | 2 |
| | | α | γ | | | γ | α | | 3 |

above, for example (and Lacan mentions this explicitly), that one can *never* find a δ in slot three if there is an α in slot one—but the table above seems to suggest that this is altogether possible!

Note that this typographical error also appears in the simpler table found in Lacan's 1956 version:

$$\alpha \quad \delta \quad \delta \quad \gamma \quad \beta \quad \beta \quad \alpha$$
$$\quad \delta \quad \delta \quad \delta \quad \beta \quad \beta \quad \beta$$

Now if we run the chain in the other direction, we see that it works just fine (table A1.10). The reader may notice that I have not reversed the excluded terms on Greek letter lines 2 and 3, they being patently nonsensical as they stand in the French *Écrits* table: before modification, Table Ω suggests, for example, that we can use two δ's to get from α to γ, and on the line below goes on to suggest that δ can never be a part of any such progression!

Table A1.10: Table Ω (modified)

|  | Slot Numbers: | | | | | | | |
|---|---|---|---|---|---|---|---|---|
|  | 1 | 2 | 3 | 4 | | | | |
| sample number line: | | | | | | | | Greek |
| 1   1 | 1 | 2 | 2 | 2 | 3 | 3 | 3 | letter lines: |
|  | α | β | β | γ | δ | δ | α | 1 |
|  |  | δ | | | | β | | 2 |
|  | α | γ | | | γ | α | | 3 |

So either Lacan intended to run this series of Greek letters from right to left instead of left to right but did not catch the erroneous inversion of δ and β in line 2 (which could perhaps explain some prohibited combinations Lacan provides at the bottom of p. 51), or else the inversion took place in line 1 itself, where the doubled δ's and β's were reversed. (One could also imagine that the extreme terms, δ and γ, were inadvertently inverted. The two series that work, in any case, are α β β γ δ δ α and the same series read right to left, α δ δ γ β β α [which, for all intents and purposes, is equivalent to γ β β α δ δ γ]). In any case, the version to which I will refer is that presented in the modified table above.

This table should by now be fairly easy to understand: δ cannot be used in an α–γ four-step combination; α cannot figure in slot 2 nor γ in slot 3; β is excluded from γ–α four-step combinations, γ being barred from slot 2 and α from slot 3. The reasons for these exlusions can be deduced in the same way as we deduced those listed in Table O. (Note that the two four-step series here can in fact follow immediately upon one another. Cf. the α, β, γ, δ Network, *Écrits*, p. 57, reproduced further on in this appendix.)

5. Though there was an imbalance in the first level matrix (table A1.11), there being twice as many possible 2 combinations as 1 or 3 combinations, the second level matrix set out to rectify this (table A1.12).

Table A1.11

| 1 | 2 | 3 |
|---|---|---|
| (identical) | (odd) | (alternating) |
| + + + | + + −   − − + | + − + |
| − − − | + − −   − + + | − + − |

Table A1.12

| α | β | γ | δ |
|---|---|---|---|
| 1_1, 1_3 | 1_2 | 2_2 | 2_1 |
| 3_3, 3_1 | 3_2 |  | 2_3 |

If we take this matrix at face value, we are inclined to think that wherever we find a 2, the combination which includes it is twice as privileged as non-2 combinations; thus a letter which does not subsume 2 combinations should have twice as many ordinary combinations as one which does (α, for example, subsumes twice as many triplets as β). And if a triplet includes two 2s, it seems it is twice as likely to show up as a triplet with but one 2.

Probability in fact bears out this calculation, but not exactly in this way. First we return to our Greek Letter Matrix II where we listed the entire combinatory (table A1.13).

Table A1.13

| α | β | γ | δ |
|---|---|---|---|
| 111, 123 | 112, 122 | 212, 232 | 221, 211 |
| 333, 321 | 332, 322 | 222 | 223, 233 |

Normally there would be twenty-seven triplets possible for such a three-slot, three-number combinatory ($3^3$), but twelve of them have been eliminated here because of our 1–3, 3–1 restriction (i.e., 1 and 3 cannot be immediate successors), and because 3 cannot be immediately followed by a 2 and then 3 (two 2s necessarily being interpolated between two 3s); nor can 1 be immediately followed by 2 and then 1 again.

To give an example, the triplet 111's probability must be calculated as followed: the first 1 has one chance out of four of turning up (1/4). The second 1, however, occupies a slot which only 1 or 2 can occupy, 3 being barred here; now 2 can show up just as often as 1 (in the case of the 1 combination +++, a + can just as easily follow a −), and thus 1's probability is one in two here. The third 1, as it also follows directly upon a 1, also has a one in two chance of showing up. We thus have $1/4 \times 1/2 \times 1/2 = 1/16$.

In fact all but one of the triplets in the completed matrix have a probability of 1/16. The 222 triplet under γ, however, has a 1/8 probability, thus balancing out the seemingly unequal distribution of triplets. This can be checked with a flow chart which, starting with two branches (+ and −), is extended by splitting each branch continually into two, adding a plus to one branch and a minus to the other (see table A1.8). One finds that 222 combinations come out twice as often as any other, and that the various Greek letters have, in effect, exactly the same probability of turning up.

6. I am indebted to Thijs Berman for helping me crack this additional code.

7. Let it be noted here for the record that, even if one were to take 1 as "different" and 0 as "same," 01 and 10 would still be inverted. The only way we could suppose them to be correct as they stand would be to assume that the toss-result chain goes right to left, each new plus or minus being added on the left instead of on the right.

8. We *could*, if we really wanted to, also make the 1–3 Network work in accordance with an odd-even interpretation: grouping plus and minus signs by twos, we term "even" any instance in which two identical signs appear side by side, "odd" any in-

stance which includes one (i.e., an odd number) of each sign. Odd-even coding would obviously be a bit farfetched here.

9. If we go on to simplify the designations "symmetrical" and "asymmetrical" to refer to *pairs* (instead of triplets) of identical signs and pairs of different signs, respectively, we obviously find, in examining the 1–3 Network, the same results as we found above by defining 1 as "same" and 0 as "different."

10. See the flow-chart provided in table A1.8, which can also generate Lacan's α, β, γ, δ Network.

11. But, strangely enough, the process cannot be repeated yet again: one cannot once again recode the three-slot 1/0 sequences into two-slot 1/0 sequences to try to situate everything on the old 1–3 Network. Two applications are the maximum allowed here.

## Appendix 2
## Stalking the Cause

1. See *Écrits*, p. 193, and Seminar II, p. 109.

2. Should we be presented with a string of minuses, the numeric matrix line will read exactly as in the above example. The reader can also easily confirm that if we begin with a uniformly alternating string, the numeric matrix line will read 33333212, and as all Greek letters here are in any case defined in terms of going from odd to odd, odd to even, even to odd, or even to even, the Greek letter matrix line will always be the same. This is equally true in the examples which follow.

3. As Lacan says that the parentheses here may be altogether empty, we might think we need to take into account the situation below:

$$+ \ + \ + \ + \ + \ + \ + \ -$$
$$1 \ \ 1 \ \ 1 \ \ 1 \ \ 1 \ \ 2$$
$$\alpha \ \ \alpha \ \ \alpha \ \ \beta \ \ \delta \ \ \alpha \ \ \alpha \ \ \alpha$$
$$\mathbf{1 \ \ 1 \ \ 1 \ \ ( \ \ ) \ \ 1 \ \ 1 \ \ 1}$$

But as it is forbidden by the syntax generated—δ cannot be in position three if there is an α in position one—we can leave it aside here.

4. "[T]here is no devouring fantasy that we cannot consider to result, at some moment in its own inversion, from . . . the fantasy of being devoured" (Seminar XII, January 20, 1965).

5. The L Chain also clearly indicates that the object here is contained within the subject, at least within one of his or her folds or linings. Cf. Lacan's claim that object (a), as breast for example, belongs to the child and not to the mother, being in a sense part of its body: that part of its body which is attached or "tacked on" to her.

Lacan's use of the term "quotes" (*guillemets*) to designate the double parenthesis within which we find the subject («subject») reminds us that, for Lacan, "the subject is never more than supposed" (Seminar XXIII, December 16, 1975). The subject is not something that can, in any sense, be directly observed; it is rather an assumption or supposition on our part (albeit a necessary one), and one must always check to see whether anything really corresponds to this supposed subject.

But these quotation marks go a step further as well, suggesting both the registers of speech and writing. The subject is spoken about, and quotes often designate *something previously said*, something enunciated elsewhere at another time—and generally by someone else. The subject is thus dependent on what some other has always already said about him. Moreover, quotes cannot be seen in speech (though they are often mimicked with gestures, indicated by the particular stress placed on a word, or explicitly announced "quote, subject, unquote"), being essentially typographical in nature. For Lacan, the relation between writing—the letter—and being is of the utmost importance, and our bracketed subject's being seems altogether dependent on these marks which "set him or her off"; one might go so far as to say that the subject has no other being but as mark, or as being set off.

# Bibliography

**Jacques Lacan**

*Écrits*. Paris: Seuil, 1966. *Écrits: A Selection*. Translated by Alan Sheridan. New York: Norton, 1977. New complete translation by Bruce Fink. New York: Norton, forthcoming.

| | |
|---|---|
| Seminar I | *Les écrits techniques de Freud* (1953–54). Text established by Jacques-Alain Miller. Paris: Seuil, 1975. *Freud's Papers on Technique: 1953–1954*. Translated by John Forrester. New York: Norton, 1988. |
| Seminar II | *Le moi dans la théorie de Freud et dans la technique de la psychanalyse* (1954–55). Text established by Jacques-Alain Miller. Paris: Seuil, 1978. *The Ego in Freud's Theory and in the Technique of Psychoanalysis: 1954–1955*. Translated by Sylvana Tomaselli, with notes by John Forrester. New York: Norton, 1988. |
| Seminar III | *Les psychoses* (1955–56). Text established by Jacques-Alain Miller. Paris: Seuil, 1981. *The Psychoses*. Translated by Russell Grigg. New York: Norton, 1993. |
| Seminar IV | *La relation d'objet*. Text established by Jacques-Alain Miller. Paris: Seuil, 1994. |
| Seminar V | *Les formations de l'inconscient* (1957–58). Unpublished. |
| Seminar VI | *Le désir et son interprétation* (1958–59). Text established by Jacques-Alain Miller (seven sessions). *Ornicar?* 24 (1981): 7–31; 25 (1982): 13–36; and 26/27 (1983): 7–44. Final three sessions translated by James Hulbert as "Desire and the Interpretation of Desire in *Hamlet*." *Yale French Studies* 55/56 (1977): 11–52. |
| Seminar VII | *L'éthique de la psychanalyse* (1959–60). Text established by Jacques-Alain Miller. Paris: Seuil, 1986. *The Ethics of Psychoanalysis*. Translated by Dennis Porter. New York: Norton, 1992. |
| Seminar VIII | *Le transfert* (1960–61). Text established by Jacques-Alain Miller. Paris: Seuil, 1991. Translated by Bruce Fink. New York: Norton, forthcoming. |
| Seminar IX | *L'identification* (1961–62). Unpublished. |
| Seminar X | *L'angoisse* (1962–63). Unpublished. |
| Seminar XI | *Les quatre concepts fondamentaux de la psychanalyse* (1964). Text established by Jacques-Alain Miller. Paris: Seuil, 1973. *The Four Fundamental Concepts of Psychoanalysis*. Translated by Alan Sheridan. New York: Norton, 1978. |
| Seminar XII | *Problèmes cruciaux pour la psychanalyse* (1964–65). Unpublished. |
| Seminar XIII | *L'objet de la psychanalyse* (1965–66). Unpublished. |
| Seminar XIV | *La logique du fantasme* (1966–67). Unpublished. |
| Seminar XV | *L'acte psychanalytique* (1967–68). Unpublished. |
| Seminar XVI | *D'un Autre à l'autre* (1968–69). Unpublished. |

Seminar XVII       *L'envers de la psychanalyse* (1969–70). Text established by
                   Jacques-Alain Miller. Paris: Seuil, 1991. Translated by Russell
                   Grigg. New York: Norton, forthcoming.
Seminar XVIII      *D'un discours qui ne serait pas du semblant* (1970–71). Unpub-
                   lished.
Seminar XIX        . . . *ou pire* (1971–72). Unpublished.
Seminar XX         *Encore* (1972–73). Text established by Jacques-Alain Miller.
                   Paris: Seuil, 1975. Two classes translated by Jacqueline Rose in
                   *Feminine Sexuality*, 137–61. Complete translation by Bruce Fink.
                   New York: Norton, forthcoming.
Seminar XXI        *Les non-dupes errent* (1973–74). Unpublished.
Seminar XXII       *R.S.I.* (1974–75). Text established by Jacques-Alain Miller. *Orni-
                   car?* 2 (1975): 87–105; 3 (1975): 95–110; 4 (1975): 91–106; and 5
                   (1975): 15–66. One class translated by Jacqueline Rose in *Femi-
                   nine Sexuality*, 162–71.
Seminar XXIII      *Le sinthome* (1975–76). Text established by Jacques-Alain Miller.
                   *Ornicar?* 6 (1976): 3–20; 7 (1976): 3–18; 8 (1976): 6–20; 9 (1977):
                   32–40; 10 (1977): 5–12; and 11 (1977): 2–9.
Seminar XXIV       *L'insu que sait de l'une-bévue, s'aile a mourre* (1976–77). Text
                   established by Jacques-Alain Miller. *Ornicar?* 12/13 (1977): 4–16;
                   14 (1978): 4–9; 15 (1978): 5–9; 16 (1978): 7–13; and 17/18 (1979):
                   7–23.
Seminar XXV        *Le moment de conclure* (1977–78). Text established by Jacques-
                   Alain Miller (one session). *Ornicar?* 19 (1979): 5–9.
Seminar XXVI       *La topologie et le temps* (1978–79). Unpublished.
Seminar XXVII      *Dissolution!* (1980). *Ornicar?* 20/21 (1980): 9–20 and 22/23
                   (1981): 714. Partially translated by Jeffrey Mehlman as "Letter of
                   Dissolution" and "The Other Is Missing." In *Television*, 128–33.
*De la psychose paranoïaque dans ses rapports avec la personnalité* (1932). Paris:
   Seuil, 1980.
"L'Étourdit" (1972). *Scilicet* 4 (1973): 5–52.
*Feminine Sexuality*. Edited by Juliet Mitchell and Jacqueline Rose. Translated by Jac-
   queline Rose. New York: Norton, 1982.
"Joyce le symptôme I" (1975) and "Joyce le symptôme II" (1979). In *Joyce avec Lacan*.
   Edited by Jacques Aubert. Paris: Navarin, 1987.
"Logical Time and the Assertion of Anticipated Certainty." Translated by Bruce Fink
   and Marc Silver. *Newsletter of the Freudian Field* 2 (1988): 4–22.
"Metaphor of the Subject." Translated by Bruce Fink. *Newsletter of the Freudian Field*
   5 (1991): 10–15.
"Position of the Unconscious." Translated by Bruce Fink. In *Reading Seminar XI:
   Lacan's Four Fundamental Concepts of Psychoanalysis*. Edited by Bruce Fink,
   Richard Feldstein, and Maire Jaanus. Albany: SUNY Press, 1995.
"Proposition du 9 octobre 1967 sur le psychanalyste de l'École." *Scilicet* 1 (1968).
"Propos sur l'hystérie." *Quarto* (1977).
"Radiophonie." *Scilicet* 2/3 (1970).
"Science and Truth." Translated by Bruce Fink. *Newsletter of the Freudian Field* 3
   (1989): 4–29.

"Séminaire sur la lettre volée." *La Psychanalyse* 2 (1956).
*Télévision*. Paris: Seuil, 1974. *Television*. Translated by Denis Hollier, Rosalind Krauss, and Annette Michelson. New York: Norton, 1990.


**Jacques-Alain Miller**

*Orientation lacanienne*. Unpublished seminars given under the auspices of the University of Paris VIII at Saint-Denis starting in 1981. See, above all, *1,2,3,4*, 1984–85.
"H$_2$0." Translated by Bruce Fink. In *Hystoria*. Edited by Helena Schulz-Keil. New York: Lacan Study Notes, 1988.
"An Introduction to Lacan's Clinical Perspectives." In *Reading Seminars I & II: Lacan's Return to Freud*. Edited by Bruce Fink, Richard Feldstein, and Maire Jaanus. Albany: SUNY Press, 1995.


**Sigmund Freud**

*Collected Papers*. New York: Basic Books, 1959.
*The Origins of Psychoanalysis*. Edited by Marie Bonaparte, Anna Freud, and Ernst Kris. Translated by Eric Mosbacher and James Strachey. New York: Basic Books, 1954.
*The Standard Edition of the Works of Sigmund Freud*. Edited by James Strachey. New York: Norton, 1953–74.
*Studienausgabe*. Vol. 3. Frankfurt: Fischer Taschenbuch Verlag, 1975.


**Other Authors**

Badiou, Alain. *Manifeste pour la philosophie*. Paris: Seuil, 1989.
Barthes, Roland. *Elements of Semiology*. New York: Hill and Wang, 1967.
Berger, Peter and Thomas Luckmann. *The Social Construction of Reality*. Garden City: Doubleday, 1966.
Bergson, Henri. "Laughter." In *Comedy*. Edited by Wylie Sypher. New York: Doubleday, 1956.
Chodorow, Nancy. *Feminism and Psychoanalytic Theory*. New Haven: Yale University Press, 1989.
Damourette, Jacques and Edouard Pichon. *Des mots à la pensée : Essai de grammaire de la langue française*. 7 vol. Paris: Bibliothèque du français moderne, 1932–51.
Descartes, René. *Philosophical Writings*. Translated by J. Cottingham. Cambridge: Cambridge University Press, 1986.
Fink, Bruce. "Alienation and Separation: Logical Moments of Lacan's Dialectic of Desire." *Newsletter of the Freudian Field* 4 (1990): 78–119.
——— *A Clinical Introduction to Lacanian Psychoanalysis*. Cambridge: Harvard University Press, 1996.
——— "Logical Time and the Precipitation of Subjectivity." In *Reading Seminars I & II: Lacan's Return to Freud*. Edited by Bruce Fink, Richard Feldstein, and Maire Jaanus. Albany: SUNY Press, 1995.
——— *Modern Day Hysteria*. Albany: SUNY Press, forthcoming.

————— "The Nature of Unconscious Thought or Why No One Ever Reads Lacan's Postface to the 'Seminar on "The Purloined Letter."' " In *Reading Seminars I & II: Lacan's Return to Freud*. Edited by Bruce Fink, Richard Feldstein, and Maire Jaanus. Albany: SUNY Press, 1995.

————— "Reading *Hamlet* with Lacan." In *Lacan, Politics, Aesthetics*. Edited by Richard Feldstein and Willy Apollon. Albany: SUNY Press, 1995.

————— "Science and Psychoanalysis." In *Reading Seminar XI: Lacan's Four Fundamental Concepts of Psychoanalysis*. Edited by Bruce Fink, Richard Feldstein, and Maire Jaanus. Albany: SUNY Press, 1995.

————— "There's No Such Thing as a Sexual Relationship: Existence and the Formulas of Sexuation." *Newsletter of the Freudian Field* 5 (1991): 59–85.

Fourier, Charles. *The Passions of the Human Soul*. New York: Augustus M. Kelley, 1968.

Gallop, Jane. *Reading Lacan*. Ithaca: Cornell University Press, 1982.

Grosz, Elizabeth. In *A Reader in Feminist Knowledge*. Edited by Sueja Gunew. New York: Routledge, 1991.

Heidegger, Martin. *Being and Time*. Translated by John Macquarrie and Edward Robinson. Oxford: Basil Blackwell, 1980.

Irigaray, Luce. *Je, tu, nous: Towards a Culture of Difference*. Translated by Alison Martin, New York: Routledge, 1993.

Jakobson, Roman. *Selected Writings*. Vol. 2. The Hague: Mouton, 1971.

————— *Six Lectures on Sound and Meaning*. Cambridge: MIT Press, 1978.

Jay, Nancy. "Gender and Dichotomy." In *A Reader in Feminist Knowledge*. Edited by Sueja Gunew. New York: Routledge, 1991.

Jespersen, Otto. *Language: Its Nature, Development, and Origin*. New York: 1923.

Joyce, James. *Finnegans Wake*. London: Faber and Faber, 1939.

Kripke, Saul. *Naming and Necessity*. Cambridge: Harvard University Press, 1972.

Kurzweil, Raymond. *The Age of Intelligent Machines*. Cambridge: MIT Press, 1990.

Lee, Jonathan Scott. *Jacques Lacan*. Boston: Twayne Publishers, 1990.

Lévi-Strauss, Claude. *Structural Anthropology*. Translated by Claire Jacobson and Brooke Grundfest Schoepf. New York: Basic Books, 1963.

Milner, Jean-Claude. *Introduction à une science du langage*. Paris: Seuil, 1989.

————— "Lacan and the Ideal of Science." In *Lacan and the Human Sciences*. Edited by Alexandre Leupin. Lincoln: University of Nebraska Press, 1991.

Nancy, Jean-Luc and Philippe Lacoue-Labarthe. *The Title of the Letter*. Translated by David Pettigrew and François Raffoul. Albany: SUNY Press, 1992.

Nasio, J.-D. *Les Yeux de Laure. Le concept d'objet a dans la théorie de J. Lacan*. Paris: Aubier, 1987.

O'Neill, John. *Making Sense Together*. New York: Harper and Row, 1974.

Pascal. *Pensées*. Paris: Flammarion, 1976.

*The Purloined Poe*. Edited by John Muller and William Richardson. Baltimore: Johns Hopkins University Press, 1988.

*Reading Seminar XI: Lacan's Four Fundamental Concepts of Psychoanalysis*. Edited by Bruce Fink, Richard Feldstein, and Maire Jaanus. Albany: SUNY Press, 1995.

*Reading Seminars I & II: Lacan's Return to Freud*. Edited by Bruce Fink, Richard Feldstein, and Maire Jaanus. Albany: SUNY Press, 1995.

Roudinesco, Elizabeth. *Jacques Lacan & Co.: A History of Psychoanalysis in France, 1925–1985*. Translated by Jeffrey Mehlman. Chicago: University of Chicago Press, 1990.

Russell, Bertrand. *Introduction to Mathematical Philosophy*. London: Allen and Unwin, 1919.

Russell, Bertrand and Alfred North Whitehead. *Principia Mathematica*. Vol. 1. Cambridge: Cambridge University Press, 1910.

Soler, Colette. "The Symbolic Order (I)." In *Reading Seminars I & II: Lacan's Return to Freud*.

Turkle, Sherry. *Psychoanalytic Politics: Freud's French Revolution*. New York: Basic Books, 1978.

# Index

A, barred (A̶). *See* Other, lacking
Abraham, K., 93
*Agalma*, 86, 190n.13
"Agency of the Letter in the Unconscious" (Lacan), 4–9, 15
Alcibiades, 187n.8
Alienation, 3–76; castration and, 99; fantasy and, 66–68; language and, 7, 46, 50; mirror stage and, 51; needs and, 50; separation and, 47–48, 49, 61, 184n.12; subject and, 47, 130, 172; vel of, 51
Alterity. *See* Otherness
Anagrams, 8
Analysis: aporia in, 143; association in, 142; cause in, 140; confession and, 88; desire and, 90, 141; discourse of, 28, 129–31, 135–36; ethics and, 146; formalization and, 144–45; linguistics and, 139; master signifiers, 135; mathematics and, 143; metaphors of, 70; purpose of, 26, 79, 89, 92, 121, 135; science and, xiv, 138, 144–45, 177n.4; situation of, xiv, 136–37; status of, 145–46; subject in, 36; symbolic relations, 89; talking cure, 25; terms of, 36; transmissibility of, 144–45; truth of, 121–22; understanding in, 71; verbalization in, 25. *See also* Analyst
Analyst, 67; authorization of, 193n.16; desire and, 61, 66, 141; discourse of, 135–36, 142; identification with, 62; interruption by, 65, 66–67; job of, 25; knowledge of, 87; as Other, 87–88; role of, xiii, 25, 61, 86; sexless, 194n.25; speaking equivocally, 67; subject supposed to know, 87; terminating session, 65, 67
Anglo-American tradition, 62, 136
Anomaly, 29–31, 134
Anxiety, 53, 103
Aphanisis, 73
Aporia, xiii, 30, 143, 151
Artificial languages, 15–21, 153–72
Asexuality, 120, 194n.25
Assemblages, 20–22
Assumption, xii–xiii, 28–29, 61–68
Autism, 6, 75

Badiou, A., 145, 175, 200n.15
Barred A. *See* Other, lacking (A̶)

Barred S. *See* Subject barred (S̶)
Being, xii, 43–44, 61, 76–79, 182n.5
*Being and Time* (Heidegger), 183n.9
Berman, Thijs, 203n.6
*Beyond the Pleasure Principle* (Freud), 16, 181n.6
Binary systems, 15–21, 153–72, 181n.6, 197n.57
Bisexuality, 197n.56
Body image, 12, 24
Borderline category, 108
Borromean knot, 123
Breach, 72, 77–79, 184n.10
Breast, 94, 190n.23, 204n.5
"But," as signifier, 39

Capitalism, 131, 132, 137, 147, 193n.15
*Caput mortuum*, 27, 153
Castration: alienation and, 99; beyond of, 188n.18; incest taboo and, 110; jouissance and, 99, 192n.5; masculine structure and, 109; subjectivity and, 69, 72–73; symbolic, 100, 131
Cause, 27; Aristotelian, 196n.49; *caput mortuum* and, 171; desire and, 59, 91, 102; interpretation of, 28; psychoanalysis and, 140; science and, 140; signifier as, 170; structuralism and, 31; structure *vs.*, 31, 140; subjectivity and, 28, 62–66, 141
Chain. *See* Signifying chain
Child: body of, 24; ego ideals, 36; language learning, 6; Other and, 49; parental discourse and, xii, 5, 178n.15; question "why" and, 54; random experience and, 181n.6. *See also* Father; Mother
"Child is Being Beaten, A" (Freud), 35
Chodorow, N., 192
Ciphering, 16, 21, 25–26, 153–72
Class logic, 109–10
Coding, 37–38, 40, 153–72
Cogito, 43, 169
Combinatories, 16–19, 153–72
Comte, A., 133
Condensation, 4, 15
Contradictions, 135
Correspondence theory, 15
Cosmology, 187n.11

## DATE DUE

| | | | |
|---|---|---|---|
| | | | |
| | | | |
| | | | |
| | | | |
| | | | |
| | | | |
| | | | |
| | | | |
| | | | |
| | | | |
| | | | |
| | | | |
| | | | |
| | | | |
| | | | |
| | | | |
| | | | |
| | | | |
| | | | |
| | | | |